Religion and American Literature since 1950

NEW DIRECTIONS IN RELIGION AND LITERATURE

This series aims to showcase new work at the forefront of religion and literature through short studies written by leading and rising scholars in the field. Books will pursue a variety of theoretical approaches as they engage with writing from different religious and literary traditions. Collectively, the series will offer a timely critical intervention to the interdisciplinary crossover between religion and literature, speaking to wider contemporary interests and mapping out new directions for the field in the early twenty-first century.

Series editors: Emma Mason and Mark Knight

ALSO AVAILABLE IN THE SERIES:
The New Atheist Novel, Arthur Bradley and Andrew Tate
Blake. Wordsworth. Religion, Jonathan Roberts
Do the Gods Wear Capes?, Ben Saunders
England's Secular Scripture, Jo Carruthers
Victorian Parables, Susan E. Colón
The Late Walter Benjamin, John Schad
Dante and the Sense of Transgression, William Franke
The Glyph and the Gramophone, Luke Ferretter
John Cage and Buddhist Ecopoetics, Peter Jaeger
Rewriting the Old Testament in Anglo-Saxon Verse, Samantha Zacher
Forgiveness in Victorian Literature, Richard Hughes Gibson
The Gospel According to the Novelist, Magdalena Mączyńska
Jewish Feeling, Richa Dwor
Beyond the Willing Suspension of Disbelief, Michael Tomko
The Gospel According to David Foster Wallace, Adam S. Miller
Pentecostal Modernism, Stephen Shapiro and Philip Barnard
The Bible in the American Short Story, Lesleigh Cushing Stahlberg and Peter S. Hawkins
Faith in Poetry, Michael D. Hurley
Jeanette Winterson and Religion, Emily McAvan

FORTHCOMING:
Romantic Enchantment, Gavin Hopps
Esoteric Islam in Modern French Thought, Ziad Elmarsafy
Marilynne Robinson's Wordly Gospel, Ryan S. Kemp and Jordan M. Rodgers
Weird Faith in 19th Century Literature, Mark Knight and Emma Mason

Religion and American Literature since 1950

Mark Eaton

BLOOMSBURY ACADEMIC
LONDON • NEW YORK • OXFORD • NEW DELHI • SYDNEY

BLOOMSBURY ACADEMIC
Bloomsbury Publishing Plc
50 Bedford Square, London, WC1B 3DP, UK
1385 Broadway, New York, NY 10018, USA
29 Earlsfort Terrace, Dublin 2, Ireland

BLOOMSBURY, BLOOMSBURY ACADEMIC and the Diana logo
are trademarks of Bloomsbury Publishing Plc

First published in Great Britain 2020
This paperback edition published in 2021

Copyright © Mark Eaton, 2020

Mark Eaton has asserted his right under the Copyright, Designs
and Patents Act, 1988, to be identified as Author of this work.

For legal purposes the Acknowledgments on p. vi–vii constitute
an extension of this copyright page.

Cover design: Eleanor Rose
Cover photograph: People outside St Patrick's Cathedral, NYC. Circa 1950 ©
George Marks / Stringer / Getty Images

All rights reserved. No part of this publication may be reproduced
or transmitted in any form or by any means, electronic or mechanical,
including photocopying, recording, or any information storage or retrieval
system, without prior permission in writing from the publishers.

Bloomsbury Publishing Plc does not have any control over, or responsibility
for, any third-party websites referred to or in this book. All internet
addresses given in this book were correct at the time of going to press.
The author and publisher regret any inconvenience caused if addresses
have changed or sites have ceased to exist, but can accept no
responsibility for any such changes.

A catalogue record for this book is available from the British Library.

A catalogue record for this book is available from the Library of Congress.

ISBN: HB: 978-1-3501-2375-5
PB: 978-1-3502-4321-7
ePDF: 978-1-3501-2376-2
eBook: 978-1-3501-2377-9

Series: New Directions in Religion and Literature

Typeset by Integra Software Services Pvt. Ltd.

To find out more about our authors and books visit www.bloomsbury.com
and sign up for our newsletters.

Contents

Acknowledgments — vi

Introduction: Suspending Disbelief — 1
1 "Cursed with Believing": Failed Apostasy in Flannery O'Connor's Fiction — 19
2 Conversion and Storefront Pentecostalism in James Baldwin's Harlem — 61
3 Secular Theodicy: Saul Bellow, E.L. Doctorow, and Philip Roth — 111
4 Apocalypse Then: Eschatology in Don DeLillo's America — 161

Notes — 200
Bibliography — 254
Index — 272

Acknowledgments

This book began at the Rothermere American Institute (RAI), University of Oxford. Thank you to the wonderful staff of the Vere Harmsworth Library for making the RAI a productive place to work. Many thanks to Nigel Bowles, Val Bullock, Scott Bullock, Michael Burdett, Emily Burdett, Kenneth Christie, David Evans, Paul Giles, Robert Gullifer, Simon Head, Cynthia Hamilton, Matthew Jenkinson, Alister McGrath, Michèle Mendelssohn, Catherine Morley, Peter Ramsay, Stan Rosenberg, Bernie Ross, Jacinta Ross, Tessa Roynon, Jay Sexton, Ed Sudgen, Alan Wolfe, and Suke Wolton for making Oxford truly a home away from home.

This book was completed at the Center of Theological Inquiry in Princeton, NJ. I am grateful to William Storrar and Joshua Mauldin for inviting me to participate in the workshop, and to fellow participants Etin Anwar, Richard Davis, Willem Drees, Dirk Evers, Joel Hodge, Pauline Kollontai, Philip McDonagh, Paul Middleton, Peter Ochs, and Christine Schliesser.

Jack Matthews has been an extraordinary mentor from the beginning, and I'm deeply grateful for his longtime guidance. For a lasting friendship, heartfelt thanks to Peter Lurie. For enriching my intellectual life, I wish to thank Nancy Bentley, Stuart Burrows, Donna Campbell, Aaron DeRosa, Bill Deverell, Joe Dimuro, Kathleen Donegan, Chris Douglas, John Duvall, Bert Emerson, Luke Ferreter, Jeanne Follansbee, Richard Fox, Paul Gilmore, Mark Goble, David Hall, Jared Hickman, Steve Hindle, Amy Hungerford, Kendall Johnson, Bob Jackson, Colin Jager, Gavin Jones, Catherine Jurca, Katie Kodat, Katie Lofton, Chris Looby, Mark McGurl, Susan Mizruchi, Chris Noble, Will Norman, Lindsay O'Neill, Sharon Oster, John Paul Riquelme, Sarah Rivett, Donovan Schaefer, Ethan Schrum, Matt Smith, Stephanie Sobelle, Caleb Spencer, Eric Sundquist, Elisa Tamarkin, Mark Valeri, Cheryl Walker, Frederick Wegener, Cindy Weinstein, Sarah Gleeson White, and Ivy Wilson.

Acknowledgments

I am grateful to the staff of the Huntington Library for creating a small haven where reading and writing take precedence over all the other things that tend to take up our time.

Greg Jackson read the entire manuscript, and I benefitted from his keen insights about what I was up to. Many thanks to Andrew Tate for his enthusiasm and helpful suggestions. Other anonymous readers also helped improve the manuscript. I want to thank Mark Knight and Emma Mason for believing in this book and recommending it for this series at Bloomsbury Academic.

My family has been there every step of the way. I'm deeply grateful to my parents, Philip and Sharon Eaton. My mother-in-law Jeanne Hoffman Smith has been generous and supportive. I'm very blessed by my two children, Andrew and Elliot. Thank you, Victoria—for everything.

Introduction: Suspending Disbelief

In John Updike's ambitious, underappreciated novel *In the Beauty of the Lilies* (1996), Reverend Clarence Arthur Wilmot experiences a crisis of faith so profound that he "felt the last particles of faith leave him. The sensation was distinct—a visceral surrender, a set of dark sparkling bubbles escaping upward."[1] The metaphors Updike employ to describe this crisis of faith—particles leaving, bubbles escaping—make it seem like a science experiment gone wrong, though it is principally an affect that he experiences viscerally inside his body.

As the senior pastor of Fourth Presbyterian Church of Paterson, New Jersey, Clarence had always envisioned his faith not only as a vocation in the traditional religious sense of the word—God's special calling to ministry—but also as a "force of will whereby a Christian defines himself against the temptations of an age."[2] Suddenly, he suffers from a failure of nerve, and "it seemed that the invisible vestiges of the faith and the vocation he had struggled for decades to maintain against the grain of the Godless times and his own persistent rationalist suspicions now of their pulverized weightlessness lifted and wafted upstairs too," as if they had "simply evaporated," and "an immense strain of justification was at a blow lifted."[3] Sitting alone in the dining room of his parsonage house on a warm spring day in 1910 and "numbed by his sudden atheism," Updike's fictional minister cannot help but conclude: "*There is no God.*"[4]

This character's crisis of faith occurs against the backdrop of an increasingly viable atheism in the United States. Robert G. Ingersoll, the "famous atheist" whose book *Some Mistakes of Moses* (1880) the minister had read "in order to refute it for a perturbed parishioner," no doubt had some influence on Clarence's de-conversion.[5] Likewise, Clarence had been unwittingly influenced by the Higher Criticism:

"all those Germans," as the narrator puts it, "who dared to pick up the Sacred Book without reverence, as one more human volume, more curious and conglomerate than most, but the work of men."[6] Inspired by Higher Criticism, Ingersoll and other freethinkers were frankly skeptical about the Bible, which they considered a product of human beings, not a divinely inspired, much less inerrant, sacred text. In popular lectures such as "Why Am I Agnostic?" (1896), Ingersoll extolled the virtues of rationalism and boldly predicted that in the twentieth century, "science would be the engine of disbelief."[7]

Updike's novel would seem at first glance to confirm that prediction. As the narrator explains in an apt oceanic metaphor, the "inexorable … tidal wave" of such thinking "crested in mad Nietzsche," with his infamous pronouncement: God is dead.[8] Although Clarence insists that neither Ingersoll nor Nietzsche "was to blame for this collapse, this invasion of his soul by the void," and that "the failure was his own," certainly such thinkers contributed to a climate in which agnosticism had become a viable position among writers and intellectuals in this period.[9] As H.L. Mencken wrote in *The Philosophy of Friedrich Nietzsche* (1908): "Today a literal faith in the gospel narrative is confined to ecclesiastical reactionaries, pious old ladies and men about to be hanged."[10]

In a splendid essay titled "The Future of Faith," first published in *The New Yorker* in 1999, Updike himself summed up the modernist challenges to Christianity facing his character:

> By 1900, the great shocks of nineteenth-century science—Lyell's exposition of fossils and the vast extent of geologic time; Darwin's theory of evolution through natural selection; the so-called higher criticism of Biblical texts, which undermined their status as the direct word of God, plus the biographies of Jesus, by Strauss and Renan foremost, that presented Him as a mere historical mortal—had settled a commonplace atheism in the minds of the younger generations.[11]

Unable to stem the tide of unbelief, Clarence succumbs to what he calls "the virus of atheism," and the cosmos suddenly seems to him "as empty of divine content as a corroded kettle."[12]

In these darkly comic yet resonant opening scenes, Updike dramatizes what philosopher Charles Taylor has identified as the embattled predicament of religion in a secular age. By tracing the "epochal transformation of religion" from the late medieval period to the present, Taylor has excavated the genealogy of a major historical shift "from a society in which it was virtually impossible not to believe in God, to one in which faith, even for the staunchest believer, is one possibility among others."[13] When angels, spirit possession, and the supernatural were no more a matter of belief than the ground beneath our feet, belief in God (or the gods) was simply taken for granted, unquestioned, and thus in a sense ontologically different. Once this terra firma of "certainty" that long served as the bedrock of Christian faith was "largely eroded" for all sorts of reasons, according to Taylor, the grounds for incredulity were laid.[14] Belief in God would prove to be more difficult to sustain in the face of a scientific materialism, as "empiricism became an increasingly institutionalized way of organizing knowledge."[15] Henceforth, believers must confront what we might call the problem of God; they have to own their beliefs as it were.[16]

Scholars have long recognized that the secularization thesis stands in need of revision.[17] We now understand that religion and the secular are best understood less as antagonists than as interdependent partners. Certainly they "implicate each other more profoundly than we thought," as Talal Asad suggests.[18] We understand, too, that secularization is not a zero-sum game. It turns out that the end game all along had not been eradicating religion but adjudicating the boundaries between good religions and bad beliefs. Today, most scholars agree that religions are "more resilient, varied, elastic, and consequential than the secularization narrative has allowed."[19] Still, modernity entails a fundamental change in our understanding of what religion is and does. The very notion of "religion" in its current usage—that is, as a domain more or less "separate from the rest of life"—is relatively recent.[20] If nothing else, as Taylor reminds us in *A Secular Age*, "secularity" redefined "the terms in which the struggles of belief and unbelief now occur."[21] Put another way, it reconfigured the "social imaginary" in which religious beliefs are understood to be both private and optional.[22] In Wade Clark Roof's elegant formulation, privatization meant changing "from a world in which beliefs held believers to one in which believers hold beliefs."[23]

This is why the persistence of religiosity does not necessarily refute the most radical claims of the new secular studies, which hold that the secular has in large part redefined what it means to be religious in the first place.[24] Michael Warner is at the forefront of a new generation of scholars who are developing a more robust understanding of secularization "not as the absence of religion, or as an antagonist to religion," but rather "as a specific cultural formation in its own right, with its own sensibilities, rituals, constructions of knowledge, and ethical projects."[25] "This understanding of secularization does not necessarily predict a decline in belief," writes Warner: "In fact, the understanding of religion as defined primarily in terms of subjective belief could be seen as *evidence* of this larger transformation. ... Thus, it would not at all be absurd to say that U.S. society, marked by high levels of belief in God, is highly secularized precisely because mental and voluntary adherence is the principle way that religion is salient."[26] Reinhold Niebuhr noted this paradox long ago in his book *Pious and Secular America* (1958) when he observed that the United States is "at once the most religious and the most secular of Western nations."[27]

Another consequence of secularization involves a related shift in the way we understand belief as more of a position than a practice. As historian Wilfred Cantwell Smith explains:

> Indeed, one might perhaps sum up one aspect of the history of these matters over the past few centuries in the following way. The affirmation "I believe in God" used to mean: "Given the reality of God as a fact of the universe, I hereby pledge to Him my heart and soul. I committedly opt to live in loyalty to Him. I offer my life to be judged by Him, trusting His mercy." Today the statement might be taken by some as meaning: "Given the uncertainty as to whether there is a God or not, as a fact of modern life, I announce that my opinion is 'yes.'"[28]

This passage captures a move away from traditional religion as a form of belonging toward a more individualized religiosity as a form of *believing*, such that the question whether God exists looms larger than ever before as the central problem of belief.[29]

What can literary fiction add to our understanding of such historical trends? As we have seen, Updike's novel *In the Beauty of the Lilies* foregrounds the problem of belief in a secular age, the way doubt emerges as an insurmountable obstacle to faith for some people. "Believing isn't supposed to be easy," Clarence's wife Stella admonishes him. "Faith is something we *build*; it's a *habit*."[30] As if testifying to the difficulty of building and sustaining a faith in a secular age, Clarence discovers that he simply does not want to go on believing: "Yet would he call it back, his shaky half-faith, with its burden of falsity and equivocation, even if he could?"[31]

Clarence Wilmot is not the first pastor in Updike's fiction to succumb to doubt, of course. As far back as *Rabbit, Run* (1960), Updike's men of the cloth are no less susceptible to apostasy than they are to adultery. Consider Rabbit Angstrom's colorful Episcopal priest Jack Eccles:

> He steals belief from the children he is supposed to be teaching. He murders faith in the minds of any who really listen to his babble. He commits fraud with every schooled cadence in the service, mouthing Our Father when his heart knows [that] the real father he is trying to please ... [is] the God who smokes cigars.[32]

Another clergyman turned apostate is Reverend Tom Marshfield in *A Month of Sundays* (1975), banished from his Midwestern parish for sexual indiscretion. Still another is Roger Lambert in *Roger's Version* (1986), a former minister and now professor of theology at a New England college, who ridicules his student Dale Kohler's earnest efforts to prove the existence of God through computer technology. Indeed, Updike is arguably our greatest literary chronicler of the difficulties of sustaining religious faith at a time when "the presumption of unbelief has become dominant" in some milieu, such as "the academic and intellectual life, for instance."[33]

In a posthumous collection of essays titled *Higher Gossip* (2011), Updike admits that he tends to gravitate toward "the difficulties and embarrassments of faith in a disbelieving age."[34] Probing into the minds of characters who are desperately trying to hold onto their beliefs, Updike intuits Taylor's insight about the immanent frame in which such struggles with doubt now occur. With the advent of secular modernity, those who remain religious must develop strategies for evading or managing doubts. One strategy is to embrace a form of cognitive dissonance, or what T.M. Luhrmann calls interpretive drift, in which a person's beliefs are not consistent in different social contexts.[35] Attitudes and beliefs considered appropriate in one context, such as a church service or prayer group, may be seen as inappropriate in another context—an advertising agency, say, or a research university. Updike's fiction vividly evokes such strategies of cognitive dissonance and interpretive drift. To the extent that his characters keep the faith, they typically do not inhabit a "world of arrived faith and its consolations," as the author readily admits, but a "fallen world whose emptiness, perhaps, led them to make the leap of faith."[36]

Insofar as there is a critical consensus about Updike, it is undoubtedly the view that he "casts a theological eye on a Christianity in sharp decline."[37] But if Clarence Wilmot's fictional crisis of faith has emerged as a familiar trope in literature, *In the Beauty of the Lilies* confounds any expectation of a progressively more secular America. While it's true that Updike begins the novel with a story about how secularism and scientific materialism undermined religious beliefs in the first decades of the twentieth century, he also stages various forms of reconciliation and recuperation, which amount to a counter-narrative of resilience rather than religious decline. Almost immediately after Clarence's death of tuberculosis, for example, his widow Stella begins to downplay his "locally notorious apostasy."[38] She confides to her granddaughter Essie Wilmot: "Your grandfather could have gone on in the ministry—a lot of us have doubts, but we just brush them under the table and get on with the job."[39] Teddy Wilmot regards his mother's revisionism as a lesson in how "the stories of Jesus' miracles and Resurrection could have been spread across the world if they were not true."[40] Yet even Teddy, a lifelong atheist, largely agrees with Stella's assessment of his father, as he confides in a letter to his grandson Clark: "Looking back I wonder if Dad didn't believe more than he knew, and that's what made him so serene at the end."[41]

Updike's curious hint of what we might think of as Clarence's failed apostasy here, a concept I will flesh out more fully in my analysis of Flannery O'Connor's similarly anguished apostate characters in Chapter 1, is nothing compared to what happens to Clarence's descendants in the decades to follow. Within a generation, they appear to become nothing so much as seekers, which is to say the sorts of persons who might describe themselves, in the altogether common parlance of the time period, as spiritual but not religious.[42] Esther Sifford Wilmot, for instance, whose life story occupies the middle two sections of the novel, illustrates the growing popularity of therapeutic individualism and New Age spirituality in the 1950s and 1960s.[43] Never outgrowing her childhood solipsism, Essie puts it to good use as an actress, adopting the stage name Alma DeMott and embarking on a career in film and television, all the while maintaining her bland therapeutic view of the deity: "when she was a child God had watched her every move, recorded her every prayer and yearning, nothing unnoticed, the very hairs on her head numbered."[44] In contrast to her grandfather Clarence, Essie has no doubts at all about God's existence, if only because God is virtually indistinguishable from her own existence: "She, too, had her religion. She had trouble understanding how people could doubt God's existence. He was so clearly there, next to her, interwoven with her, a palpable pressure, as vital as the sensations of her skin, as dependable as her reflection in the mirror."[45]

Updike's character evokes here a brand of self-focused religiosity that sociologist Robert Bellah once labeled Sheilaism. "One person we interviewed has actually named her religion (she calls it her 'faith') after herself," Bellah explains in his book *Habits of the Heart* (1985), "a kind of radical individualism that tends to elevate the self to a cosmic principal."[46] The character Essie Wilmot's faith, like Sheila's, derives above all from an unshakable confidence in her luminous self, as if the whole point of her film career is "to offer up with a priestly reverence her image to the cameras."[47] Even the social upheavals of the 1960s and 1970s do little to undermine Essie's therapeutic faith, which looks utterly different from the one her grandfather had once espoused.

Nowhere is Updike's tracking of religious history more compelling, however, than in the novel's final section, which all too clearly invokes the resurgence of religious fundamentalisms during the 1980s and 1990s, culminating in a spectacular Waco, Texas-style standoff at the end. Clark Wilmot, Clarence's great-grandson, is working as a ski-lift operator in Colorado when he finds himself lured to a remote ranch by a young woman promising sex; there he "fell under the spell of a religious mountain-man called Jesse Smith and joins his supposedly utopian commune, called the Temple of True and Actual Faith."[48] This fictional cult descends from a branch of Adventism founded by William Miller, who first prophesied that Christ would return in 1843. Arguably "the most significant American millenarian movement of the nineteenth century," Updike includes a short history of the movement in the novel.[49] "For all the chances they gave Him," the narrator wryly observes, "Christ declined to come."[50] Updike's Jesse Smith, for his part, "is always studying Revelation, to find the exact date" of the Second Coming, for which he has prepared his flock by accumulating a cache of "shotguns, rifles, machine guns, pistols."[51] When Clark asks about all the weapons, trying to conceal his growing alarm about the sect, Jesse responds matter-of-factly, "Brother, those are for the Day of Reckoning."[52] Like some "high-ranch messiah," Jesse Smith believes he will be an instrument of Jesus's return, and the Temple of True and Actual Faith resembles many so-called doomsday cults of the time.[53] Indeed, Updike's fictional cult is based on the Branch Davidians, a religious movement led by David Koresh in Waco, Texas, that broke away from the Seventh-Day Adventist Church. The group developed a potent mix of millennialism and militarization under Koresh's leadership in the late 1980s. Finally, in 1993, a government siege of the Branch Davidian compound went horribly awry. Eighty members of the group died in the debacle, including David Koresh.

New religious movements like the Branch Davidians often "maintain a distinct identity by drawing a sharp boundary between themselves and an outside, perceptibly hostile world."[54] Mesmerized by a religious fanatic who will ultimately lead to his demise, Clark feels compelled to remain in the cult through an invisible, almost gravitational force: "He could not project for himself the moment of his conversion; in one frame he was on the outside, wondering how Hannah had tricked him into this rat-trap, and in the next he was inside, unable to leave, tied by gravity to this savior's unpredictable orbit."[55] Note the mixed metaphors: a scientific metaphor combined with a cinematic one of two frames spliced together as if in a jump cut. Updike brings readers inside the mind of a cult member who cannot really account for what led to his conversion, much less what it means to be a follower of its messianic leader: "Clark could not remember when he had decided to believe in Jesse."[56] What Clark *believes* is not all that important. What matters is whether he is inside or outside the Temple of True and Actual Faith, and whether he will do what is required when the day of reckoning comes. We have come a long way from Clarence Wilmot's mainline Fourth Presbyterian Church of Patterson, New Jersey.

Updike replaces the teleology of the secularization thesis with a *genealogy* of religious change. By tracing the circuitous routes that belief takes in the lives of Clarence's descendants, the novel discloses how various forms of religion had become more dynamic and flexible by the end of the century. These characters prove to be quite open to religion and spirituality. As such, they support Jon Butler's contention that the "story of religion in America" is one of "ascension rather than declension," and even though religion is "so complex and heterogeneous as to baffle observers and adherents alike," the United States as Updike describes it remains awash in a sea of faith.[57] The novel in some sense offers oblique testimony to Pericles Lewis's brilliant and witty remark: "If God died in the nineteenth century, he had an active afterlife in the twentieth."[58]

If Updike's novel *In the Beauty of the Lilies* began as a tale about the death of God, then, it ends up being about God's afterlives. In an unpredictable plot twist, religion comes back with a vengeance in the novel's apocalyptic conclusion, as if to underscore the author's observation that there is "a pocket in human nature" that nothing but God can fill.[59] We learn about the "sensation in Jesse Smith's balding head that God was about to act through him," setting in motion a chain of events that will lead inexorably to a final confrontation.[60] Readers may doubt the authenticity of Jesse's belief that God was about to act through him, but the narrator makes a similar claim about divine intervention when Clark Wilmot finally turns on the cult leader to save the day: "the living God had laid hold of him, the present-tense God beyond betting on."[61] In any event, Teddy is surely mistaken when he bemoans his grandson Clark's fate as "a Wilmot shot to death and charred to cinders out in some Godforsaken nowhere out west."[62] Far from a Godforsaken land, the Colorado setting in Updike's novel is a place where God still fires the imaginations of the most fervent believers. In a short preface to the first edition of the novel, Updike hinted as much when he wrote that he wanted "to tell a continuous story, of which God was the hero."[63]

In the dramatic climax of *In the Beauty of the Lilies*, Clark Wilmot finally turns against Jessie Smith. Renamed Esau to mark his conversion, Clark intervenes to save Jessie's followers. Curiously, Clark's betrayal of the cult leader unmistakably invokes his great-grandfather's crisis of faith: "A flock of sparkling dark immaterial bubbles descended into Esau, and he knew what to do. He felt his physical body existing within that electric hyperclarity that for years had come and gone in his head."[64] It is as if the same "set of dark sparkling bubbles escaping upward" from earlier in the novel now come back to strengthen Clark's resolve, and he knows what he must do:

> Jesse saw the revolver in Esau's hand now and jubilantly cried, "Take 'em to Heaven, Slick! Big Daddy needs his girls!" … Clark had always had a non-cooperative streak. "Slick," he said to Jesse, "you fucker, I'll give you Slick," and shot the false prophet twice, once in the chest and the second time in the top of the head, where it was bald, as the man doubled over. He had never liked looking at the supposed holy man's bald pate, the way the shiny skin clung to fitted plates of bone underneath like a turtle's shell. He hadn't liked his gold tooth either.[65]

Whereas Clarence lost his faith because he could not be certain that God exists, that lost faith now returns to give his descendent Clark the resolve to kill the false prophet and save his flock. Describing "the shooting that had taken place inside" to reporters at the scene, a "freckled face" woman relates "how Clark had done it to save them all."[66] This is Hannah, of course, the young woman who had seduced Clark into coming to the Temple of the True and Actual Faith in the first place. Indeed, she may well have borne his child, for the two-year-old boy who "looked up at Clark with a thin-lipped wised-up smile that seemed familiar" is almost certainly a fifth-generation Wilmot.[67] Thus, the novel ends on a hopeful note.

By following the Wilmot family saga across many decades, Updike provides us with a fascinating window—albeit filtered through the prism of literary fiction—onto some of the most important religious trends of our time. In *A Religious History of the American People* (1972), Sidney E. Ahlstrom influentially argued that the United States had entered a new "post-Protestant era," noting in particular the "fundamentally pluralistic situation" of America's "spiritual present."[68] Ahlstrom was writing, of course, in the midst of what sociologists Robert D. Putnam and David E. Campbell have described as the "seismic upheaval" of the 1960s, when "a relatively placid period of pervasive but diffuse religiosity" gave way to a "social, sexual, and political turmoil" that profoundly altered the religious landscape, making it much more diverse, if not fractured.[69] Updike's novel *In the Beauty of the Lilies* offers a capacious account of this religious landscape, exploring among other things the overall decline of liberal or mainline Protestant denominations; the rise of an ecumenical "civil religion" in mid-century America; the vogue in Eastern religions and New Age spirituality; the emergence of religious fundamentalisms and apocalyptic groups (premillennial, postmillennial); and so on. In short, the novel shows how different versions of religion and spirituality took root in the seemingly arid soil of an ever-more pluralistic nation.

What do novels know about subjectivity and history that can help us understand, and maybe even preserve, the possibilities of believing in a secular age? Working inductively through details of characterization, plot, point of view, and setting, readers of Updike's late masterpiece gain a better understanding of how religious beliefs and practices evolve over time. In turn, we can also see how fictional characters are subject to social forces beyond their control. For while religious beliefs and practices touch the deepest part of our innermost selves, they are not simply our own; rather, they are grounded in particular historical contexts. They are at once personal and historical. The reasons some characters sustain their faith, while others don't, may finally depend less on individual temperament than on whether they find a religious community of like-minded believers to serve as a sort of bulwark against the corrosive effects of skepticism.

By way of comparison, consider Marilynne Robinson's award-winning novel *Gilead* (2004), narrated as a letter written in 1956 from a Presbyterian minister, John Ames, to his son. Ames has persisted for nearly half a century as the pastor of a tiny church in Gilead, Iowa. By his own estimate, he has delivered 2,250 sermons, all written "in the deepest hope and conviction. Trying to say what was true."[70] One might suppose that the isolated, provincial setting of the novel shields pastor Ames from the modernist controversies of his day, but that would be wrong. For Ames, too, has grappled with formidable modernist thinkers of his time, such as the "famous atheist" Ludwig Feuerbach, best known for his book *The Essence of Christianity* (1841), as well as "Owen and James and Huxley and Swedenborg and, for heaven's sake, Blavatsky."[71] Whereas Clarence could not shake the conviction that such thinkers fatally undermine his faith, Ames finishes his own similar reading program with his faith intact. Ames does admit, though, that this makes him something of "a relic, an archaism" in a world of ascendant atheism.[72] He continues:

> These days there are so many people who think loyalty to religion is benighted, if not worse than benighted. I am aware of that, and I know the charges that can be brought against the churches are powerful. And I know, too, that my own experience of the church has been, in many senses, sheltered and parochial. In every sense, unless it really is a universal and transcendent life, unless the bread is the bread and the

cup is the cup everywhere, in all circumstances, and it is a time with the Lord in Gethsemane that comes for everyone, as I deeply believe."[73] Insofar as Ames is characterized as an outlier, the novel reads like a throwback to a distant age, as James Wood points out in a review aptly titled "Acts of Devotion": "*Gilead* is a beautiful work—demanding, grave and lucid—and is, if anything, more out of time than Robinson's book of essays, suffused as it is with a Protestant bareness that sometimes recalls George Herbert."[74]

Gilead is an unusually devotional novel in which Robinson's protagonist works out a remarkable rapprochement between belief and skepticism. When younger members of his flock come back to Gilead after being away at college, invariably "flummoxed by the possibility of unbelief," Ames refuses to engage in apologetics: "And they want me to defend religion, and they want me to give them 'proofs.' I just won't do it. It only confirms them in their skepticism. Because nothing true can be said about God from a posture of defense."[75] Apologetics are misguided, in his view, because any proofs of God's existence are, as he puts it, "never sufficient to the question, and they're always a little impertinent, I think, because they claim for God a place within our conceptual grasp."[76] For Ames, "it is religious experience above all that authenticates religion, for the purposes of the individual believer."[77] What matters, then, is religious experience, not belief, which can never be entirely devoid of doubt. Ames accepts God as a mystery, as befits someone who once ruminated on the "oddness of the phrase 'believe in God.'"[78] In this posture of humility, Ames becomes a fictional exemplar of how uncertainty might be a resource for Christian faith rather than a stumbling block to it. Notably, he is in effect following Robinson's own advice about how to be a good Christian: "There is something about certainty that makes Christianity un-Christian. Therefore, because I would be a good Christian, I have cultivated uncertainty, which I consider a form of reverence."[79] For my purposes, Ames's quiet, unassuming faith, which can be described as a self-consciously Midwestern Protestantism, stands in marked contrast to the mental gymnastics of Clarence Wilmot's dramatic crisis of faith. Whereas Ames arrives at a spiritual maturity through many years of diligent study and dutiful sermonizing, counseling his parishioners with patience and wisdom, Clarence's apostasy arrives almost instantaneously in one thunderclap of disbelief. Nevertheless, as novels about religion, *Gilead* and *In the Beauty of the Lilies*, have more in common than we might expect at first glance. For Robinson shares with Updike a recognition that the twentieth century witnessed not religious decline but religious revivals on a scale that would have been difficult to predict in the 1950s, even in the biblically resonant town of Gilead. Indeed, so fervent were these religious revivals that one historian has called the period following the 1950s and 1960s a fourth Great Awakening.[80]

Both novels represent an important if underappreciated segment of contemporary writing, in which religion as lived experience gets woven into narrative fiction. Much of what we can learn from fiction about religion and spirituality derives from its content and themes, of course, yet formal questions can also help us see how writers delineate religious experiences as well. Pushing up against the limits of language, writers use literary devices such as characterization, metaphor, point of view, and so on to explore various aspects of religious experience that are difficult to grasp, much less describe. Writers often portray religious affects and beliefs as something like what Raymond Williams called *structures of feeling*. He chose the word "feeling" to "emphasize a distinction from more formal concepts of 'world-view' or 'ideology'" and to describe "specifically affective elements of consciousness and relationships: not feeling against thought, but thought as felt and feeling as thought: practical consciousness of a present kind, in a living and interrelating community."[81] Literary fiction turns out to be a multifaceted and supple means of representing minds in motion, with longstanding techniques for rendering interiority like free-indirect discourse and stream of consciousness, two variations of third-person narration that were employed to startling effects by the great modernist writers. In the hands of such writers, literary fiction has likewise proven to be a means of representing history in the making, bringing events like the Branch Davidian debacle alive on the page, as we have seen. In keeping with these dual strengths of novelistic narrative, since it is equally adept at rendering interiority and historicity, fiction writers tend to represent religions both psychologically and sociologically. After all, religions are at once a crucial feature of personhood and a central fact of social life.[82] Why does literary fiction rather than, say, contemporary spiritual autobiography or the sociology of religion emerge as an especially rich, timely cultural form for reading religious phenomena? What does it mean to put religion into literary discourse in the latter half of the twentieth century, and how does literature allow writers to expand the possibilities of what it means to be religious in our time? Robinson's novel participates in a larger discursive effort to reframe doubt as something that need not preclude belief, seemingly a pressing concern for even the most devout among us. *Gilead* also invites us to cultivate uncertainty through the practice of reading itself. Because fiction requires a "voluntary suspension of disbelief," the very activity of reading fiction fosters "the suppleness, agency, and scope of disbelief itself."[83] *Gilead* is a recent example of an important trend in contemporary literary fiction, in which authors explore not only what their characters actually believe, but also what forms, habits, and rituals their beliefs take.[84]

The focus of this study is on American writers from the postwar period to the present who represent religion and spirituality with open-minded sensitivity and historical specificity, without downplaying the universalizing claims that make religion, religion.[85] Predictably anti-doctrinal and nonsectarian, most writers neither preach nor proselytize in fiction. Instead, they depict varieties of religions, spirituality, and secularisms in all their affective and social power. The chapters that follow consider the work of Flannery O'Connor, James Baldwin, Saul Bellow, Philip Roth, E.L. Doctorow, Don DeLillo, and others through four major keywords drawn from religious studies and theology: apostasy, conversion, theodicy, and eschatology. These terms have been somewhat neglected in literary criticism, yet without them, our terminology for thinking about religions is impoverished.[86] Employing such terms may well present hazards of its own, but my hypothesis is that language specific to faith traditions will enlarge our vocabulary and enliven our discussions.

My approach is not theological, however, but rather literary-critical and socio-historical. Building on the work of scholars in religious studies, I want to bring an understanding of "lived religion" to bear upon how writers represent religion and spirituality in their fiction. "The study of lived religion," as Robert A. Orsi explains, tries to understand religion "within a more broadly conceived and described lifeworld, the domain of everyday existence, practical activity, and shared understandings, with all its crises, surprises, satisfactions, frustrations, joys, desires, hopes, fears, and limitations."[87] Adapting this approach to the study of literature will require a delicate balancing act. If the new sociology of literature attempts "to coordinate the literary with the social," as James F. English puts it, my methodology tries to coordinate the literary with the religious.[88] I am also interested in moving beyond belief to consider the affective dimensions of religion, an approach that should already be clear from my analyses of how religious experience registers as bodily affect in Updike and Robinson. Finally, my work is indebted to a literary-critical method best described as historical formalism, a method that attends to aesthetics and historical contexts to uncover the social power of forms.[89] My purpose in applying these disparate methodologies to literary representations of religion is to divulge how a select group of contemporary writers seeks to grasp and understand, perhaps even to expand, the possibility of sustaining faith commitments in a not quite secular America.

The writers examined in this study are not necessarily religious themselves, but whether Catholic or Protestant, Jewish or Buddhist, agnostic or believer, all of them are as fascinated as they are puzzled by what John Updike called the "welter of religious phenomena" in America.[90] Indeed, "the very multiplicity and variety suggest that none of it is true, other than manifesting an undoubted human tendency," but if "the reasons for doubt in God's existence are easily come by" at the end "of a century that has the Holocaust at its center," then how do we explain why so many religions have not only survived, but actually thrive in this supposed "age of post-faith?"[91]

The writer E.L. Doctorow (born one year later than Updike in 1932) likewise marvels at the "virtual supermarket of spiritual choice" in an ostensibly secular yet "God-soaked country."[92] Far from being dismissive or intolerant of religion, he simply wants to understand what drives religious others. A self-described nonobservant Jew, he concludes that, taken together, "our religions or religious cults testify to the deeply serious American thirst for celestial connection. We want a spiritual release from the society we have made out of our secular humanism."[93] These comments appear in the Massey lectures that Doctorow gave at Harvard, subsequently published under the title *Reporting the Universe* (2003). Portions of the lectures were lifted almost verbatim from his brilliant novel *City of God* (2000), as I will show in more detail in Chapter 3. What does it mean that Doctorow in effect stole the words of his own protagonists (without indicating that they are anything other than his own point of view) when lecturing on the subject of religion? Let me be clear: I am not suggesting that he has committed plagiarism, since he clearly invented the words his characters used in the first place. But this glaring instance of pilfering from his novel suggests that literary fiction is peculiarly suited to imagining religion. By fleshing out various kinds of believers in their fiction, and by inviting readers to inhabit their faiths and fictional worlds, if only momentarily and vicariously, contemporary writers can help us understand the lived experience of religion and perhaps enliven the possibilities for pluralism.

"Does the leap of faith ever land?" Doctorow once mischievously asked.[94] To anyone who has been paying attention to religion in the twentieth and early twenty-first centuries, the answer must surely be no. But if the leap of faith never lands, does it not remain suspended over an abyss of doubts? Let us therefore leave Doctorow's quizzical question hanging, like the leap of faith itself, over the pages that follow.

1

"Cursed with Believing": Failed Apostasy in Flannery O'Connor's Fiction

Flannery O'Connor was a believer her entire life. She remained in the Catholic Church. Yet throughout her short career as a writer—truncated, of course, by her early death of lupus—the author worked under the assumption that most readers did not share her religious beliefs. In book reviews, essays, and letters she presumes again and again that for a majority of her readers the pervasive secularism of the mid-twentieth century had taken a toll on religion, to the point that, as O'Connor puts it, "the dissolution of belief is eventually inevitable."[1] In her view, even many self-identified Christians were at best only nominally Christian, either because they rejected doctrinal orthodoxy or because they had allowed their faith to become watered down. Others abandoned faith altogether. But there were still others like herself who took their faith seriously enough to examine it more carefully in light of what she called our unbelieving age:

> We live in an unbelieving age but one which is markedly and lopsidedly spiritual. ... At its best our age is an age of searchers and discoverers, and, at its worst, an age that has domesticated despair and learned to live with it happily. ... These unbelieving searchers have their effect even upon those of us who do believe. We begin to examine our own religious notions, to sound them for genuineness, to purify them in the heat of our unbelieving neighbor's anguish.[2]

In a posthumously published essay titled "The Catholic Novelist in the Protestant South" (1966), a lecture she delivered at Georgetown University in October 1963 (less than a year before she died), O'Connor again points out the precariousness of an essentially privatized, uprooted faith: "We live now in an age which doubts both fact and value, which is moved this way and that by momentary convictions, which regards religion as a purely private matter."[3] Unmoored from the Church and its traditions, she implies, believers would be hard-pressed to withstand the winds of change. Nor were they alone in this predicament. More than most writers, O'Connor understood that if religion was now a purely private matter, a religious writer could simply no longer assume that readers share a common faith: "Instead of reflecting a balance from the world around him, the novelist now has to *achieve* one by being a counterweight to the prevailing heresy."[4]

O'Connor elaborates on these insights in another essay titled "Novelist and Believer," written for a symposium on Religion and the Arts held at Sweet Briar College in March 1963 and reprinted, posthumously, in her book *Mystery and Manners: Occasional Prose* (1969). Here, O'Connor describes the conditions for holding *any* beliefs, whether religious or secular beliefs, in strikingly similar terms as Charles Taylor does in his important book *A Secular Age* (2007). "For the last few centuries," she writes, "we have lived in a world which has been increasingly convinced that the reaches of reality end very close to the surface, that there is no ultimate divine source, that the things of the world do not pour forth from God."[5] The supernatural had been discredited by the epistemological and metaphysical revolutions of modern science: "The supernatural is an embarrassment today even to many of the churches. The naturalistic bias has so well saturated our society that the reader doesn't realize that he has to shift his sights to read fiction which treats of an encounter with God."[6] For O'Connor, writing about religion now faced challenges that were not present for earlier writers. The immanent frame of a secular age made belief optional, and to some extent superfluous: "the believer no longer stands with his faith amid the concrete, actual world, and he no longer rediscovers that world by faith."[7]

The essay "Novelist and Believer" reflects how O'Connor responded to that predicament. Apparently, the invitation to speak at the 1963 symposium came with an admonition for invited participants to "conceive religion broadly as an expression of man's ultimate concern rather than identify it with institutional Judaism or Christianity or with 'going to church.'"[8] Such anti-institutionalism was all too common in the early 1960s, yet O'Connor predictably took umbrage at the implicit rejection of institutional religion. In a letter to her friends Robert and Sally Fitzgerald, with whom she had lived in Connecticut for two years starting in 1949 while working on *Wise Blood* (1952), O'Connor wrote, "I have just got back from the Symposium on Religion & Art at Sweet Briar and boy do I have a stomach full of liberal religion! The Devil had his day there ... but I waded in and gave them a nasty dose of orthodoxy, which I am sure they thought was pretty quaint."[9] O'Connor took the symposium as an opportunity to, as she puts it in her lecture, "enlarge your ideas of what religion is and of how the religious need may be expressed in the art of our time."[10] Speaking of two monotheistic religions, Judaism and Christianity, she insists that they remain important for understanding today's world: "The Judaeo-Christian tradition has formed us in the west; we are bound to it by ties which may often be invisible, but which are there nevertheless. It has formed the shape of our secularism; it has formed even the shape of our modern atheism."[11] The Judeo-Christian tradition concept emerged out of the religious pluralism of the period, yet O'Connor felt the specificity of these two Abrahamic religions was certainly worth preserving.[12] In other words, she did not accept the premise that institutionalized religion would be off limits: "For my part, I shall have to remain well within the Judaeo-Christian tradition. I shall have to speak, without apology, of the Church, even when the Church is absent; of Christ, even when Christ is not recognized."[13]

The lecture at Sweet Briar College highlights O'Connor's defiance against secularism, her determination to speak forthrightly about the Church and about Christ even though it was considered unfashionable ("quaint") to do so, for "nothing in this world lends itself to quick vaporization so much as the religious concern."[14] She evidently hoped to serve as a counterweight to liberalizing trends by giving her audience a nasty dose of orthodoxy, though she did concede some ground to the pluralist spirit of the conference by using the phrase

"Judeo-Christian tradition." In her private correspondence about the symposium, O'Connor curiously reverts back to the unabashedly enchanted language of spiritual warfare ("the devil had his day there"). Elsewhere, O'Connor similarly spoke about giving the devil his due "to an audience which does not believe in evil, or better, in the reality of a personal devil, in principalities and in powers."[15] Steeped in the Bible and Catholic theology, especially Thomas Aquinas, O'Connor often thought she would have felt more at home in the Middle Ages; she once likened herself to a "thirteenth century" Catholic, and later, even as she was dying of lupus, she joked that her crutches were like "flying buttresses," a startling metaphor that makes of her ailing body a gothic cathedral.[16] In short, she took on the burden of a strong believer in the age of disbelief.[17]

But if O'Connor was in one sense a walking anachronism—a medieval Catholic living in the modern Protestant South—she was at the same time a profoundly modern, reflexive believer. Responding to a student who had seen her give a lecture at Emory University in 1962 and who confessed in a letter that he was having doubts about his faith, O'Connor wrote: "I think that this experience you are having of losing your faith, or as you think, of having lost it, is an experience that in the long run belongs to faith."[18] She reassures him that one can hardly go on believing without coming to terms with doubt: "I don't know how the kind of faith required of the Christian living in the twentieth century can be at all if it is not grounded in this experience you are having right now of unbelief."[19] While she took the viability of unbelief in a secular age seriously, she insisted that doubt had always been an intrinsic part of faith, as evidenced by Saint Peter's "foundational prayer" of Christian faith: "Lord, I believe; help my unbelief."[20]

O'Connor counted herself among those believers who were trying, against all odds it often seemed, to stave off the inevitable dissolution of belief that she saw everywhere around her. She had a secret weapon in that effort, however. She would shore up belief by developing a remarkably coherent artistic and theological vision. As literary critic Jay Watson summarizes it:

Boiled down to its theological essentials, that vision rested on two elements. The first was a cosmological and epistemological emphasis on mystery, a conviction that the workings of the universe were ultimately unknowable, exceeding the limits of human perception and reason. The second was a deep belief in the radical incompleteness and dependence of humanity, a condition of ontological lack remediable only by and through otherness, an outside agency she identified with God's grace.[21]

O'Connor was especially concerned that Christians should be open and receptive to God's grace, and the major stumbling block to such receptivity, as she saw it, was a sense of self-sufficiency: "That human beings characteristically disavow their vulnerability and limitations, preferring to see themselves as self-actuating, coherent, and in control, was merely another symptom of their brokenness and imperfection."[22] More often than not, hubris proved fatal to grace.[23]

This vision remains consistent throughout her literary career. O'Connor wants to write short stories and novels that resist being subsumed under secular assumptions about art and life. Yet she always insisted that writers should not impose their views on readers: "I don't believe that you can impose orthodoxy on fiction. I do believe that you can deepen your own orthodoxy by reading if you are not afraid of strange visions."[24] The strange visions in her fiction are intended to deepen the mysteries of faith, not to resolve them.[25] Convinced that "we don't live in an age of settled belief" anymore, she envisioned herself as a sort of prophet of unsettled belief, an artist uniquely qualified to make belief believable or credible.[26] In a sense, secularism sanctioned rather than undermined O'Connor's highly religious artistic project, since she was writing against the grain. "Making belief believable to the contemporary reader is the almost insurmountable problem of the novelist who writes from the standpoint of Christian orthodoxy," O'Connor wrote in a review of Caroline Gordon's novel *The Malefactors* (1956).[27] And in the essay "Novelist and Believer" she repeats more or less the same point, although here she elaborates on *why* she considers the problem almost (but not quite) an insurmountable one:

> The problem of the novelist who wishes to write about a man's encounter with this God is how he shall make the experience—which is both natural and supernatural—understandable, and credible, to his reader. In any age this would be a problem, but in our own, it is a well-nigh insurmountable one. Today's audience is one in which religious feeling has become, if not atrophied, at least vaporous and sentimental.[28]

O'Connor wanted to make literary fiction reflect a stronger version of religious faith than the vaporous and sentimental forms of faith she found so prevalent even among those who might well have counted themselves among the faithful. "I am no disbeliever in spiritual purpose and no vague believer," she declared. "I see from the standpoint of Christian orthodoxy. This means that for me the meaning of life is centered in our Redemption by Christ and that what I see in the world I see in its relation to that. I don't think this is a position that can be taken halfway or one that is particularly easy in these times to make transparent in fiction."[29]

To make redemption transparent in fiction, while putting the requisite limitations on omniscience, O'Connor developed what many scholars have described as an incarnational or sacramental approach in which she attempts to render the supernatural immanent in her fiction.[30] Consider the following statement from her essay "The Church and the Fiction Writer" (1957):

> Many well-grounded complaints have been made about religious literature on the score that it tends to minimize the importance and dignity of life here and now in favor of life in the next world or in favor of the miraculous manifestations of grace. When fiction is made according to its nature, it should reinforce our sense of the supernatural by grounding it in concrete reality.[31]

This gets to the heart of O'Connor's approach to fiction, her artistic statement of faith, as it were. Far from trying "to prove the truth of the Faith" or "to prove the existence of the supernatural," O'Connor believes "that fiction can transcend its limitations only by staying within them."[32] Declaring allegiance to "the concrete" or what she calls the "what-is" as the "medium of fiction," she felt that supernatural or transcendent realities will "grow out of the necessities that lie in the material itself and these will generally be more rigorous than any religion could impose."[33]

Flannery O'Connor came of age as a writer at a moment when formalist New Criticism was being institutionalized as a critical practice, even as Creative Writing programs modeled on the Iowa Writers Workshop were sprouting up everywhere, as Mark McGurl has shown. No wonder she regarded that influential textbook of the period, *Understanding Fiction* (1943/1959) by Cleanth Brooks and Robert Penn Warren, as what she "resonantly" called a "bible" of sorts.[34] By training and temperament, she understood the "experiential intensity" that could be gained from third-person limited omniscient narration, and her greatest achievement, argues McGurl, was "to maximize the ironic distance between her focalizing characters and her disembodied narrators, and to attest thereby to the cognitive limits of any embodied life, including certainly the author's fragilely embodied own."[35] Insisting that there was something *beyond* our cognitive limitations, however, O'Connor's "third-person narration aspires to the unimaginable condition of 'fourth person' narration—narration from a higher dimension."[36] In the slim volume *A Prayer Journal* (2013), which she kept between 1946 and 1947 while a student at the University of Iowa, O'Connor wrote: "Please let Christian principles permeate my writing, and please let there be enough of my writing (published) for Christian principles to permeate."[37]

Like the conservative, evangelical movement that was at least in part a reaction against the countercultural and secularizing trends of this period, O'Connor learned to make the most of her opposition to the putatively secular culture surrounding her. The author's insistence that the culture *was* secular resonated with evangelicals themselves, even as the evangelical movement and the revivals associated with it in many ways belied that assessment. O'Connor's aesthetic approach aligned with the "write what you know" and "show don't tell" imperatives of postwar Creative Writing programs, yet the religious framework she employed to describe her approach would also appeal to a wide range of audiences. Generations of students discovered her fiction in high school and college classrooms and found it not only ready-made for close reading, but also amenable to their own sense of alienation from the dominant culture. Finally, and paradoxically, Christian evangelical readers embraced O'Connor as one of their own, despite her Catholicism.[38]

Secularization and Revival

In one of many letters to her friend Elizabeth "Betty" Hester, who is identified simply as "A" throughout the published correspondence, O'Connor complained, "One of the awful things about writing when you are a Christian is that for you the ultimate reality is the Incarnation, the present reality is the Incarnation, and nobody believes in the Incarnation; that is, nobody in your audience. My audience are the people who think God is dead. At least these are the people I am conscious of writing for."[39] The author surely knew that some readers believed in the doctrine of Incarnation—readers like her frequent interlocutor and fellow Catholic Betty Hester, for example—but they were not the people she was writing for; instead, she self-consciously wrote her novels and short stories for a skeptical if not downright "hostile audience."[40] This meant that she could not assume her readers would even know what she was talking about, much less agree with her. The challenge was to "produce something a little more palatable to the modern temper," without compromising her religious convictions or her religious vision.[41] The author summed up her oppositional approach in another letter to Betty Hester: "You have to push as hard as the age that pushes against you."[42]

O'Connor once wrote in a book review that the writer in question "seems able to assume an audience which has not lost its belief in Christian doctrine."[43] The implication is that she herself was not so naive; for her, readers were at best indifferent to and at worst ignorant of doctrine. We might wonder if the author's often-repeated claims about writing for a secular, unbelieving audience are somehow necessary for her fiction to work in the way she wants it to—namely, as a countervailing force against a dominant secularism. While critics generally take such claims at face value, in my view it is worth asking why she is so wedded to an oppositional stance.[44] What advantages did she gain by writing against the grain of the dominant culture?

I believe this posture allowed O'Connor to have her cake and eat it, too, which is to say that it allowed her to appear intellectually respectable for secular critics and readers while at the same time remaining suitably and strenuously doctrinal for her more religious-minded readers. O'Connor sometimes found occasion to portray herself as seasoned by modernist philosophies. "I am a Catholic peculiarly possessed of the modern consciousness," she wrote. "To possess this *within* the Church is to bear a burden, the necessary burden for the conscious Catholic."[45] Thomas Merton considered her to be one of our most existentialist writers: "I can think of no other American writer who has made a more devastating use of existentialist institutions."[46] She took pride in being open to new ideas—the necessary burden for the conscious Catholic—for "belief in fixed dogma cannot fix what goes on in life or blind the believer to it."[47]

There were a number of reasons for O'Connor to assume that religion was under duress when she began her career in the aftermath of the Second World War. She was certainly not alone in calling attention to a growing secularism among intellectuals of the postwar period. One Catholic theologian whom O'Connor much admired, Romano Guardini, wrote in his book *The End of the Modern World: A Search for Orientation* (1956) that many people had lost their way amidst the "fogs of secularism" that now clouded everything.[48] In a world rent asunder by atomic weapons, genocide, and totalitarianism, it was not difficult to view religion as irrelevant if not obsolete.

Whatever the reasons for the "negative appearance" of religion in the period, however, O'Connor was convinced that "if you live today you breathe in nihilism. In or out of the Church, it's the gas you breathe."[49] It is difficult not to sense that the gas chambers at Auschwitz might lie behind this startling metaphor. Like many writers and intellectuals, O'Connor certainly understood that the Nazi concentration camps dealt a singularly devastating blow to faith in God, placing a special burden on believers to confront the age-old problem of theodicy: how could a benevolent, sovereign God allow such suffering? Referring to Hannah Arendt's account of Nazi war criminal Adolf Eichmann's trial in 1961, which appeared in *The New Yorker* in March 1963 and was subsequently published as *Eichmann in Jerusalem* (1963), O'Connor was stunned by the sheer scale of suffering in the Holocaust: "I am reading Eichmann in Jerusalem. Anything is credible after such a period of history. I've always been haunted by the boxcars, but they were actually the least of it."[50]

In O'Connor's early story "The Displaced Person," published in *Sewanee Review* in 1954 and included in her first short story collection *A Good Man Is Hard to Find* (1955), the priest has brought a Polish family displaced by the war to work for Mrs. McIntyre, who comes out of the house to greet them "wearing her best clothes and a string of beads" as the woman's other hired help, Mrs. Shortley, watches the scene.[51] In a passage that slides into free-indirect discourse, O'Connor characteristically undercuts the knowing self-assurance of Mrs. Shortley:

> Mrs. Shortley recalled a newsreel she had seen once of a small room piled high with bodies of dead naked people all in a heap, their arms and legs tangled together. ... Before you could realize that it was real and take it into your head, the picture changed and a hollow-sounding voice was saying, "Time marches on!" This was the kind of thing that was happening every day in Europe where they had not advanced as in this country, and watching from her vantage point, Mrs. Shortley had the sudden intuition that the Gobblehooks, like rats with typhoid fleas, could have carried all those murderous ways over the water with them directly to this place. If they had come from where that kind of thing was done to them, who was to say they were not the kind that would also do it to others? The width and breadth of this question nearly shook her. Her stomach trembled as if there had been a slight quake in the heart of the mountain and automatically she moved down

from her elevation and went forward to be introduced to them, as if she meant to find out at once what they were capable of.[52]

O'Connor was self-aware enough to know that she was far removed from the European theater; hence she was not in the best position to grapple with the full implications of the Holocaust. The question about what effects such "murderous ways" would have on those who witnessed them was not to be taken lightly; Mrs. Shortley's smug moral superiority is the wrong response. While O'Connor obviously witnessed the Second World War from the relative security of her home in the South, it is clear that the devastating events of the war compelled her to reconsider her own way of life: "So far as I am concerned as a novelist, a bomb on Hiroshima affects my judgment of life in rural Georgia."[53] Indeed, they led her to question everything she took for granted. Writing in the aftermath of the war, her "gravest concern" as she once put it was how to portray "the conflict between an attraction for the Holy and the disbelief in it we breathe in with the air of the times. It's hard to believe always but more so in the world we live in now."[54]

This conviction that unbelief permeated the very air we breathe derives more from her sympathy with intellectual trends of the day, however, than from actual declines in religious adherence, at least in the United States. Indeed, religious identification was increasing in the 1950s when her fiction first appeared, not waning. According to sociologist Will Herberg, in 1953 fully 95 percent of Americans declared themselves to be either Protestants, Catholics, or Jews, and only 5percent chose "no preference" as their religious affiliation; moreover, church membership was at "an all-time high in the nation's history," at nearly 60 percent of the population.[55] In his widely read *Protestant-Catholic-Jew* (1955), Herberg argued that a "new religiosity pervading America" basically validated "the social patterns and cultural values associated with the American Way of Life," amounting to nothing less than a sort of "national messianism" that lent evangelical fervor to the desire on the part of many to spread democracy "to every corner of the globe."[56]

The interplay between America's religiosity and its most cherished values—not least the deeply held notion that capitalism was superior to Communism—also gave rise to a remarkable reinsertion of religion into the public sphere. This public religiosity was decidedly nonsectarian. A month before his inauguration as president, Dwight D. Eisenhower declared, "Our form of Government has no sense unless it is founded in a deeply felt religious faith—and I don't care what it is."[57] For President Eisenhower, the problem was how to make our religious differences a source of unity rather than division, and the answer was a stronger form of religious pluralism. "In our fundamental faith we are all one," he declared in 1953. "Whatever our individual church, whatever our personal creed, our common faith in God is a common bond among us."[58]

Eisenhower's advocacy of religious pluralism reflects a growing trend toward nonsectarian, interdenominational, or nondenominational religious organizations such as the National Council of Churches, which was founded in 1950 to promote "greater unity" among different denominations and religions.[59] There were those who refused to let their beliefs be "dissolved into an over-all American religion," including orthodox Catholics and the "many holiness, Pentecostal and millenarian sects," who regarded such efforts as an emptying out of faith.[60] Yet Eisenhower rejoiced in the fact that the nation was growing more religious, not less, a fact he admitted might seem counterintuitive to those who assumed that secularism was more and more dominant. "Contrary to what many people think," Eisenhower told an assembly of the World Council of Churches in 1954, "the percentage of our population belonging to churches steadily increases."[61] George Gallup, Jr., corroborates Eisenhower's claim, describing the "religious revival" of the 1950s as a time of rapid growth in church membership: "Modern American religious belief and practice attained its peak during the 1950s, before the social upheavals of the 1960s and 1970s took their toll on most institutions, including religion."[62]

Against the backdrop of the Cold War, assertions of religious vitality were politicized. "The world is divided into two camps!" Billy Graham thundered. "Communism ... has declared war against God, against Christ, against the Bible, and against all religion! ... Unless the Western world has an old-fashioned revival, we cannot last!"[63] What distinguishes this broad national religious revival from earlier ones is that it occurred during a time when pluralism and secularism exerted greater influence. Religious practice was more robust, as church attendance surged, yet it was compartmentalized and privatized. A therapeutic search for self and success increasingly severed religion from its historical roots. Billy Graham's so-called crusades may have invoked the Middle Ages in name, but they were not the tent revivals of old-time religion. Beginning in Los Angeles in 1949, they were distinctly modern and forward-looking. By 1957, Graham presided over a mass religious revival that attracted some 2.3 million attendees and ran for sixteen weeks at Madison Square Garden and Yankee stadium. The most famous evangelist since Billy Sunday, he appeared on the cover of *Time* magazine in 1954, and two years later he was a cofounder of *Christianity Today* magazine, whose title signals its ecumenical orientation. Exploiting the mass media, Graham was a modern evangelist whose movement contributed to even as it reflected a larger shift away from church-centered religious practices toward a more eclectic, therapeutic spirituality. As Graham himself once wrote, "The greatest need in America at the moment is for a moral and spiritual renewal. This comes, I believe, *only* as we turn in repentance and faith to the living God, Who stands ready to forgive and renew us from within."[64] Graham's emphasis on personal renewal fostered a new nondenominational evangelicalism.[65]

The postwar period also saw the emergence of new religious movements, which sought to capitalize on "elective affinity" as a pressing concern for many people in choosing their religion. The Church of Scientology, founded in Los Angeles in 1953, was fueled, in part, by L. Ron Hubbard's bestselling book *Dianetics: The Modern Science of Mental Health* (1950). "In the early phase of Dianetics," writes Hugh B. Urban, "Hubbard made no attempt to define his new science of the mind as anything having to do with religion. Yet throughout the 1950s, '60s, and '70s, in response to a variety of internal and external pressures, Hubbard began to increasingly pursue what he called the 'religion angle.'"[66] Indeed, Hubbard basically invented a new religion.

Both a revitalized American Protestantism and new religious movements exemplify an inward turn or privatization of religion, even if these phenomena appear to be public in nature. In another highly popular book, *Gift from the Sea* (1955), Anne Morrow Lindberg urged readers "to realize that the kingdom of heaven is within."[67] While church attendance offered the nation a "great centering force," Lindberg stressed that churchgoing provided an insufficient barrier to counteract the eroding influences of mass culture: "How can a single weekly hour of church, helpful as it may be, counteract the many daily hours of distraction that surround it?"[68] To meet their spiritual needs, Americans would have to look elsewhere, and for Lindberg that meant looking inward: "The cell of self-knowledge is the stall in which the pilgrim must be reborn."[69]

How could so many different forms of religion and spirituality thrive in what to most cultural observers appeared to be a more distracted, restless, and predominantly secular culture? Cultural responses to the powerful secularizing trends of the period varied widely, to be sure. Whereas conservative churches doubled down on anti-modernist populism, liberal churches were "irresistibly pulled toward values and attitudes prevalent in the academic world."[70] Like Updike, O'Connor was prescient about how liberal Protestants capitulated to therapeutic individualism:

> One of the effects of modern liberal Protestantism has been gradually to turn religion into poetry and therapy, to make truth vaguer and vaguer and more and more relative, to banish intellectual distinctions, to depend on feeling instead of thought and gradually to come to believe that God has no power, that he cannot communicate with us, cannot reveal himself to us, indeed has not done so, and that religion is our own sweet invention.[71]

O'Connor's criticism was couched in her trademark humor, but it was trenchant nonetheless. "Scratch an Episcopalian and you're liable to find most anything," she remarked with evident relish to a priest.[72]

Yet she did not exempt Catholics from her withering sarcasm: "If the average Catholic reader could be tracked down through the swamps of letters-to-the-editor and other places where he momentarily reveals himself, he would be found more of a Manichean than the Church permits. By separating nature and grace as much as possible, he has reduced his conception of the supernatural to a pious cliché."[73] Whether disoriented by the fogs of secularism or bogged down in the swamps of sanctimonious letters to the editor, Protestants and Catholics alike were guilty, albeit in different ways, of allowing their convictions to devolve into nothing more than pious clichés. Echoing O'Connor's bleak diagnosis, Will Herberg argued that the "religion which actually prevails among Americans today has lost much of its authentic Christian (or Jewish) content," becoming "so empty and contentless, so conformist, so utilitarian, so sentimental, so individualistic, and so self-righteous" as to be unrecognizable as religion.[74]

Watered-down versions of religious faith were driven in part by an underlying anxiety of doubt. Paul Tillich, the most famous theologian of the period, argued in the last sentence of his influential book *The Courage to Be* (1952) that religiously inclined people must rediscover their faith "in the God who appears when God has disappeared in the anxiety of doubt."[75] Tillich later appeared on the cover of *Time* magazine in 1959 under the banner "A Theology for Protestants," yet his theology was thoroughly ecumenical. Over the course of his storied career as a professor and public theologian, he developed what we might call a theology of doubt, bringing faith to the faithless and doubt to the faithful. He also took his message to the masses. In his essay "The Lost Dimension in Religion" (1958), which appeared in the popular magazine *The Saturday Evening Post*, Tillich wrote: "Such an idea of religion makes religion universally human. But it certainly differs from what is usually called religion. It does not describe religion as the belief in gods or one God, and as a set of activities and institutions for the sake of relating oneself to these beings in thought, devotion and obedience." Tillich mines the same anti-institutional vein here that O'Connor will object to in her speech at Sweet Briar College three years later. He insists that many people "take the question of the meaning of their life infinitely seriously and reject any historical religion just for this reason. ... They are religious while rejecting the religions." This was a rapidly expanding demographic category in the period, yet Tillich believed that a concern for meaning was actually diminishing. Hence the "lost dimension" that he points to in his title: "Man in our time has lost such infinite concern. And the resurgence of religion is nothing but a desperate and mostly futile attempt to regain what has been lost."[76] Tillich wants to recover some depth in our religious concerns, but without recourse to religion in the narrower sense of theism.

Notwithstanding historical evidence of religious resilience and revival in America, then, O'Connor put her finger on some troubling trends. She took the secular tenor of the times to mean that religiosity in all its manifestations was being tested and transformed. Ironically, her fiction has been perhaps most celebrated by Christian readers—Catholic and Protestant alike—who regard her as one of the preeminent religious writers in American literature. The irony of this embrace by the Christian literati would not have been lost on the author, who had a wicked sense of humor and cultivated a deeply antagonistic relationship with her readers. In a visit to Notre Dame at the invitation of Robert Fitzgerald, for instance, she complained that she felt like a "displaced person" among the "Cathlick interleckchuls."[77] We might assume that she would have felt comfortable at a Catholic university; surely this would be one place where, in the words of her biographer Brad Gooch, "she could unveil her Christian subtext."[78] This visit was the occasion for one of her best-known speeches about being a Catholic writer. "When you can assume that your audience holds the same beliefs you do," she remarked, "you can relax a little and use more normal means of talking to it; when you have to assume that it does not, then you have to make your vision apparent by shock—to the hard of hearing you shout, and for the almost-blind you draw large and startling figures."[79]

As this often-quoted statement suggests, O'Connor developed a kind of aesthetic shock treatment. Drawing from the gothic mode in much Southern fiction, she infused her stories with grotesque humor and horrific violence.[80] "In my own experience," she informs us, "everything funny I have written is more terrible than it is funny, or only funny because it is terrible, or only terrible because it is funny."[81] What distinguishes O'Connor's Southern gothic is not just its dark comedy, but also the fact that it is so insistently religious. She herself insisted that "writers who see by the light of their Christian faith will have, in these times, the sharpest eyes for the grotesque, for the perverse, and for the unacceptable."[82] Given the evident gulf between the predominantly secular world and the spiritually charged atmosphere of her fiction, her characters may seem willfully perverse. In a 1962 "Author's Note" to the second edition of *Wise Blood* (1952), O'Connor writes about one consequence of such a disparity: "That belief in Christ is to some a matter of life and death has been a stumbling block for readers who would prefer to think of it as a matter of no great consequence."[83] In a world where belief doesn't really matter much, it is the anomaly that has to be explained. As O'Connor declares elsewhere:

> A secular society understands the religious mind less and less. It becomes more and more difficult in America to make belief believable, which is what the novelist has to do. It takes less and less belief acted upon to make one appear a fanatic. When you create a character who believes vigorously in Christ, you have to explain his aberration.[84]

Making belief believable: if strong forms of religious belief had come to seem like an aberration, then believers will necessarily look like fanatics or freaks. This helps explain why O'Connor saw her characters' blatant fanaticism as "a reproach" and "not merely an eccentricity."[85] The question is: a reproach for what, exactly?[86]

Preaching Blasphemy

O'Connor's first novel *Wise Blood* established the gothic mode, Southern settings, and obsession with religious doubt that would become a hallmark of much of her subsequent fiction. Published when the author was twenty-seven years old, *Wise Blood* features as its protagonist one Hazel Motes, a misanthropic would-be preacher who takes umbrage at being mistaken for a minister. With "eyes the color of pecan shells, set deep in his sockets," a suit of "glaring blue" that cost him $11.98, and a hat like that of "an elderly country preacher," Hazel Motes looks like nothing so much as an itinerant Southern preacher.[87] "You look like a preacher," the taxi driver tells him matter-of-factly when he arrives in the city. "That hat looks like a preacher's hat."[88] Motes flatly rejects the identification: "'Listen,' he said, 'get this: I don't believe in anything.'"[89] Curiously, the driver doesn't accept his denial: "That's the trouble with you preachers. … You've all got too good to believe in anything."[90] Later, when the driver drops him off at Mrs. Leora Watts's house, he seems puzzled by the fact that, as he puts it, "She don't usually have no preachers for company."[91] The driver's misidentification of Hazel Motes as a preacher anticipates the difficulty that readers will have in making sense of this enigmatic character, the first of many misfits in O'Connor's work. But it may also reflect changing cultural expectations about what preachers are supposed to believe and how they are expected to behave in the South.

Hazel Motes's fanaticism stands in stark contrast to the bland, complacent religiosity of other characters. "Do you think I believe in Jesus?" he asks a stranger on the train. "Well, I wouldn't even if he existed. Even if he was on this train."[92] The woman's response to this unsolicited provocation is telling. In a "poisonous Eastern voice," she replies, "who said you had to?"[93] Like the taxi driver and Mrs. Watts, this woman too is nonplussed by Hazel Motes's atheism. Considering the novel's Bible-belt setting, it seems reasonable to ask whether these characters would have taken such aggressive protestations of atheism so lightly. Yet as the narrator's offhand reference to the woman's "poisonous Eastern voice" suggests, O'Connor needed such characters to represent a growing apathy about religious matters, not least among intellectuals. For O'Connor, religion was in jeopardy not just because of serious challenges to Christian faith from recent historical events or existential philosophy, but also because of a growing discomfort with dogmatism, as the woman's nonchalance about whether he believes or not surely hints. Motes envisions his own ministry as an affront to emerging middle-class norms that viewed religious adherence less as a guarantee of right belief than as a measure of social propriety: it's not whether you believe that mattered, but whether or not you look like you do. Hazel Motes wants to disabuse everyone he encounters of such unexamined social conformity.[94]

The historical and psychological origins of Hazel Motes's atheism are not hard to find.[95] From his upbringing, he acquires "a deep black wordless conviction in him that the way to avoid Jesus was to avoid sin."[96] His grandfather was an itinerant preacher, "with Jesus hidden in his head like a stinger," and a young Hazel Motes used to accompany him as they "traveled three counties in a Ford automobile," asking everyone they met the same question, "Did they doubt?"[97] Hazel Motes will later insist that doubt disqualifies him from being a preacher. During his time as a solider during the First World War, he meets other men who are openly hostile to religion. When he tries to articulate his fundamentalist views about salvation, one soldier bitterly replies, "Nobody was interested in his goddamn soul unless it was the priest."[98] By the time he gets back from Europe, Motes is "thoroughly convinced" that he no longer believes in Christianity, and "he saw that this was something he had always known."[99]

These formative early experiences provide Hazel Motes with a model for his own brand of evangelism, which he adapts for a different purpose: to establish a new anti-religious church. Motes is curiously somewhat like the linoleum prints that O'Connor created in her early work as a cartoonist, for as Barry Moser tells us in his introduction to a collection of her cartoon work, linoleum prints involve "working backward" by cutting away the negative space to reveal the intended image.[100] Similarly, Motes is the negative space that reveals a positive image for readers with eyes to see it. When a writer "has a freak for his hero," O'Connor explains in a different context, "he is not simply showing us what we are, but what we have been and what we could become. His prophet-freak is an image of himself."[101] In her essay "Some

Remarks on the Grotesque in Southern Fiction," she elaborates that freaks "can be very fierce and instructive. ... [I]t is when the freak can be sensed as a figure for our essential displacement that he attains some depth in literature."[102] Not all readers will recognize her prophet freaks as figures for our essential displacement, however; some readers will simply regard them as freaks. "There is a moment in every great story," as she puts it, "in which the presence of grace can be felt as it waits to be accepted or rejected, even though the reader may not recognize this moment."[103] One character mistakes Hazel Motes for a preacher and therefore has no interest in what he has to say, but she is wrong about him, since preachers in the South did not try to convert people to atheism. She does not perceive that this cartoonish prophet freak represents our "essential displacement," which is to say that in our fallen condition as humans we are utterly dependent on God's grace.

In *Wise Blood*, O'Connor stages a sort of old-time tent revival in a small Southern town, in which several sidewalk preachers compete against each other to attract followers. A makeshift and improvised affair, this fictional tent revival is nothing like Billy Graham's massive crusades. In May 1952, the same month *Wise Blood* was published, Billy Graham took his campaign on the road, staging revivals in Florida, Texas, and Mississippi. O'Connor's fictional preachers have neither the charisma nor the charm that made Graham the most famous evangelist in the world. Like other literary representations of revivalism, such as Sinclair Lewis's *Elmer Gantry* (1927), *Wise Blood* is a scathing critique of revivalism, as O'Connor's preachers are basically hucksters. The apparently blind preacher Asa Hawks, whom we later discover is not blind, first puts Hazel Motes's apostasy to the test when he confronts him outside the movie theater with the statement, "Jesus is a fact," to which the Motes responds: "Nothing matters but that Jesus don't exist."[104]

Hazel Motes inaugurates his own evangelistic ministry outside a movie theater, where he confronts moviegoers coming out of the theater with odd questions like, "Where has the blood you think you been redeemed by touched you?"[105] When a boy replies that he attends the Church of Christ, Hazel seizes upon the name for his own church, which he calls the Holy Church of Christ Without Christ. Unlike the Church of Christ, however, the Holy Church of Christ Without Christ is one that, as Motes insists from the start of his ministry, "the blood of Jesus don't foul with redemption."[106] In other words, what Hazel Motes preaches is a peculiarly fundamentalist brand of modern disbelief: "I preach there are all kinds of truth, your truth and somebody else's, but behind all of them, there's only one truth and that's the truth that there is no truth."[107] As in a photographic negative, this is precisely the inverse of what one would expect of a preacher. Hazel Motes is peddling a frankly anti-religious message.

This message is surely meant to be as confrontational and off-putting as possible, in contrast to the soft-pedaling of religious doctrines and moral obligations promulgated by others in the novel. Another equally shady character is Hoover Shoats, for example, who goes by the name of Onnie Jay Holy. Like Motes, he has no formal education or special calling to ministry, and his message is also similar to that of Motes, except that Holy emphasizes the undemanding, no-strings-attached quality of his ministry. As Onnie Jay Holy tells the crowd that has assembled around him, "I wouldn't have you believe nothing you can't feel in your own hearts."[108] This version of affective or experiential faith strikes a chord with many listeners. It resembles the radical subjectivism of the postwar "gospel of self-realization" disseminated by Norman Vincent Peal in his best-selling book *The Power of Positive Thinking* (1952), published the same year as *Wise Blood*, even as it also presages the essentially pluralistic idea that everyone is entitled to his or her own version of truth.[109] Perhaps unsurprisingly, Hazel Motes takes issue with this idea. "Blasphemy is the way to truth," he insists, "whether you understand it or not."[110]

Sabbath Lily Hawks is another character in *Wise Blood* trying to make sense of what O'Connor rightly perceived as an emergent therapeutic individualism in mid-twentieth-century America. Early in the novel, Sabbath tells Motes that she had once written to advice columnist Mary Brittle about whether necking was acceptable, because she herself was an illegitimate child and cannot "enter the kingdom of heaven anyway so I don't see what difference it makes."[111] The advice columnist responds: "Your real problem is one of adjustment to the modern world. Perhaps you ought to re-examine your religious values to see if they meet your needs in Life. A religious experience can be a beautiful addition to living if you put it in proper perspective and do not let it warp you. Read some books on Ethical Culture."[112] The passage clearly satirizes the therapeutic ethos that influenced even the most traditional forms of religion at mid-century.

O'Connor is not content merely to satirize that ethos; she wants to offer alternatives. In Hazel Motes's earnest and tortured struggle with his religious background, she provides readers with glimpses of what a more authentic faith, or at least a less superficial one, might look like. The author seems determined to make Hazel Motes confront his own demons. As if unable to outrun the proverbial Hound of Heaven, the character cannot escape his fate. When his mother once admonished him, "Jesus died to redeem you," Motes had replied, "I never ast him."[113] In an early review that appeared in the Catholic journal, *Commonweal*, John W. Simon interestingly described *Wise Blood* as "a kind of Southern-Baptist version of *The Hound of Heaven*," referring to Francis Thompson's beloved 1909 poem about a man being relentlessly pursued by God, but he then mistakenly claims: "Nobody here is redeemed because there is nobody to redeem."[114] The claim is mistaken because redemption is precisely what O'Connor has in mind for the novel. "I don't intend the tone of the book to be pessimistic," she remarked in a letter to Helen Greene, one of her former professors at the Georgia State College for Women. "It is after all a story about redemption and if you don't admit redemption, you are no pessimist. The gist of the story is that H. Motes couldn't really believe that he hadn't been redeemed."[115]

In what would become O'Connor's trademark plot device, violence brings redemption. The crisis occurs when Onnie Jay Holy brings along another preacher of sorts, Solace Layfield, to help win converts to their fledgling church. Motes antagonizes this newly hired prophet by accusing him of hypocrisy. For Motes, the question of belief is paramount—you either believe or you don't. Other characters vacillate, sliding easily between belief and unbelief. Hazel accuses the preacher of denying what he actually believes: "You ain't true. ... You believe in Jesus."[116] Recall the Presbyterian minister Clarence Wilmot's personal agony after suffering a crisis of faith in the opening pages of John Updike's *In the Beauty of the Lilies* (1996): how can he go on preaching when he is no longer a believer? Here, the question Motes puts to Solace Layfield is something like: how can you preach the opposite of what you in fact believe? Motes simply cannot abide this hypocrisy, obsessed as he is with being true to one's beliefs: "Two things I can't stand," Haze said, "—a man that ain't true and one that mocks what is. You shouldn't have tampered with me if you didn't want what you got."[117] He murders the false prophet by running over him in his newly acquired Essex automobile, an act of unaccountable violence that compels him to undertake gruesome penance at the end by gouging out his eyes. This horrific ending has tripped up more than a few critics, who fail to grasp that from a Catholic point of view, his only chance for atonement is through penance.[118]

What ultimately saves Hazel Motes is that he cannot deny the existence of God. That is, he is a failed apostate who blasphemes against God but cannot finally evade God's claim on him. When Motes drives by a billboard announcing "Jesus Died for YOU," he looks at it but refuses to register its true import, "he saw and deliberately did not read it," a moment of willed disbelief that encapsulates his entire career as a would-be prophet.[119] Like the billboard receding in his rearview mirror, God remains a felt presence hovering over Motes even as he forsakes Him. God is ever present, watching his every move. Try as he might, Motes just cannot get rid of God.

Early reviewers did not perceive the novel's religious content for what it was. As Brian Wilkie observes, "Almost no reviewer read the novel as any kind of religious affirmation."[120] More precisely, they did not grasp that Motes's failed apostasy was in fact a form of redemption. Sounding somewhat exasperated, O'Connor found herself explaining to one perplexed reader:

> Let me assure you that no one but a Catholic could have written Wise Blood even though it is about a kind of Protestant saint. … And of course no unbeliever or agnostic could have written it because it is entirely Redemption-centered in thought. Not too many people are willing to see this, and perhaps it is hard to see because H. Motes is such an admirable nihilist. His nihilism leads him back to the fact of his Redemption, which is what he would have liked so much to get away from.[121]

Ten years later, in the "Author's Note to the Second Edition" of *Wise Blood* I mentioned earlier, O'Connor was still at pains to instruct readers on how to make sense of the horrific self-blinding that occurs, Oedipus-like, in the novel's conclusion. It was a mistake to think that Hazel Motes would be enlightened if he could only escape his fundamentalist views. For readers who see him as benighted,

> Hazel Motes' integrity lies in his trying with such vigor to get rid of the ragged figure who moves from tree to tree in the back of his mind. For the author Hazel's integrity lies in his not being able to. Does one's integrity ever lie in what he is not able to do? I think that usually it does, for free will does not mean one will, but many wills conflicting in one man.[122]

With the publication of her first short story collection *A Good Man Is Hard to Find* in June 1955, O'Connor's reputation as a writer became more closely associated with her religion. Above all, though, it was paratexts such as prefaces, essays, and letters that shaped how her fiction is read.

Heresy and the Art of Fiction

Trained at the fabled University of Iowa Writers Workshop, where she absorbed the narrative techniques and presuppositions about literature promulgated by the New Criticism, O'Connor employed limited omniscience to great effect as a means of exploring what I have called suspending disbelief, a sort of cognitive dissonance that allows someone to believe and disbelieve at the same time. "Suspending disbelief" is an apt term to describe the dialectic between belief and unbelief at work in these stories, for faith in O'Connor's fiction often sneaks up on her characters even as they try to fight it. Faith arrives unbidden at the most inopportune moments, often after enduring some terrifying ordeal, or experiencing a sudden, shocking event that shakes them out of their smug complacency. "Flannery O'Connor wrote many stories about people who are convinced that they are not believers but stumble onto God on their way somewhere else," Cheryl Walker has observed. "In O'Connor's world people are stalked by the Lord, who inevitably gets them in the end since the unconscious, for O'Connor, always seems to harbor the Holy Ghost, and the Hound of Heaven is relentless."[123]

In much of O'Connor's short fiction, written in the span of less than two decades and collected in two masterful short story collections published during her lifetime, she continues to probe into the recesses of her characters' minds to reveal all manner of delusions, foibles, and deeply troubled psyches. Far from empathetic, much less heroic, O'Connor's characters tend to be fairly despicable on the whole, as if to throw readers off the trail of redemption that may or may not come their way. How any of these characters could be made in the image of God, one might ask. Her penchant for writing about freaks is well known. Less noted is her theological conviction that every human being, no matter how unworthy, is eligible for unconditional grace. She regarded her backwoods prophets, Michael Mears Bruner tells us, with an "almost primal, filial empathy as a fellow sufferer on the road to redemption."[124] The only question worth asking, for the author, is whether they are willing to accept God's grace.[125]

In "A Good Man Is Hard to Find," the title story of her debut collection of short stories, the Misfit cannot bring himself to believe in Jesus because he did not witness the resurrection in person. "Before encountering the grandmother," writes Thomas Hill Schaub, "the Misfit had developed a logic by which he could live, but it was a logic that required disbelief."[126] Like so many of O'Connor's apostate characters, however, the Misfit cannot help but take Christianity seriously, and he fully understands what is at stake in his decision: "If He did what He said, then it's nothing for you to do but thow away everything and follow Him, and if He didn't, then it's nothing for you to do but enjoy the few minutes you got left the best way you can—by killing somebody or burning down his house or doing some other meanness to him."[127] In the end, the Misfit chooses to reject it: "He shouldn't have done it. He thown everything off balance."[128]

Unaware of the Misfit's uncompromising position, the grandmother insists that he is a gentleman who would never murder a "lady" like herself, following the moral code of chivalry.[129] Then, in a remarkable and unaccountable gesture of compassion, she reaches out to touch him, causing the Misfit to spring back "as if a snake had bitten him."[130] The grandmother's gesture is the most redemptive thing she has ever done: "Her head clears for an instant and she realizes, even in her limited way, that she is responsible for the man before her and joined to him by ties of kinship which have their roots deep in the mystery she has merely been prattling about so far."[131] O'Connor elaborates on the theological implications of this scene:

> There is a moment of grace in most of the stories, or a moment where it is offered, and is usually rejected. Like when the Grandmother recognizes the Misfit as one of her own children and reaches out to touch him. It's the moment of grace for her anyway—a silly old woman—but it leads him to shoot her. This moment of grace excites the devil to frenzy.[132]

Typical of her work, it takes a harrowing encounter with the Misfit for the grandmother to arrive at such a moment of clarity. As she once told an audience at Hollins College in Virginia in 1962: "I have found that violence is strangely capable of returning my characters to reality and preparing them to accept their moment of grace."[133] Bringing her characters face to face with such brutal acts of violence, O'Connor sought to jar them out of their self-sufficiency.

Critical attention to "A Good Man Is Hard to Find," O'Connor's most anthologized story, benefitted from a better understanding of the author's religious intentions. More informed than her earliest reviewers of *Wise Blood*, literary critics were less likely to miss—or simply dismiss—the story's obvious theological content. "The Grandmother's gesture testifies to her belief," Schaub rightly observes, and moreover it "violates the consistency of the Misfit's protective logic and removes his last line of defense against the mystery of existence."[134] David Williams argues that the grandmother's social conformity may be more troubling to the author than the Misfit's fanaticism: "O'Connor's perspicuous critique of modern society reveals that few disbelievers go as far in their convictions as the Misfit and that most believers, like the Grandmother, are really make-believe believers content to observe the social conventions that include religion, as long as religion is kept in its place."[135] Counterpoised with such "make-believe believers," prophet freaks raise the stakes of belief considerably. By murdering the grandmother and her family, the Misfit assures his damnation, yet his apostasy is nonetheless an affront to weak belief, as if O'Connor hoped to beat the heretics at their own game. Of course, she was also theologically sophisticated enough to understand that the antidote to heresy was not more heresy but humility.

One of the great psychopaths in American literature, the Misfit is quite possibly the only apostate figure in O'Connor's fiction who remains one. Yet neither the Misfit's nihilism nor his brutal, cold-blooded murder of the grandmother at point-blank range is the real crux of the story. The story's true purpose is not even to give the petty grandmother her comeuppance. Rather, it is her acceptance of grace. The story is a prime example of how O'Connor often accomplishes her purposes indirectly, at the risk of obscuring the all-important theological subtext. In this instance, O'Connor perhaps unwittingly made the Misfit a far more fascinating figure than she intended.

"Remember that you don't write a story because you have an idea," she would respond, "but because you have a believable character."[136] This gets to the heart of O'Connor's aesthetics. She was not a dogmatist, and she sought to make her fiction similarly nondogmatic, even as she also tried to embody truths about religious faith and human experience in her fiction. "Although I am a Catholic writer," she once wrote, "I don't care to get labeled as such in the popular sense of it, as it is then assumed that you have some religious axe to grind."[137]

As a corollary to her insistence that writers must not have an axe to grind, O'Connor also felt that readers should favor literal meanings over symbolic meanings. "The meaning of a story has to be embodied in it, has to be made concrete in it," she declared. "The meaning of fiction is not abstract meaning but experienced meaning."[138] Thus, O'Connor berated one well-meaning professor who wrote to ask her whether the Misfit exists only in Bailey's imagination:

> Bailey, we believe, imagines the appearance of the Misfit. ... Bailey, we further believe, identifies himself with the Misfit and so plays two roles in the imaginary last half of the story. But we cannot, after great effort, determine the point at which reality fades into illusion or reverie. Does the accident literally occur, or is it part of Bailey's dream?[139]

O'Connor did not mince words: "The interpretation of your ninety students and three teachers is fantastic and about as far from my intentions as it could get to be."[140] "If it were a legitimate interpretation," she adds, "the story would be little more than a trick and its interest would be simply for abnormal psychology. I am not interested in abnormal psychology. ... My tone is not meant to be obnoxious. I am in a state of shock."[141] O'Connor felt that fiction should be interpreted literally and straightforwardly. "Everything has to operate first on the literal level," she insisted. "Too much interpretation is certainly worse than too little, and where feeling for a story is absent, theory will not supply it."[142] The danger of over-interpretation arises whenever the reader overlooks the obvious meanings and goes in search of symbolic meanings. Writing to yet another hapless English teacher, O'Connor resorted to a curious culinary metaphor for interpretive overreach, "I think you folks sometimes strain the soup too thin."[143] O'Connor could be equally critical of readers who missed important cues in her fiction, however. She called out a critic for lacking basic religious literacy: "Can it be possible that a man with this much learning knows so little about Christianity?"[144] By including biblical allusions or spiritually supercharged moments in her fiction, she dared readers to recognize them as such.

Consider the short story "Good Country People," also from *A Good Man Is Hard to Find*. Having lost her leg in a hunting accident when she was no more than a child, Joy Hopewell now lives with her mother, Mrs. Hopewell, with whom she has a contentious relationship at best. The story almost certainly reflects O'Connor's experience upon returning to live with her mother at the farmhouse Andalusia in Georgia after she was diagnosed with lupus and she was undergoing treatment. "Hulga believes herself to be her mother's opposite," Williams points out, yet her "hard-bitten intellectualism is every bit as trite and clichéd as her mother's moralism."[145] With a PhD philosophy, the agnostic Joy is condescending toward everyone, especially her mother. As O'Connor once observed about the character, if she had any faith to begin with, it "has been over-ridden by pride of intellect through her fine education."[146] To spite her mother, Joy changes her name to Hulga.

Thinking herself in control of a situation in which she means to seduce and corrupt the Bible salesman Manley Pointer, Joy/Hulga turns out to have a relatively fragile self-image as the latter begins to probe her innermost feelings and fears. Her pride does not serve her well in the contest of wills that ensues. When Manly Pointer asks Hulga if she will remove her artificial leg, the author represents this moment of vulnerability in language that invokes Christian salvation: "This boy, with an instinct that came from beyond wisdom, had touched the truth about her. When after a minute, she said in a hoarse high voice, 'All right,' it was like surrendering to him completely. It was like losing her own life and finding it again, miraculously, in his."[147] By deliberately alluding to Christian salvation, O'Connor makes the fraudulent Bible salesman a surrogate Jesus and Hulga a figure for the leap of faith required to surrender her life to Christ.[148]

O'Connor's protagonist undergoes a similar self-surrender, analogous to but not identical to that required for her salvation. She is no longer wholly self-sufficient and becomes vulnerable, if not utterly dependent on the Bible salesman. Yet Manley Pointer, it turns out, is not nearly as innocent and naive as Hulga thinks. "You ain't so smart," he sneers. "I been believing in nothing ever since I was born."[149] It turns out that the young boy is not a believer, after all. Indeed, he surpasses Hulga at her own atheist game; he is a fraud and a thoroughly disillusioned nihilist. Joy/Hulga finally gets her comeuppance at the hands of the Bible salesman, but it is not entirely clear whether the point of the story is to satirize her pride or to affirm that she acknowledges it.[150] This story may not follow the pattern of failed apostasy I have been tracking as closely.

That pattern can be found in O'Connor's second novel *The Violent Bear It Away* (1960), however, in which the middle-aged schoolteacher George Rayber also espouses his materialist worldview with the same dogmatic intensity as Hazel Motes in *Wise Blood*. O'Connor called *The Violent Bear It Away* "a more ambitious undertaking" than *Wise Blood*, because the "boy doesn't just get himself saved by the skin of his teeth, he in the end prepares to be a prophet himself."[151] The schoolteacher takes it upon himself to save young Tarwater from the seemingly simplistic backwoods religion of his father, ironically a kind of secular salvation that he takes no less seriously than the old-time evangelists he despises. Having been raised in the same backwoods environment as Tarwater, and having long since rejected the old man's faith, Rayber now wants to disabuse young Tarwater of the faith, which the schoolteacher views as a form of child abuse: "A child can't defend himself. ... Children are cursed with believing."[152] Cursed with believing: this is the passage from which I have taken the title for this chapter, because it articulates the notion that runs throughout O'Connor's fiction, namely that religious belief in a secular age is in some sense both a burden and a curse. Rayber recalls his own memorable experience when, at age seven, he had come to old Tarwater's camp at Powderhead and heard, for the first time, the man's talk about redemption and salvation: "the calamity was I believed him. For five or six years I had nothing else but that. I waited on the Lord Jesus."[153] This experience has stuck with him ever since as an instance of brainwashing.

Readers are no doubt inclined to agree with Rayber that the young Tarwater would be better off growing up in the city with a trained schoolteacher than with an illiterate and indeed crazy backwoods preacher. Yet O'Connor, ever the iconoclast, insisted that being raised by the preacher is preferable, again emphasizing that readers, by virtue of their antipathy to fanaticism, are liable to misread the novel: "the modern reader will identify himself with the schoolteacher but it is the old man who speaks for me."[154] This is a remarkable claim, considering the fact that the old man, Mason Tarwater, is given to apocalyptic Jeremiads such as the following:

> He had been called in his early youth and had set out for the city to proclaim the destruction awaiting a world that had abandoned its Savior. He proclaimed from the midst of his fury that the world would see the sun burst in blood and fire and while he raged and waited, it rose every morning, calm and contained in itself, as if not only the world, but the Lord Himself had failed to hear the prophet's message.[155]

Embracing an apocalyptic rhetoric that is sure to alarm O'Connor's modern readers all the more, Old Tarwater rages against apostasy ("a world that had abandoned its Savior") even as he also registers a gnawing doubt about God's inexplicable silence. O'Connor articulates her critique of the modern indifference to religion, then, through the mad ravings of a crazy prophet of doom.

But if Mason Tarwater represents something closer to the iconoclastic spirit of the author, Rayber might be read as a caricature of the modern intellectual. For is he not something of a foil? The need to write for secular readers even as she antagonizes them creates a note of ambivalence in her fiction (an attitude that I described earlier as an instance of having her cake and eating it). Readers who identify with Rayber are implicated in her critique of his intellectual sophistication. O'Connor once claimed that when intellectuals "lose their faith in Christ," they often "substitute a swollen faith in themselves."[156] Nothing was more contemptible to O'Connor than an inflated sense of self-worth. Susan Srigley rightly emphasizes that "O'Connor is not critical of the fact that Rayber is an intellectual; her criticism is focused on his belief that rationality is autonomous and completely within his control."[157] To the extent that O'Connor's unbelieving characters share some of the same inflated self-regard as her fanatical ones, her fiction minimizes the difference between their ideological investments in atheism and religious faith, respectively. For whatever today's intellectuals may "gain in sensibility" compared to those who blindly accept their faith, they lose in perspective, or "vision," about what really matters in life.[158]

The Violent Bear It Away turns on the tête-à-tête between the apparently brainwashed Tarwater and the supposedly enlightened but equally dogmatic Rayber, which gives O'Connor a chance to dispel once and for all the idea that religions have cornered the market on dogmatism. The two characters pass what the narrator describes a sort of Pentecostal "tabernacle" with the words "UNLESS YE BE BORN AGAIN YE SHALL NOT HAVE EVERLASTING LIFE" posted over the door.[159] This sign recalls the one Hazel Motes passes while driving out of Taulkinham after running over Solace Layfield in his Essex. What do these roadside religious exhortations have in common? Together they furnish indirect evidence of a thriving evangelical movement. The use of the word "Pentecostal" alone points readers to one of the fastest-growing religious movements of the twentieth century, Pentecostalism, which I examine more fully in the next chapter. Perhaps it is telling that these characters either dismiss or fail to notice these signs.

Readers are surely meant to criticize Rayber condescension even if they share his views: "all such people have in life … is the conviction that they'll rise again," he comments on the sign, and the "profound finality in his tone" is O'Connor's way of undercutting his point.[160] But if what Rayber offers Tarwater is a secular upbringing free from religion, then why does he characterize the difference it will make as nothing so much as a conversion? Rayber not only gives him a new name (Frankie instead of Tarwater) but also a set of "new clothes to indicate a new life."[161] You have to be "born again," he tells him, "back to the real world where there's no savior but yourself," thus expunging the "backdrag of belief" that has been pounded into the boy since childhood, through

Tarwater's indoctrination.[162] A kind of secular evangelist, Rayber imagines himself in grandiose terms as the savior of all the children who have been indoctrinated into Christianity: "You still believe in all that crap he taught you. ... You need to be saved right here and now from the old man and everything he stands for."[163] The young Frankie needs to be saved, we might say, from the curse of believing.

While directing his wrath at old Tarwater for being "prey" to all kinds of "superstitions," however, Rayber in fact "looked like a fanatical country preacher. His eyes glistened."[164] This is just the sort of religious-secular reversal that had always intrigued O'Connor, yet she apparently was worried that she hadn't gotten Rayber quite right. She told the literary critic Richard Gilman, "I don't reckon he'd be very convincing to you folks in New York."[165] Again, she alerts us to an opposition between her own religious sensibility and the presumably secular one of folks in New York, between Southern religiosity and Northeastern secularism. My argument has been that this opposition is constitutive of her self-understanding and of her fiction.[166] If George Rayber represents the secular views of her imagined audience, the author undercuts him at every turn, while serving up yet another gothic tale of religious violence.

As if in confirmation of the novel's title, the path to redemption is strewn with violence.[167] The boy first kills old Tarwater and burns down his barn, and then, "with all the old man's fancie burned out of him," he drowns Rayber's son in the lake and "scorns the Resurrection and the Life."[168] His apostasy is short-lived, as "his destiny forced him on to a final revelation."[169] Like so many characters in O'Connor's fiction, Tarwater is another failed apostate, and in the closing pages she sets the stage for a final miraculous occurrence: "A deep quiet pervaded everything. The encroaching dusk seemed to come softly in deference to some mystery that resided there."[170] Then the revelation occurs: "He threw himself on the ground and with his face against the dirt of the grave, he heard the command GO WARN THE CHILDREN OF GOD OF THE TERRIBLE SPEED OF MERCY."[171] Marked like Hazel Motes with "wise blood," Tarwater moves "toward the dark city, where the children of God lay sleeping."[172] There he will obey God's command, which had come to him as if from a "burning bush," and by taking on the role of a prophet, he will now begin to convert the children of the secular city.[173]

The supernatural climax of *The Violent Bear It Away* alone should alert readers that we are no longer dealing with a disenchanted world. O'Connor's late fiction seems more and more drawn to the supernatural. Consider the astonishingly grand eschatological vision at the end of "Revelation," from her final short story collection *Everything That Rises Must Converge* (1965), where she departs from her usual focus on the immanent, quotidian world and describes a vision that comes to the supremely self-absorbed, unsympathetic character Ruby Turpin in a dream, though again the tone is difficult to pin down. Are we to read this vision as a delusion on the part of an unselfconscious character or as a true revelation from God as the title of the story suggests? The author's unabashed belief in the supernatural meant that she had no difficulty seeing "the natural things of this world as vehicles or instruments for God's grace."[174] More often than not, though, violence rather than some sort of supernatural intervention is the vehicle for God's grace.

In "Greenleaf," another story from *Everything That Rises Must Converge*, O'Connor reveals the ways that even the most tepid believers can find their beliefs tested in a trial by fire. The character Mrs. May thinks of herself as "a good Christian woman with a large respect for religion, though she did not, of course, believe any of it was true."[175] A skeptic though not an atheist, she wanted like many upwardly mobile Christians then as now to keep religion compartmentalized, safely cordoned off in the private sphere. "She thought the word, Jesus, should be kept inside the church building like other words inside the bedroom."[176]

In contrast, the eponymous character Mrs. Greenleaf is a fanatic who collects "morbid stories out of the newspaper" and buries them in the woods, engaging in a practice she calls "prayer healing": "then she fell on the ground over them and mumbled and groaned for an hour or so, moving her arms back and forth under her and out again and finally just lying down flat and, Mrs. May suspected, going to sleep in the dirt."[177] Mrs. May reproves of Mrs. Greenleaf's fanatical behavior and extols the virtue of moderation, which sounds like reasonable advice, except that in O'Connor's fiction, the characters are nothing if not *immoderate* in their beliefs.[178] Those who uphold the value of moderation in everything, including religion, are quite often the ones most likely to be jolted out of their self-assured complacency, and by violence if necessary.

This is exactly what happens at the end of "Greenleaf," when Mrs. May faces down a stray bull on her property that she had sent her faithful employee Mr. Greenleaf to shoot and kill:

> She looked back and saw that the bull, his head lowered, was racing toward her. She remained perfectly still, not in fright, but in a freezing unbelief. She stared at the violent black streak bounding toward her as if she had no sense of distance, as if she could not decide at once what his intention was, and the bull had buried his head in her lap, like a wild tormented lover, before her expression had changed ... and she had the look of a person whose sight has been suddenly restored but who finds the light unbearable.[179]

Impaled on the wild bull's horns, Mrs. May experiences an unlikely conversion at the moment of death, in which her sight is restored, like Saul on the road to Damascus. She meets her demise at the horns of a charging bull: "One of his horns sank until it pierced her heart and the other curved around her side and held her in an unbreakable grip."[180] By coming face to face with extremity and violence, her decorous and above all superficial faith is replaced with something much darker if not ineffable, "some last discovery" she now imparts, "bent over whispering ... into the animal's ear."[181]

O'Connor employs violence in order to shock readers into confronting the difficulty of maintaining their religious convictions amidst the de-facto secularism of postwar America. The novelist John Hawkes was being deliberately provocative when he suggested that O'Connor "was rather too enamored of the Devil she professed to warn her readers against" and "seemed a little too fond of the demonic to claim to be" a genuine believer.[182] Literary critic Harold Bloom was apparently not exaggerating when he wrote that a "ferocious religious zeal" was O'Connor's greatest liability, without which she "would have bequeathed us even stronger novels and stories, of the eminence of Faulkner's, if she had been able to restrain her spiritual tendentiousness."[183]

Both Hawks and Bloom seem to assume that religious commitments prevent O'Connor from attaining a properly neutral stance. O'Connor took issue with the assumption that belief necessarily entailed bias or blindness; properly understood, belief actually allowed one to see. "It is popular to believe that in order to see clearly one must believe nothing," she once observed. "This may work well enough if you are observing cells under a microscope. It will not work if you are writing fiction. For the fiction writer, to believe nothing is to see nothing."[184] O'Connor entertains the idea that far from limiting one's vision, belief may actually enhance it: "belief, in my own case anyway, is the engine that makes perception operate."[185] As the writer Joyce Carol Oates astutely observed, "O'Connor's unfashionable religious sensibility" was at odds with "a mid-twentieth-century secular, materialist literary culture largely indifferent to conservative Christian belief of the kind that seems to have shaped every aspect of her life."[186]

There is a telling anecdote from relatively early in O'Connor's career that speaks to her sense of estrangement from the literary establishment. Writing to a sympathetic correspondent, Betty Hester, O'Connor recounts a dinner party she attended several years earlier hosted by the Catholic writer Mary McCarthy, who in O'Connor's words had "departed the Church at the age of 15 and is a Big Intellectual." Robert Lowell and his then wife Elizabeth Hardwick were also there, and the conversation after dinner continued well into the early morning hours. "I hadn't opened my mouth once, there being nothing for me in such company to say," O'Connor recalls. "Having me there was like having a dog present who had been trained to say a few words but overcome with inadequacy had forgotten them," but when the conversation suddenly turned to the subject of the Eucharist, about which she had definite ideas, she felt compelled to speak up:

Well, toward morning the conversation turned on the Eucharist, which I, being the Catholic, was obviously supposed to defend. Mrs. Broadwater [Mary McCarthy] said when she was a child and received the Host, she thought of it as the Holy Ghost, He being the "most portable" person of the Trinity; now she thought of it as a symbol and implied that it was a pretty good one. I then said, in a very shaky voice, "Well, if it's a symbol, to hell with it." That was all the defense I was capable of but I realize now that this is all I will ever be able to say about it, outside of a story, except that it is the center of existence for me; all the rest is expendable.[187]

Yet the implications of this anecdote become more complicated when we consider that she was writing to a close friend with whom she had in common not only their shared Catholic faith but also a mutual disdain for intellectual pretentiousness. We know that O'Connor also counted among her friends some of the foremost figures of the postwar literary scene, not only Robert Lowell and Elizabeth Hardwick, who had taken O'Connor to the dinner party that night, but also Robert and Sally Fitzgerald, whom she met through Lowell and whose farmhouse in Connecticut became her frequent refuge, as well as Allen Tate and his wife Caroline Gordon, the publisher Robert Giroux, and many other writers and critics including Randall Jarrell, Malcolm Cowley, Van Wyck Brooks, Elizabeth Bishop, Katherine Ann Porter, Eudora Welty, and Cleanth Brooks.[188] Obviously, the author's roots were thoroughly Southern and, if you include the Iowa Writers Workshop period, Midwestern, and this had some bearing on the path of her early career. She was first published in *The Kenyon Review* by Southern Agrarian John Crowe Ransom and in *The Sewanee Review*. Although Philip Rahv published her work in *The Partisan Review*, early champions of O'Connor, with the exception of Alfed Kazin, by and large were not Jewish, and she never attracted a substantial following among the most prominent Jewish intellectuals.[189] Writing in *The New Yorker*, Hilton Als has claimed that she remained largely an outsider to that world: "O'Connor had little exposure to European immigrants, to intellectual debate as a form of socializing, or agnosticism."[190] Could it be that her cherished outsider status led her to project the secular worldview of the Big Intellectuals onto the proverbial general readers of her fiction?[191]

In her lecture "Novelist and Believer" (1963), which she gave the year before her death, O'Connor reiterates a claim about her audience that had become a recurring theme:

> Today's audience is one in which religious feeling has become, if not atrophied, at least vaporous and sentimental. When Emerson decided, in 1832, that he could no longer celebrate the Lord's Supper unless the bread and wine were removed, an important step in the vaporization of religion in America was taken, and the spirit of that step has continued apace.[192]

Following the author's lead, critics have mostly read her work in terms of this secular-religious binary. Writing in 1980, the psychologist Robert Coles noted O'Connor's oppositional stance: "She favored detachment in a world whose assumptions she often challenged strenuously."[193] Literary critic Christina Bieber Lake articulates what amounts to the current critical consensus: "Flannery O'Connor saw herself as a prophet called to push violently against the spirit of the age. She believed that our religious and philosophical thinkers alike have become secular and Gnostic."[194] Yet O'Connor's own statements about her artistic project undoubtedly need to be considered within the larger context of the postwar period, when a newly legitimized secularism was accompanied by widespread religious revivals. In light of what we now know about uneven secularization, this approach to O'Connor stands in need of revaluation.[195] As Christian Smith reminds us, "*secularization is itself culturally and historically relative and specific*, so that exactly what qualifies as secularization in one context may not in other situations."[196] Pluralism "can undermine religions by fostering doubts among practitioners about the probability and truth of their own religion," for example, but it can also strengthen religions "by prompting some religious actors to mobilize resources to promote their religions in the face of competition."[197]

O'Connor was not altogether wrong about the secular outlook of literary critics and public intellectuals. By the mid-twentieth century, critics like J. Hillis Miller and Cleanth Brooks regarded the death of God and the eclipse of religion as more or less axiomatic. In his influential book *The Disappearance of God* (1963), Miller writes that for many writers in the nineteenth and twentieth centuries, it seems God "can only be experienced negatively, as a terrifying absence."[198] In *The Hidden God* (1963), Brooks likewise observes that despite the "continuing importance of a substratum of Christianity" in US society, most writers "frankly put themselves down as agnostics or atheists," and even "those who are avowed Christians will, as a matter of necessity, reflect some of the difficulties of belief" under "the pressure of a secular culture."[199] In much American literary criticism of the 1960s, then, the consensus was that "cultural pluralism" and "secularization" were the dominant trends of the day, not revivals or religious orthodoxy; indeed, according to Howard Mumford Jones in his book *Belief and Disbelief in American Literature* (1967), virtually the entire span of US literary history "chronicles the almost continuous failure of religious orthodoxy in America to appeal to the serious literary imagination."[200]

But there was also a return to orthodoxy, or "neo-orthodoxy," among public intellectuals like Will Herberg and Reinhold Neibuhr in the mid-twentieth century.[201] Speaking before a national convention of Catholics in 1965, a year after O'Connor's death, Herberg criticized the Second Vatican Council for attempting to

> slough off its old ways and bring itself up to date by adjusting itself to the spirit of the age. I say just the opposite: in all that is important, the Church must stand firm in its witness to the truth that is eternal and unchanging. ... If it is to remain true to its vocation, it must take its stand against the world, against the age, against the spirit of the age—because the world and the age are always, to a degree, to an important degree, in rebellion against God.[202]

O'Connor herself addressed this renewed interest in religion two years earlier: "I have said a great deal about the religious sense that the modern audience lacks, and by way of objection to this, you may point out to me that there is a real return of intellectuals in our time to an interest in and a respect for religion."[203] But while she acknowledges that a "new spirit of ecumenism" had become "fashionable" among some intellectuals, she was skeptical that this trend will "herald a new religious age."[204] "We live in an unbelieving age but one which is markedly and lopsidedly spiritual," she once wrote, as if trying to put her finger on how religious revivals could be occurring under conditions of an ecumenical, pluralistic, and secular public culture that made even the most committed believers feel defensive and marginalized.[205]

O'Connor was a keen observer of the signs of the times, even if the modernist milieu of intellectual life led her to overestimate secularism's reach into the lives of average Americans. Worth noting is that the Southern Baptist Church gained 300,000 new members between 1945 and 1949, for example, just as O'Connor was launching her career (she obtained her Master's in Fine Arts degree in 1947 from the Iowa Writers Workshop).[206] Still, she was prescient about a number of things, including a decline in the centrality and dominance of mainline Protestantism, the rise of an ecumenical civil religion at mid-century, and the nascent new religious movements. If she felt drawn to fanatical characters, it was because they resisted the drift toward relativism:

> The true prophet is inspired by the Holy Ghost, not necessarily by the dominant religion of his region. Further, the traditional Protestant bodies of the South are evaporating into secularism and respectability and are being replaced on the grass roots level by all sorts of strange sects that bear not much resemblance to traditional Protestantism— Jehovah's witnesses, snake-handlers, Free Thinking Christians, Independent Prophets, the swindlers, the mad, and sometimes the genuinely inspired.[207]

Perhaps her affinity for fanatics—the snake-handlers and swindlers of the American landscape—can be attributed to her attraction to and fascination with more robust forms of faith. Why then did she view fanaticism as a reproach and not merely an eccentricity? O'Connor's apostates were meant as a reproach to those who took religious faith too much for granted, and to those who had become much too comfortable in their ivory towers, looking down their noses on everyone else.

Believers and unbelievers alike had grown far too comfortable and complacent for her tastes, so she set out to rattle the cages of all those who simply did not take their beliefs seriously enough. "We have to have stories," she insisted. "It takes a story of mythic dimensions ... one in which everybody is able to recognize the hand of God and imagine its descent upon himself."[208]

As we have seen, O'Connor returned again and again to a small repertoire of ideas: that secularism was now dominant, that religious points of views were marginalized, that being true to Christian orthodoxy was in effect countercultural, and that art could somehow make people recognize the hand of God at work in their lives. Attuned as she was to the possibilities of belief in a secular age, she often compared the experience of faith to the ebb and flow of ocean tides: "Faith comes and goes. It rises and falls like the tides of an invisible ocean."[209] In 1962, two years before her death, she wrote to a college student named Alfred Corn who, like the author herself some twenty-five years earlier, was struggling with doubts. She encouraged him to make doubt a resource rather than a stumbling block to her faith: "if you are going to stand up intellectually to agnostics," then "intellectual difficulties will have to be met," she tells him, "and you will be meeting them for the rest of your life."[210]

O'Connor had been meeting such intellectual difficulties all her life, yet she took courage from the fact that "faith is what you have in the absence of knowledge."[211] In an entry from *A Prayer Journal*, she speculated that you cannot really be an atheist unless you know everything: "No one can be an atheist who does not know all things. Only God is an atheist. The devil is the greatest believer & he has his reasons."[212] She clung to this paradoxical idea as a consolation for the vicissitudes of uncertain faith. She apparently really believed it. Little wonder, then, that her unbelieving characters are not atheists, but failed apostates who can never fully shirk their faith.

2

Conversion and Storefront Pentecostalism in James Baldwin's Harlem

In April 1959, Flannery O'Connor refused a request from a friend to meet the African American writer James Baldwin, whose first novel *Go Tell It on the Mountain* (1953) had been published within a year of *Wise Blood* (1952). O'Connor's friend Maryat Lee, a playwright from Kentucky who was then living in New York and "Flannery's foil" on matters pertaining to race, in the words of her biographer Brad Gooch, had recently encountered Baldwin on a street corner, and Lee took it upon herself to inquire whether O'Connor would care to meet him at her home in Milledgeville, Georgia, during his trip to the South.[1] "No I can't see James Baldwin in Georgia," she demurred: "It would cause the greatest trouble and disturbance and disunion. In New York it would be nice to meet him; here it would not. I observe the traditions of the society I feed on—it's only fair. Might as well expect a mule to fly as me to see James Baldwin in Georgia."[2]

O'Connor hastens to add that her refusal does not reflect an uncharitable view of Baldwin's work: "I have read one of his stories and it was a good one."[3] Rather, it stems from her deference to social customs that she felt she could not transgress, as her use of the loaded term "disunion" suggests. "She grew up in a world defined by segregation," writes literary critic Hilton Als, and although she "was herself part of a minority," she knew that "belonging was provisional, and society was fueled by exclusion and hatred."[4] She also tells Maryat that she is simply tired of socializing: "I am just back from Vanderbilt and have had enough of writers for a while, black or white."[5] In the same letter, she reports that she knows another white Southern writer "who is writing a novel set in inter-racial circles in New York," a writer who would very much "like to meet James Baldwin I am sure." Yet when the writer in question was visiting New York, he "wasn't able to meet one Negro socially. Well, at least down here we are benighted over the table not under it."⁶ Hinting that inhospitality may go both ways, O'Connor evidently preferred to wear her own benightedness on her sleeve.⁷

O'Connor's relationship to the race question, like Faulkner's and indeed like Baldwin's, was conflicted. Although she claimed to be an "integrationist," she nonetheless opposed forced busing to create "racially balanced" schools, which she felt would "do nothing to help the race situation."⁸ On the other hand, when a group burned a cross in protest against desegregation, O'Connor remarked with lethal sarcasm: "The people who burned the cross couldn't have gone past the fourth grade but, for the time, they were mighty interested in education."⁹

In her fiction, of course, O'Connor satirized white Southerners with unrelenting irony. Consider the scene in "A Good Man Is Hard to Find" (1955) when the grandmother observes a black child standing in the door of a shack beside the road: "Oh look at the cute little pickaninny! … Wouldn't that make a picture now?"¹⁰ Or consider Julian's mother in "Everything That Rises Must Converge" (1960), who is opposed to desegregation but insists that she is on friendly terms with Negroes. "I've always had great respect for my colored friends," she says. "I'd do anything in the world for them."¹¹ The older generation sublimates racism into condescension and paternalism, yet the younger generation, which is ostensibly more accepting of social equality, turns out to be equally troubled by desegregation. "If you have to live next to them," Tanner's daughter in "Judgment Day" (1960) remarks when a black family moves in next door: "just you mind your business and they'll mind theirs."¹² As insightful as these stories are about the blatant if often unconscious racism of her white Southern characters, O'Connor's investigations of race can seem forced at times. As Joyce Carol Oates points out,

> O'Connor's favorite among her stories, "The Artificial Nigger," has become virtually unteachable as a consequence of its blunt pseudo-racist title. Ironically, O'Connor had intended the "artificial nigger"—a

crude blackface lawn ornament observed in a Southern town by the back-country Mr. Head and his grandson Nelson—to be a simulacrum of Jesus Christ and the story to evoke a tender sort of redemption unexpected in O'Connor's *oeuvre*.[13]

In some ways, O'Connor managed to ride the fence on racial issues. In a letter of 1963, the same year as Martin Luther King, Jr.'s "I Have a Dream Speech," she wrote: "I feel very good about those changes in the South that have been long overdue—the whole racial picture. I think it is improving by the minute, particularly in Georgia, and I don't see how anybody could feel otherwise than good about that."[14] In another letter the same year she sounds rather exasperated about Eudora Welty's short story "Where Is the Voice Coming From?" (1963): "What I hate most is its being in the *New Yorker* with all the stupid Yankee liberals smacking their lips over typical life in the dear old dirty Southland."[15] The Welty short story confirms her suspicion that writing about race is to be avoided, if only because it might occasion gloating in the North about the benighted South, "The topical is poison. I got away with it in 'Everything that Rises' but only because I say a plague on everybody's house as far as the race business goes."[16]

A year later, O'Connor was still vexed about the race business. In a letter to Maryat Lee dated May 21, 1964, just weeks before the Civil Rights Act was signed, she wrote the following:

> About the Negroes, the kind I don't like is the philosophizing prophesying pontificating kind, the James Baldwin kind. Very ignorant but never silent. Baldwin can tell us what it feels like to be a Negro in Harlam [*sic*] but he tries to tell us everything else too. M.L. King I don't think is the age's great saint but he's at least doing what he can do & has to do. Don't know anything about Ossie Davis except you like him but you probably like them all. My question is usually would this person be endurable if white. If Baldwin were white nobody would stand him a minute.[17]

She goes on in this vein for some time. I suppose these comments might seem less egregious if we could attribute them to a sort of country bumpkin persona she adopted for some interlocutors, as Maryat Lee suggests when she writes in O'Connor's defense: "Flannery permanently became devil's advocate with me in matters of race, as I was with her in matters of religion. Underneath the often ugly caricatures of herself ... I could only believe that she shared with me the sense of frustration and betrayal and impotency over the dilemma of the white South."[18]

Baldwin himself was having none of it. He points up the evasiveness of such convoluted Southern attitudes about race in a brilliant essay titled "Faulkner and Desegregation" (1956):

> What seems to define the Southerner, in his own mind at any rate, is his relationship to the North, ... a relationship which can at the very best be described as uneasy. It is apparently very difficult to be at once a Southerner and an American; so difficult that many of the South's most independent minds are forced into the American exile. ... The difficulty, perhaps, is that the Southerner clings to two entirely antithetical doctrines, two legends, two histories. ... He is, on the one hand, the proud citizen of a free society and, on the other, is committed to a society which has not yet dared to free itself of the necessity of naked and brutal oppression.[19]

This diagnosis certainly resonates with O'Connor's apparently uneasy relationship to the North.

During the same journey through the South in 1959 on which O'Connor snubbed him, Baldwin began writing the essay titled "Nobody Knows My Name: A Letter from the South," which he published later that year in *Partisan Review* and subsequently included in his masterful collection of essays, *Nobody Knows My Name: More Notes of a Native Son* (1961). In this essay, Baldwin writes from the point of view of a city-born black boy who visits the South for the first time, notably a Great Migration in reverse. Born to a mother who had only recently arrived in Harlem from the South, Baldwin was among the first-generation city-born African Americans that Richard Wright spoke of in his book *12 Million Black Voices* (1941). "We are the children of black sharecroppers," Wright wrote, "the first born of the city tenements."[20] Baldwin tells us in his first book titled *Notes of a Native Son* (1955) that he, too, belonged to "that generation which had never seen the landscape of what Negroes sometimes call the Old Country."[21]

When Baldwin finally made a pilgrimage to see the Old Country for himself, he felt an odd sense of déjà vu, as if he'd been there before even though he was visiting it for the first time: "A Negro born in the North who finds himself in the South is in a position similar to that of the son of the Italian emigrant who finds himself in Italy, near the village where his father first saw the light of day. Both are in countries they have never seen, but which they cannot fail to recognize."[22] Like the son or daughter of immigrants to the New World, the young Harlem-born African American feels at once estranged from and connected to the Old Country. "Everywhere he turns," Baldwin writes, "the revenant finds himself reflected" in the landscape:

> He sees himself as he was before he was born, perhaps; or as the man he would have become, had he actually been born in this place. He sees the world, from an angle odd indeed, in which his fathers awaited his arrival, perhaps in the very house in which he narrowly avoided being born. He sees, in effect, his ancestors, who, in everything they do and are, proclaim his inescapable identity.[23]

The Great Migration doubled the double consciousness famously described by W.E.B. DuBois, creating in effect a sort of quadruple consciousness: African American-Southerner-city dweller. As if unlocking the key to this complex identity, Baldwin concludes by saying: "I was, in short, but one generation removed from the South."[24]

Like his creator, Baldwin's protagonist John Grimes from his first novel *Go Tell It on the Mountain* is also but one generation removed from the South, part of a generation of African Americans whose experience of the South was not direct but mediated. Surrounded by elders who were by turns nostalgic for and haunted by the South, these young African Americans may well have wondered, as Milkman Dead wonders in Toni Morrison's novel *Song of Solomon* (1977), "why black people had ever left the South."[25] Baldwin's *Go Tell It on the Mountain* delves into some of the reasons why black people left the South, as well as how these migrants and their progeny adapted to Harlem once they got there.[26]

The complex role that Christianity played in the lives of these transplanted Southerners is one aspect of Baldwin's story that needs further explication, especially in light of recent work on religion's outsized role in the Great Migration.[27] Many African Americans were bolstered by their conviction that God himself was guiding them in a present-day exodus, which they viewed as a contemporary analogue to the biblical Exodus.[28] For the most part, Southern migrants were astonishingly resilient in adapting their religious beliefs and traditions to new urban conditions. Albert J. Raboteau, a leading authority on African American religion, has argued that there was a great deal of religious diversification in many Northern cities as a result of the Great Migration:

> Besides increasing the size and number of black urban churches, migration also increased the variety of black religious life by exposing people to new religious choices. Accustomed to deciding between Baptist, Methodist, and perhaps Holiness-Pentecostal churches back home, migrants to the cities encountered black Jews, black Muslims, black Catholics, black Spiritualists (people who believed that the living could communicate with the dead), and black disciples of charismatic religious figures like Daddy Grace, the founder of a church called the Universal House of Prayer for All People.[29]

Another charismatic religious leader was the self-styled prophet Father Divine, who had visited the 1906 Azusa Street Revival in Los Angeles—now widely regarded as the founding event of Pentecostalism—and then in 1914 brought this new style of revivalism to Brooklyn, New York, where he began preaching on street corners as Father Major Jealous Divine and founded a small religious community that practiced abstinence from alcohol, drugs, profanity, and sex. At one point, Father Divine had even claimed to be the Second Coming of Christ.[30] Figures like Daddy Grace and Father Divine testify to the fact that New York was fertile ground for new religious movements and offered plenty of opportunities for religious experimentation and syncretism.[31]

While some migrants managed to retain their Southern religious traditions in the North, others sought out different forms of religious practice or launched new religious movements.[32] Still others rejected their religious heritage altogether.[33] Richard Wright is one example of this. Baptized in a Methodist church at his mother's insistence, Wright was raised in a highly religious household and attended a Seventh-Day Adventist school in the South, but he soon found himself "at odds" with his aunt Addie, a "strict disciplinarian" who enforced the dietary restrictions of her Seventh-Day Adventist tradition and forbade her nephew (only nine years her junior) from reading secular literature, until Wright rebelled "against the rules and practices of the religion."[34] After leaving the South at age nineteen, Wright was increasingly drawn to leftist politics and literature. In *12 Million Black Voices*, he claims that churches had done virtually nothing to ameliorate the "cultural devastation" brought about by "slavery, physical suffering, unrequited longing, abrupt emancipation, migration, disillusionment, bewilderment, joblessness, and insecurity."[35] Wright acknowledges that African American churches continued to play a vital role as "centers of social and community life," however, insofar as they allowed newly arrived migrants from the South to retain their "ardent religious emotionalism … on the fervid levels of the plantation revival."[36]

In *Go Tell It on the Mountain*, his most overtly religious novel, Baldwin captures this religious diversity as Pentecostalism and other new religious movements proliferated in Harlem. The novel also registers the complex processes of individual, social, and religious transformation at a time of rapid historical change. The resiliency of religious groups from the Great Migration to the Civil Rights movement is one of the more surprising stories in American religious history. Baldwin's novel sheds light on that story, reworking in narrative form some important aspects of what occurred at the larger social and historical level. At the individual and psychological level, the novel shows how religion continued to influence migrants even when they rejected the faith. Baldwin himself continued to be influenced by it and make use of it even after he lost his faith: "The church in which I was born operates in one way in *Go Tell It on the*

Mountain, mainly as a presence, I think, as a weight, as a kind of affliction for all those people who are in it, who are in fact trapped in it and don't know how to get out."[37]

At the beginning of what is arguably his crowning literary achievement, *The Fire Next Time* (1963), Baldwin counseled his nephew (and namesake) James: "Know whence you came. If you know whence you came, there is really no limit to where you can go."[38] Baldwin took this advice to heart. Early in his career, he collaborated with the photographer Theodore Pelatowski on a book "about the store-front churches in Harlem."[39] He was also working on his first play around the same time, *The Amen Corner* (1955), about a storefront church modeled on the Mount Calvary Pentecostal Assembly Hall of the Pentecostal Faith of All Nations that he attended in his youth. Finally, as we have seen, his first novel *Go Tell It on the Mountain* is a semiautobiographical narrative derived largely from his experiences as a Young Minister in that church. He initially planned to call the book *Crying Holy* before settling on *Go Tell It on the Mountain*. Both titles, of course, derive from slave spirituals. When he submitted the manuscript to a publisher, one shortsighted editor objected to its overt religious content. "What about all that come-to-Jesus stuff? Don't you think you ought to take it out?"[40] But as Baldwin acknowledges in his essay "Autobiographical Notes," the King James Bible and "the rhetoric of the store-front church" were among the most formative "influences" on his literary imagination from the start.[41] Without them, *Go Tell It* would be an entirely different book. Still, surprisingly few critics focus specifically on the holiness or sanctified Pentecostal storefront church in the novel.[42]

Baldwin neither rejected nor fully relinquished his religious upbringing.[43] "The church was very exciting," he recalls in "Down at the Cross," first published in *The New Yorker* in 1962 and reprinted in *The Fire Next Time*:

> It took a long time for me to disengage myself from this excitement, and on the blindest, most visceral level, I never really have, and never will. There is no music like that music, no drama like the drama of the saints rejoicing, the sinners moaning, the tambourines racing, and all those voices coming together and crying holy unto the Lord.[44]

Baldwin recreates the drama and intensity of Pentecostal worship services in his novel, although he was also highly critical of the church, as when he writes of "all the prohibitions, crimes, and hypocrisies of the Christian church. If the concept of God has any validity or any use, it can only be to make us larger, freer, and more loving. If God cannot do this, then it is time we got rid of Him."[45] The novel itself embodies the author's ambivalence about the church. On the one hand, it offers community; it is a place of refuge from the pressures of city life. On the other hand, its members must uphold strict standards of personal piety. When the protagonist John Grimes is slain in the spirit, however, he is momentarily freed both from his father's abuse and from the church's strict doctrinal regime. In effect, the book rescues the church from its worst tendencies.

From his own strict religious upbringing, Baldwin fashioned an aesthetic-political vision that ultimately made him an important moral voice in the United States. Ivy G. Wilson has analyzed the way African American writers developed a "political aesthetics," using literature "to engender and sustain collectivities of social belonging."[46] By recreating the social belonging offered by Pentecostal churches, Baldwin developed a similar form of religious aesthetics in literary works. In a lecture at Kalamazoo College in 1960, Baldwin outlined his own sort of liberation theology:

> I suggest that the role of the Negro in American life has something to do with our concept of what God is, and from my point of view, this concept is not big enough. It has got to be made much bigger than it is because God is, after all, not anybody's toy. To be with God is really to be involved with some enormous, overwhelming desire, and joy, and power which you cannot control, which controls you. I conceive of my own life as a journey toward something I do not understand, which in the going toward, makes me better. I conceive of God, in fact, as a means of liberation and not a means to control others.[47]

Baldwin emphasizes liberation, reconciliation, and also reciprocity. He goes on to say, "Whether I like it or not, whether you like it or not, we are bound together forever. We are part of each other."[48] As a sort of modern-day Jeremiah, he called upon all Americans, black and white, to transform the country. In another address that same year titled "Notes for a Hypothetical Novel," he writes: "Now, this country is going to be transformed. It will not be transformed by an act of God, but by all of us, by you and me. I don't believe any longer that we can afford to say that it is entirely out of our hands. We made the world we're living in and we have to make it over."[49] Baldwin transmuted the rich religious heritage of his upbringing into a new prophetic vision with which to confront the seemingly intractable problem of race at the dawn of the Civil Rights era.[50]

Exodus: Movement of the People

Read in the context of US religious history, *Go Tell It on the Mountain* opens a window onto the fascinating world of storefront Pentecostalism in the early twentieth century. The novel thus testifies to the resourcefulness and resiliency of African American religion as it evolves in response to changing social and historical conditions, for Baldwin understood that religion was "in a perpetual state of change and fermentation, being perpetually driven, God knows where, by forces within and without."[51] In a remarkable 1958 photo-essay, *Life* magazine writers identified Pentecostalism as "the fastest-growing Christian movement in the world today, one so dynamic that it stands with Catholicism and historic Protestantism as a third force in Christendom," with some 8.5 million followers in the United States alone.[52] The article continues: "This third force is made up of groups sometimes called 'fringe sects'—those marked, in the extreme, by shouting revivalists, puritanical preachers of doomsday, faith healers, jazzy gospel singers."[53] By the end of the twentieth century, the number of Pentecostals would grow to nearly 11 million in the US; Worldwide, the number of Pentecostals is estimated to be 280 million.[54] To be sure, we cannot predict such rapid growth from the pages of *Go Tell It on the Mountain*. What we can learn from the novel is something about the profoundly moving experiences of Pentecostal worship. Indeed, most critics assume that the novel's main character, John Grimes, will follow the author's path to apostasy by ultimately disavowing his faith, despite John's powerful conversion experience at the end, yet the astonishing growth of Pentecostalism perhaps suggests a different outcome.

Pentecostalism has roots in the late-eighteenth- and early-nineteenth-century religious revivals of the second Great Awakening, but its emergence as a religious movement in its own right can be traced to the beginning of the twentieth century. On January 1, 1901, a woman in Topeka, Kansas, began speaking in tongues during a prayer vigil and did not let up for three days. This outpouring of the spirit occurred at a small Bible school founded by Charles Fox Parham. Within a year, Parham closed the school and began traveling a revival circuit throughout Kansas and neighboring Missouri. In 1905, Parham moved to Houston, Texas, and founded another Bible-training school, where one of his students was a young African American minister named William J. Seymour. Seymour then moved to Los Angeles, where he presided over a series of revival meetings that began on April 8, 1906, in a small house on North Bonnie Bray Street. Within a week, some 300 people were showing up to experience for themselves the outpouring of the Spirit that was rumored to be taking place there, and the Los Angeles Police Department told them they would need to disperse or find a larger location. The revivals then moved to the Apostolic Faith Gospel Mission, a larger structure on Azusa Street beginning on April 16, 1906. In a front-page account of these meetings on April 18, 1906, the same day of the devastating San Francisco earthquake, *The Los Angeles Daily* headlines described a "wild scene last night on Azusa Street" in which a "new sect of fanatics is breaking loose":

> Breathing strange utterances and mouthing a creed which it would seem no sane mortal could understand, the newest religious sect has started in Los Angeles. Meetings are held in a tumble-down shack on Azusa Street, near San Pedro Street, and devotees of the weird doctrine practice the most fanatical rites, preach the wildest theories and work themselves into a state of mad excitement in their peculiar zeal.[55]

The writer of this account is troubled not only by the "Weird Babel of Tongues," as the headline suggests, but also by the racially integrated meetings: "Colored people and a sprinkling of whites compose the congregation, and night is made hideous in the neighborhood by the howlings of the worshippers, who spend hours swaying forth and back in a nerve-racking attitude of prayer and supplication. They claim to have the 'gift of tongues' and be able to understand the babel."[56]

The Azusa Street Revival marks the birth of modern Pentecostalism, which combines "evangelical revivalism" with a new emphasis on so-called gifts of the spirit, especially glossolalia, or speaking in tongues.[57] Glossolalia derives from a modern interpretation of a passage in the Acts of the Apostles, in which the disciples speak in unknown tongues at the feast of Pentecost (held each year fifty days after Passover)—hence the name for the movement itself. In addition to glossolalia, Pentecostalism also emphasizes "spirit baptism" or spirit possession; antiphonal or "call-and-response" participation during worship; and personal piety, or "getting right with God."[58] In his book *The Fire Spreads: Holiness and Pentecostalism in the American South* (2008), Randall J. Stephens observes that the movement spread quickly: "Within months, the 'Pentecost' in the West had captivated the attention of holiness folk in the South. Initiates from the West Coast revival transmitted the radical doctrines and practices of Pentecostalism not only by re-creating the event in the South but also through an elaborate print culture."[59]

Pentecostalism found fertile ground in the North as well. In what historian Grant Wacker calls "one of the great religious migrations of modern times," at first "hundreds, then thousands, then tens of thousands" of black people left their "natal churches" in the South and often joined new upstart churches with names like Pillar of Fire, Shiloh, or Fire-Baptized Holiness Church.[60] Associated with the "four-fold" gospel of personal salvation, Holy Ghost baptism, and the Second Coming, Pentecostals were dubbed "holy rollers" by adherents and detractors alike; however, the real "genius" of Pentecostalism was that it combined "turbid emotionalism" and sheer physical abandon with a more practical concern for the contingencies of everyday life, since the conviction that nearly everything in life was predicated on the work of the Holy Spirit, according to Wacker, "freed them from self-doubt, legitimated reasonable accommodations to modern culture, and released boundless energy for feats of worldly enterprise."[61]

The Great Migration brought about "a more mixed religious culture" in urban areas.[62] African Americans traditionally belonged to two major denominations, Baptist and Methodist. Holiness and Pentecostal churches, collectively known as "Sanctified" churches, attracted many newly arrived migrants from the South, making African American religious culture more diverse. In *Gods of the City: Religion and the American Urban Landscape* (1999), Robert A. Orsi writes:

> African American migrants from the South ... built a complex religious culture in northern cities that included Pentecostal practice and experience, New Thought and other metaphysical schools, vernacular healing idioms, the revitalization and reorganization of long-established Protestant denominations touched now by the rhythms and ways of southern migrants, cosmologically derived dietary regimes, African nationalisms, and new faiths such as the Black Jews of Harlem or the Nation of Islam.[63]

Baldwin captures this promiscuous mixing of religious cultures in "The Harlem Ghetto," first published in *Commentary* in February 1948 and later included in *Notes of a Native Son* (1955): "There are probably more churches in Harlem than in any other ghetto in this city and they are going full blast every night and some of them are filled with praying people every day."[64] He calls attention not only to the sheer number of churches in Harlem, but also to their diversity: "These churches range from the august and publicized Abyssinian Baptist Church on West 138th Street to resolutely unclassifiable lofts, basements, store-fronts, and even private dwellings."[65] The people who gathered for worship were themselves diverse, for as Baldwin notes elsewhere, "Seventh Day Adventists and Methodists and Spiritualists seemed to be hobnobbing with Holyrollers and they were all, alike, entangled with the most flagrant disbelievers."[66] Of course, for Baldwin the proliferation of churches could also be viewed as a "fairly desperate emotional business," a sort of coping mechanism that helped to mitigate the "pressure of life in Harlem."[67]

Religious diversity was not lost on other prominent African American writers at the time. Ralph Ellison's *Invisible Man* (1952) captures not only the religious diversity of New York City, for instance, but also the way that storefront churches competed for adherents with organizations like the Brotherhood, Ellison's caricature of the John Reed Club, a national literary organization sponsored by the Communist Party. Near the end of *Invisible Man*, Ellison's eponymous hero becomes disillusioned with the Brotherhood for what he views as their heartless, opportunistic response to his friend Tod Clifton's death, and while trying to escape from a young woman who mistakes him for the Brotherhood leader Rinehart, he takes refuge in a storefront church with a neon sign on the marquee that reads in part, "HOLY WAY STATION/BEHOLD THE LIVING GOD."[68] "It hung above a store that had been converted into a church," Ellison writes,

> Behind me I heard the rise and fall of an old-fashioned prayer such as I hadn't heard since leaving the campus; and then only when visiting country preachers were asked to pray. The voice rose and fell in a rhythmical, dreamlike recital—part enumeration of earthly trials undergone by the congregation, part rapt display of vocal virtuosity, part appeal to God.[69]

The Invisible Man is astonished to discover that the Marxist revolutionary Rinehart has evidently reinvented himself as a Pentecostal preacher, the Reverend B.P. Rinehart, according to handbills being passed out by two black boys outside the church: "I wanted to tell them that Rinehart was a fraud, but now there came a shout from inside the church and I heard a burst of music."[70] As the doors close and the service begins, the Invisible Man remains outside the church, astonished by the protean transformation of Rinehart: "The world in which we lived was without boundaries. ... Perhaps the truth was always a lie."[71] Ellison attributes the appeal of Pentecostalism not only to heightened emotionalism and rapturous music, but also to the promise of self-transformation.

Storefront Pentecostal churches were often criticized for lacking any set rules for ordination.[72]

Arguably the greatest migration novel of all, Ellison's *Invisible Man* also draws attention to the ways in which the Great Migration transformed religious practices and communities. This aspect of the novel has not been fully appreciated, perhaps because Rinehart's self-fashioning as a spiritual technologist comes late in the novel and seems incidental to the main plot involving the Brotherhood. Yet the scene outside Rinehart's church is in fact the inciting incident for the Invisible Man's major epiphany about his essential anonymity and invisibility in the city, an epiphany that will drive his decision to go underground. "In the South everybody knew you," the Invisible Man muses, "but coming North was a jump into the unknown. How many days could you walk the streets of the big city without encountering anyone who knew you, and how many nights? ... You could actually make yourself anew. ... And sitting there trembling I caught a brief glimpse of the possibilities posed by Rinehart's multiple personalities and turned away."[73] As he walks away from the church, however, a woman mistakes him for Reverend Rinehart and informs him that she once heard him preach years ago, "You was just a lil' ole twelve-year-ole boy, back in Virginia. And here I come North and find you, praise God, still preaching the gospel, doing the Lord's work. Still preaching the ole time religion here in this wicked city."[74] The woman is doubly mistaken, of course, for the boy she heard preach in Virginia was neither the Invisible Man nor Rinehart. Nonetheless, her misrecognition speaks to the ways in which Southern blacks in the city hoped to replicate the religious traditions they observed back home.

Rinehart's church is similar to the type of storefront Pentecostal church that will be the central focus of Baldwin's novel *Go Tell It on the Mountain*, published only one year later. Many elements associated with holiness-Pentecostal churches find expression in *Go Tell It*, not only in the flashback scenes set in the South but also in Baldwin's fictional Fire of the Temple Baptized, a storefront church where glossolalia is a regular occurrence. The young pastor's nephew Elisha, for instance, who "had but lately arrived from Georgia," suddenly begins speaking in tongues at an all-night church service: "Elisha, from the floor, began to speak in a tongue of fire, under the power of the Holy Ghost. John and his father stared at each other, struck dumb and still and with something come to life between them—while the Holy Ghost spoke."[75] Elisha's "tongue of fire" signals that he has the gift of tongues, which makes him a very influential member in the church. The gift of tongues is regarded as a form of bodily possession by the Holy Spirit. In Pentecostal theology, traditional or sacramental baptism is often followed by a second Holy Spirit baptism.[76] The novel's representation of Pentecostalism culminates in John's baptism in the Holy Spirit, of course, a literary tour de force that creates a palpable sense of what such an experience feels like.

Before attending to John's conversion experience in greater detail, let us take a detour to consider the Southern origins of the novel's major characters. In this brilliantly structured novel, the author ends Part 1 with his characters all converging on the Temple of the Fire Baptized for a Saturday night tarry service, so-called because members of the congregation tarry, or wait, for as long as it takes until the Holy Spirit speaks to them and through them. Part 2, titled "Prayers of the Saints," is comprised of a series of flashbacks rendered through free indirect discourse as the tarry service is taking place. In these prayers, members of John's extended family—first his aunt Florence, then his stepfather Gabriel, whom he believes to be his biological father, and finally his mother Elizabeth—recall their Southern upbringing, what brought them to the North, and so on. Employing a narrative technique that M.M. Bakhtin called polyphony, Baldwin represents each of these character's experiences in the Great Migration and the church through multiple voices.[77] Yet all roads lead to the Temple of the Fire Baptized in Harlem on a particular Saturday night, which will turn out to be a spectacularly eventful one for John Grimes. His aunt, interestingly, had never set foot in the church before: "John knew that it was the hand of the Lord that had led her to this place, and his heart grew cold. The Lord was riding on the wind tonight. What might that wind have spoken before morning came?"⁷⁸ As if by some mysterious gravitational force, each major character finds his or her way to the church to see what, indeed, the Lord had in store.

Gabriel's story begins in Georgia, where his full-immersion baptism at a camp meeting in Georgia when he is twelve marks the beginning of his conversion, which comes in fits and starts:

> On the banks of a river, under the violent light of noon, confessed believers and children of Gabriel's age waited to be led into the water. Standing out, waist-deep and robed in white, was the preacher, who would hold their heads briefly under water, crying out to Heaven as the baptized held his breath. ... They came up from the water, visibly under the power of the Lord, and on the shore the saints awaited them, beating their tambourines.⁷⁹

In one of the novel's few comical moments, however, Gabriel resists his baptism by kicking and screaming as he goes under, as if to suggest that he is a reluctant convert at best: "Gabriel began to kick and sputter, nearly throwing the preacher off balance; and though at first they thought that it was the power of the Lord that worked in him, they realized as he rose, still kicking and with his eyes tightly shut, that it was only fury, and too much water in his nose."⁸⁰ Indeed, his resistance arguably foreshadows the fact that he is susceptible to backsliding throughout his life. A more genuine conversion experience comes later when, on his way home from a tryst with a young woman in his flock, Gabriel suddenly falls against a tree, like Saint Augustine before him, and repents for his sins. Gabriel describes this moment as "the beginning of his life as a man."⁸¹

Gabriel's personal story intersects with the history of evangelical revivalism in the South. He makes an auspicious debut as a preacher at a "monster revival meeting" called the Twenty-Four Elders Revival Meeting, where the men do all the preaching, while the women serve as cooks and helpers. When it comes time for Gabriel to preach—on one of twenty-four successive nights—he takes the stage in "the great, lighted lodge hall ... that the saints had rented for the duration of the revival."⁸² Looking out at the sea of eager faces before him, "He saw joy in those faces, and holy excitement, and belief—they all looked up to him."[83] Then, a tall boy in the back row gets up and marches "down the long, bright aisle" toward the dais to become Gabriel's first convert: "The boy knelt, sobbing, at the mercy seat, and the church began to sing."[84] Like many preachers before and since, Gabriel becomes addicted to this kind of adulation and influence over his flock. Because he thinks of other preachers as his rivals in the race to win converts, he comes to regard them as "stumbling-stones in the path of the true believer."[85] Baldwin's fictional revival meeting accurately portrays the way Pentecostalism "stressed an experiential conversion of the heart," and such heightened emotionalism no doubt helps account for its rapid growth.[86] Yet the novel also portrays how such revivals were in effect an unregulated, commercialized religious industry: "they might easily have been, Gabriel thought, highly paid circus-performers, each with his own special dazzling gift. Gabriel discovered that they spoke, jokingly, of the comparative number of souls each of them had saved, as though they were keeping score in a pool-room."[87] However, Gabriel's reputation as a revivalist preacher does not follow him to New York, where he loses much of the intoxicating adoration he once enjoyed from his flock. Whereas he once had "his name printed large on placards that advertised the coming of a man of God," in Harlem he has been relegated to the role of "a kind of fill-in speaker, a holy handyman" for the church:[88] "His father no longer, as he had once done, led great revival meetings," John tells us. "His father had once had a mighty reputation, but all this, it seemed, had changed since he had left the South."[89]

Gabriel is based on the author's stepfather David Baldwin, who once declared that his stepson was "the ugliest boy he had ever seen."[90] Baldwin portrays this "proud, bitter, lust-driven preacher" as a hypocrite who redirects his bitterness about racial injustice onto his loved ones.[91] When a young woman, Esther, unexpectedly comes to his church one night, Gabriel takes it upon himself to admonish her for her sins: "This was not belief but unbelief, not humility but pride."[92] Esther resists Gabriel's clumsy attempt to convert her. "I just don't feel it *here,"* she tells him, putting his hand on her breast.[93] With this gesture, she implies that belief is a matter of the heart, yet she is also seducing him, of course, and Gabriel proves unable to resist. Later, Esther wants nothing to do with religion—or with Gabriel—after he abandons her and their illegitimate child.

Baldwin's preacher character is not entirely unsympathetic, however, especially when it comes to the racial oppression and injustice that accounts for his bitterness and drives him North. Gabriel encounters his estranged son Royal, for instance, immediately after a gruesome lynching has occurred: "Night had not yet fallen and the streets were gray and empty—save that here and there, polished in the light that spilled outward from a pool-room or a tavern, white men stood in groups of half a dozen. As he passed each group, silence fell, and they watched him insolently, itching to kill."[94] If Gabriel is relatively safe from harm in this scene of palpable racial terror, it is only because they know him to be a preacher, but any other black man is by no means safe:

> There were no black men on the streets at all, save him. There had been found that morning, just outside of town, the dead body of a soldier. ... He lay face downward at the base of a tree, his fingernails digging into the scuffed earth. When he was turned over, his eyeballs stared upward in amazement and horror ... his trousers, soaked with blood, were torn open, and exposed to the cold, white air of morning the thick hairs of his groin, matted together, black and rust-red, and the wound that seemed to be throbbing still.[95]

As Philip Dray observes in his study of lynching, *At the Hands of Persons Unknown* (2002): "Hovering just beyond all the other daily indignities of life in the region was lynching, and even where a lynching never occurred it sat, a brooding possibility, over all aspirations Southern blacks might have. Running afoul of any one of a number of Southern racial codes could instantly put one's children, husband, or other relatives in lethal jeopardy."[96] As the novel suggests, racial discrimination only begins to describe the veritable reign of terror that many blacks endured under Jim Crow laws, and the lynching epidemic of the first two decades of the twentieth century alone must have been proof enough, if any was needed by then, that the South was inhospitable to free African Americans. In an essay, Baldwin is very clear on this point: "They had been driven north by the sheer impossibility of remaining in the South. They came with nothing. And the good Lord knows it was a hard journey."[97]

Other characters in the novel have somewhat different motivations for leaving the South. Gabriel's sister Florence, for instance, leaves the South largely to escape the indignities she faces as a single woman. The responsibility of taking care of her aging mother falls entirely upon her, and as a single woman Florence is expected to sacrifice her own aspirations for her brother. Yet one day, while working as a servant for a prominent white family, her employer propositions her, hinting that she should "become his concubine," and Florence realizes she must flee the South.[98] "She left her employment that day," the narrator tells us, "and bought a railroad ticket for New York."[99] Griffin has noted Baldwin's sensitivity to the gender politics of black migration, arguing that women often had quite different reasons for leaving than men did: "For Florence, the South is a place where black women are subjugated in the black family and where they are subject to sexual abuse by white men."[100] Florence and Deborah share "a terrible belief" about men: that they "lived to gratify on the bodies of women their brutal and humiliating needs."[101]

An interesting exchange between Florence and her mother speaks to way that Southerners often couched their decision to leave in religious terms even if other factors were also involved. "God's everywhere, ma. Ain't no need to worry," Florence assures her mother the night before she leaves on the train, even as she worries that she is just "mouthing words" of reassurance.[102] And it turns out that she is merely appeasing her mother here, for once she arrives in New York, Florence severs all ties to the church. This is why when she makes her first appearance in church at the all-night tarry service for John's birthday, her brother stares at her in "astonished triumph that his sister should at last be humbled."[103] Gabriel's self-righteous gloating seems all the more uncharitable insofar as Florence genuinely seeks grace and forgiveness, and although "she had forgotten how to pray," she suddenly recalls a phrase from the Bible that helps put words to her thoughts: "Lord, help my unbelief."[104] This is the line spoken by the father of the epileptic who brings his son to Jesus to be healed, and it is worth noting that Jesus rewards him for his honesty. Hence there is little reason to question Florence's contrition: "Her thoughts were all on God."[105]

Another character who struggles to sustain her faith is John's mother Elizabeth, the final member of the trinity of family members surrounding the protagonist in "Prayers of the Saints." Elizabeth also represents yet another reason why black women migrated away from the South. Like Florence, Elizabeth's "pretext for coming to New York was to take advantage of the greater opportunities the North offered colored people," but in fact she had fallen in love with Richard, who "hated the South" and wanted to try his luck elsewhere.[106] A demur Southern woman who is shocked that "people might live in the same building for years and never speak to one another," Harlem is a difficult adjustment for Elizabeth.[107] She often wonders if she had migrated "out of the South, and into the city of destruction."[108] As this last phrase suggests, Elizabeth remains beholden to the religious language of her upbringing, yet like Florence, she too finds her beliefs tested in the city, first by her doubts about the transferability of Southern folkways to the harsh conditions of Harlem, and second by Richard's determination to flaunt his rejection of religion. Richard and Elizabeth do not seek out a church community like so many migrants did to ease their adjustment to city life. Nor does Elizabeth adhere to traditional forms of spiritual practice like prayer: "In those days, had the Lord Himself descended from Heaven with trumpets telling her to turn back, she could scarcely have heard Him, and could certainly not have heeded."[109]

Isolated from other believers who might sustain her faith, Elizabeth drifts away from it. "Neither Richard nor his friends," literary critic Horace A. Porter writes, "ever go to Church."[110] Indeed, they are "hard drinking, hard talking" men, "and in their hearts they all cursed God."[111] Richard goes so far as to blaspheme God: when Elizabeth "timidly mentioned the love of Jesus," he fairly seethes with rage: "You can tell that puking bastard to kiss my big black ass."[112] While Richard directs his anger toward religion, the true source of his rage is systemic racial injustice in a world where black people are routinely incarcerated without cause or killed with impunity.

Meanwhile, Elizabeth reflects that she felt like she had been "forced to choose between Richard and God," and she now wonders if "this was why God had taken him away from her."[113] Whereas Richard seems haunted by a God he doesn't believe in, Elizabeth is troubled by the possibility that God is punishing her for her apostasy. In both cases, a religious understanding persists among Southerners transplanted to the ostensibly secular world of the city.

The three sections containing flashbacks of their pasts—Gabriel's, Florence's, and Elizabeth's—offer various reasons why African Americans felt compelled to leave the South. The sections also show how the Great Migration changed each character's beliefs and identity. Through free indirect discourse, readers enter into the minds of these characters as they struggle to reconcile their former selves with the people they have become in an utterly new environment. Part of that struggle involves figuring out what relevance their religious beliefs still have, if any, to city life. For those who belonged to sanctified churches like the Temple of the Fire Baptized, of course, religion was all-encompassing, a way of life that made God the center of everything. "The Sanctified churches are congregations of saints, an ethical designation members apply to themselves, as an indication of their collective response to the call to holiness," Sanders explains. "The saints follow the holiness mandate in worship, personal morality, and in society, based upon a dialectical exilic identity of being 'in the world, but not of it.'"[114] For others, religion could seem little more than a distant memory from an altogether different way of life, suited to the rural and fiercely traditional South, perhaps, but not the fast-paced urban milieu. Even so, religion continued to fire the imaginations of these migrants whatever their status in the church. Not for nothing does Baldwin call these retrospective chapters in Part 2 the Prayers of the Saints.

Temple of the Fire Baptized

Baldwin experienced the transformation of black religious culture following the Great Migration firsthand. His mother and stepfather were migrants from the South who had difficulty adjusting to city life. Baldwin's stepfather David Baldwin, who married his mother Emma Berdis Jones in 1927 when Jimmy was two years old, was himself an uneducated clergyman from the South, and the young Baldwin, too, became a preacher after his own conversion as an adolescent. He spent some three years as a boy preacher—from fourteen to seventeen—before rejecting his faith and leaving his family behind to live first in Greenwich Village and then in France, where he started working on a bildungsroman based on these experiences. From Paris, he found his way to a small village in Switzerland, where, as he later recalls, "in that alabaster landscape, armed with two Bessie Smith records and a typewriter, I began to try to recreate the life that I had first known as a child and from which I had spent so many years in flight."[115] Peeling away the "self-protective veils" he had placed between himself and his past, he tried to find a language that "might be made to bear upon the burden of my experience."[116] He found that language by combining two sources: the Bible and the blues.[117] Baldwin once wrote that the blues "are an historical creation produced by the confrontation precisely between the pagan, the black pagan from Africa, and the alabaster cross."[118] Syncretism is at the heart of African American religion no less than African American music. *Go Tell It on the Mountain* is Baldwin's great blues novel.

Gospel music was an integral part of religious life in Harlem, and Baldwin drew from this musical tradition as well. "Harlem is filled with churches," he recalled, "and on Sundays it gives the impression of being filled with music."[119] According to one estimate, nearly two-thirds of the roughly 140 churches in Harlem during the 1920s and 1930s when Baldwin was a child were of "the 'storefront' type."[120] In *The Promised Land* (1991), Nicholas Leman describes this type as "rickety two-room buildings or former small retail establishments that opened directly onto the sidewalk, with crude hand-lettered signs out front."[121] Gospel music was a focal point of worship in all of these churches, no doubt, just as it is in Baldwin's fictional Temple of the Fire Baptized.

Baldwin himself attended the Abyssinian Baptist Church on West 138th Street in Harlem. This was not a storefront church, in fact, but rather a magnificent gothic revival church built in the early 1920s. Known for his "charisma" and "spellbinding" preaching, pastor Adam Clayton Powell, Sr., had attracted a large congregation to some 13,000 members by 1930, making it by far the largest African American congregation and, indeed, the largest Baptist church in the United States.[122]

When Dietrich Bonhoeffer came to New York in 1930 to study with Reinhold Niebuhr at Union Theological Seminary, a black classmate from Alabama invited him to attend Abyssinian Baptist Church. "He was entirely captivated," writes Eric Metaxas, "and for the rest of his time in New York, he was there every Sunday to worship and to teach a Sunday school class of boys."[123] Baldwin was likely one of those boys; he was six years old at the time and Bonhoeffer taught the Sunday school class for a period of six months before returning to Berlin in June 1931. In any event, the Abyssinian Baptist Church had an indelible impact on Bonhoeffer's theology. "In contrast to the didactic style of White churches," he recorded in his diary later that summer. "I believe that the Gospel in Black Churches truly preaches the Black Christ. The Black Christ is preached with rapturous passion and vision."[124]

The Abyssinian Baptist Church continued to prosper throughout Baldwin's adolescence. Powell's son Adam Clayton Powell, Jr., took over from his father as senior pastor in 1937, the year before Baldwin entered high school. Forty years later, Baldwin would write this about his former pastor:

> I knew about Adam only that he was the son of the "old" Adam, the pastor of the Abyssinian Baptist Church, of which church we had been members when I was little; and that he had been instrumental, in the wake of the 1935 Harlem riot, in getting black people hired—for the first time—in the stores on 125th Street where we spent so much of our money.[125]

Baldwin began his own ministry, however, in a storefront church: the Mount Calvary Assembly Hall of the Pentecostal Faith of All Nations. Its founder and minister was a woman, Rosa Artimas Horn, who was born in South Carolina and worked as a dressmaker in Georgia before coming to New York after her husband's death. There she developed a reputation as a dynamic preacher in many holiness-Pentecostal churches. Calvary Assembly Hall was very much of the storefront type: a second-floor worship space above a dance club that attracted as many as 3,000 worshippers. This helps explain why Rosa Horn "vigorously campaigned," as Clarence E. Hardy notes, "against the many pool halls and other night establishments that dotted the Harlem landscape."[126] Baldwin's association with Calvary began when his friend from Frederick Douglass Junior High, Arthur Moore, the model for Elisha in *Go Tell It on the Mountain*, invited him to attend his family's church. Baldwin recalls his first encounter with Mother Horn in the essay "Down at the Cross." With her "marvelous smile," she greeted this visitor to her church by asking him, "Whose little boy are you?" and he responded, "Why, yours."[127] The correct answer is God's, but the anecdote speaks to her warm welcome of him.

Baldwin had a conversion experience at Calvary Assembly Hall not long after this first meeting with Mother Horn. Baldwin's decision to join a different church than the Abyssinian Baptist Church was motivated in part, he tells us, by a desire to beat his father at his own game:

> I did not join the church of which my father was a member and in which he preached. ... I was saved. But at the same time, out of a deep, adolescent cunning I do not pretend to understand, I realized immediately that I could not remain in the church merely as another worshipper. I would have to give myself something to do, in order not to be bored and find myself among all the wretched unsaved of the Avenue. And I don't doubt that I also intended to best my father on his own ground. Anyway, very shortly after I joined the church, I became a preacher—a Young Minister—and remained in the pulpit for more than three years.[128]

The fictional Temple of the Fire Baptized is modeled on Mount Calvary Assembly Hall of the Pentecostal Faith of All Nations, Mother

Horn's church in which he preached and worshipped. The author also drew from his short-lived experience attending another storefront church, the Fireside Pentecostal Assembly, which Arthur Moore's family began attending after an apparent falling out with Mother Horn, which prompted someone at Mount Calvary to accuse young Jimmy of "walking disorderly" for being disloyal to the church in which he had been saved.[129]

At the beginning of *Go Tell It on the Mountain*, the narrator describes the Temple of the Fire Baptized as "a storefront church" that stood "on the corner of this sinful avenue":

> The saints, arriving, had rented this abandoned store and taken out the fixtures; had painted the walls and built a pulpit, moved in a piano and camp chairs, and bought the biggest Bible they could find. They put white curtains in the show window, and painted across this window TEMPLE OF THE FIRE BAPTIZED. Then they were ready to do the Lord's work.[130]

Located on Lenox Avenue, the Temple of the Fire Baptized sits directly across the street from Harlem Hospital where Baldwin was born in 1924; indeed, the proximity of the temple and the hospital lends irony to the author's remark that "I was practically born in the church."[131]

The church was also located next to other sorts of establishments in the curious mixture of sacred and profane that made up the urban landscape. As the fictional Grimes family goes to church on Sunday morning, they invariably pass "men and women ... who had spent the night in bars, or in cat houses, or on the streets."[132] The celebrated Harlem nightclubs offered a highly popular source of entertainment.[133] When a young Ralph Ellison first arrived in New York from Oklahoma City by way of the Tuskegee Institute, he was struck by "the power and variety of the black church, the vigor of its responses to the unique challenges of Harlem—from the stiff Episcopalian propriety of wealthy St. Philip's to the Pentecostal exuberance of the storefront chapels of the poor," but as a serious musician himself, Ellison was also drawn to what his biographer Arnold Rampersad has called "the rival authority of the dancehalls and cabarets, ... where one sometimes heard even more amazing music."[134] In his book *When Harlem Was in Vogue* (1981), David Levering Lewis observes that "sober and hardworking" African Americans who "spurned" the nightclubs did so "from religious or moral certainty that the devil himself was the club proprietor," yet they often found themselves on the way to church "before the last revelers had careened homeward."[135] The contrast was not lost on churchgoers who were called upon to practice temperance and maintain piety at all times. "All churches within the Sanctified church tradition," according to Sanders, "adhere to the doctrine of sanctification in some form and historically have embraced an ascetic ethic forbidding alcohol, tobacco, or other addictive substances, gambling, secular dancing, and immodest apparel."[136] Consequently, they "are fully aware of their marginalized status within the dominant culture," and they accept this "exilic consciousness" as a condition of their faith.[137]

We see this kind of exilic consciousness in the character John Grimes, who is painfully aware of his difference from other city dwellers. When he ventures outside Harlem, for instance, he views midtown with mixed fascination and horror as a kind of Babylon: "It was the roar of the damned that filled Broadway ... the marks of Satan could be found in the faces of the people who waited at the doors of movie houses; his words were printed on the great movie posters that invited people to sin."[138] John accepts the invitation to sin: sitting in the darkened movie theater "which was so like the gloom of Hell," he "waited for this darkness to be shattered by the light of the second coming, ... for every eye to see, the chariots of fire on which descended a wrathful God and all the host of heaven."[139] On coming out of the theater he is again reminded of the stark choice "between the way that led to life everlasting and the way that ended in the pit."[140] John "struggled to find a compromise" between the two paths, but then he remembers how his parents had always tried "to save him from this city, where, they said, his soul would find perdition."[141]

Pentecostal churches feared corruption from two principal sources: sex and the city. In his essay "Down at the Cross," Baldwin recalls: "What I saw around me that summer in Harlem was what I had always seen; nothing had changed. But now, without any warning, the whores and pimps and racketeers on the Avenue had become a personal menace."[142] In the hothouse world of storefront Pentecostalism, the church was under siege, and the secular city surrounding it was nothing less than a battleground for the soul. Orsi describes this mapping of the city well:

> The young James Baldwin ... constantly scanned the horizon of avenues, temples, bars, beauty parlors, churches, and candy stores of Harlem for clues to who he was; in the process, he created a distinctly religious sense of the city for himself. His fears and desires shaped what he saw, and what he was seeing in turn oriented his fears and desires. ... Pentecostal mappings of the city constitute a disciplinary cartography.[143]

In this extreme form of anti-modernism, the city figures as a site of sin and temptation—a city "howling with sin," as Hassan puts it, "in which good and evil clash with apocalyptic fury."[144] It was, in short, a Manichean struggle for survival. "For the wages of sin were visible everywhere," Baldwin writes, "in every wine-stained and urine-splashed hallway, in every clanging ambulance bell, in every scar on the faces of the pimps and their whores, in every helpless, newborn baby being brought into this danger."[145] For his part, Baldwin found refuge in the church: "Some went on wine or whiskey or the needle, and are still on it. And others, like me, fled into the church."[146]

In *Go Tell It on the Mountain*, John Grimes tries to find some middle ground between the demands of his strict religious upbringing and the temptations of the city. He continually worries, however, about his erotic attraction to Elisha. Baldwin himself has described the confusion he felt when the onset of puberty around age fourteen had awakened mysterious sexual urges in him that seemed innocent enough at first but were strongly condemned by the church. Indeed, there were those who seemed to regard "virtually all sexual feelings and activity, even that between spouses, as in some way impure and wrong, and it instills in most members a deep sense of guilt and shame."¹⁴⁷ Because almost every character cannot help but succumb to temptations of the flesh, feelings of guilt abound in the novel. Elisha is publicly chastised for "walking disorderly," although it seems clear to the reader that he has done nothing more than innocently court Ella Mae.¹⁴⁸ And John has clearly internalized the church's dire warnings about sexual temptation. He feels a tremendous sense of guilt about having an erection, for example, which torments him. "Were his thoughts, his bed, his body foul?" he wonders, "What were his dreams?"¹⁴⁹ Here, John vigilantly polices his own thoughts for signs of transgression. An early masturbation scene shows that John has internalized the church's prohibitions against same-sex desire and self-stimulation:

> He had sinned. In spite of the saints, his mother and his father, the warnings he had heard from his earliest beginnings, he had sinned with his hands a sin that was hard to forgive. In the school lavatory, alone, thinking of the boys, older, bigger, braver, who made bets with each other as to whose urine could arch higher, he had watched a transformation of which he would never dare to speak.¹⁵⁰

Late in the novel, he is still obsessing over that furtive act of masturbating when he recalls again: "Yes, he had sinned: one morning, alone, in the dirty bathroom, in the square, dirt-gray cupboard that was filled with the stink of his father. ... Then the voice, terrified, it seemed of no depth, no darkness, demanded of John, scornfully, if he believed that he was cursed."¹⁵¹ All this tension culminates in a dramatic conversion on the threshing floor of the Temple of the Fire Baptized, Baldwin's fictional version of a Pentecostal black church.

The name of Baldwin's fictional church invokes two holiness-Pentecostal denominations: the Fire-Baptized Holiness Church, founded in 1905 by Reverend Benjamin Hardin Irwin, and the Fire-Baptized Holiness Church of God of the Americas, founded in South Carolina in 1908 by African American members who split from the integrated Fire-Baptized Holiness Church to start their own denomination.¹⁵² The fire-baptized moniker derives from the purgative fire of the Holy Spirit prophesied by John the Baptist in Matthew 3:11: "I indeed baptize you with water unto repentance: but he that cometh after me is mightier than I, whose shoes I am not worthy to bear: he shall baptize you with the Holy Ghost, and with fire." In 1895, B.H. Irwin claimed to have received what he called a "baptism of fire," and he began to spread this "third blessing" as a circuit-preacher throughout the Midwest.[153] By 1900, the movement had grown to seventy-five churches, two-thirds of them African American, and it would continue to grow, especially after the Azusa Street Revival of 1906. "Fire-Baptized believers possessed a hyperbolic religious imagination," writes Stephens, and Baldwin probably had this movement in mind for his fictional church.[154]

The Temple of the Fire Baptized features a call-and-response style of worship, in which the congregation talks back to the preacher during the sermon, as when Father James calls out: "Let the church cry amen to this! And they cried: 'Amen! Amen!'"[155] Whether spontaneous or cued, such exchanges are a hallmark of African American churches. Preachers collaborate with the congregation on their sermons by eliciting responses. Baldwin once remarked in an interview with the *Paris Review* that this style of preaching has affinities with jazz: "I would improvise from the texts, like a jazz musician improvises from a theme. I never wrote a sermon—I studied the texts. I've never written a speech. I can't read a speech. It's kind of give and take. You have to sense the people you're talking to. You have to respond to what they hear."[156]

Always a significant component of African American religion, gospel music reaches a kind of apotheosis in Pentecostalism, where it serves a crucial role in transporting congregations. The narrator describes how Elisha prompts worshippers to sing, clap their hands, and dance:

> The Sunday morning service began when Brother Elisha sat down at the piano and raised a song. This moment and this music had been with John, so it seemed, since he had first drawn breath. It seemed that there had never been a time when he had not known this moment of waiting while the packed church paused and the rustling and whispering ceased and the children were quiet; perhaps someone coughed ... then Elisha hit the keys, beginning at once to sing, and everybody joined him, clapping their hands, and rising, and beating the tambourines.[157]

The congregation waits until the song begins, then stands and joins in as Elisha's piano playing builds to a crescendo, as if only through the intensely physical and sonic experience of singing and dancing can they experience the otherworldly or transcendent realm of the spirit. "They sang with all the strength that was in them, and clapped their hands for joy," the narrator tells us. "Something happened to their faces and their voices, the rhythm of their bodies, and to the air they breathed; it was as though wherever they might be, became the upper room, and the Holy Ghost were riding on the air."[158] They have been transported somewhere else: the upper room.

The music of storefront churches offers a unique affective experience that was otherwise seemingly denied to congregants, at least according to the asceticism and self-denial that was all too often preached from the pulpit. Consider what happens when Elisha stops playing the piano:

> He struck on the piano one last, wild note, and threw up his hands, palms upward, stretched wide apart. The tambourines raced to fill the vacuum left by his silent piano, and his cry drew answering cries. Then he was on his feet, turning, blind, his face congested, contorted with this rage, and the muscles leaping and swelling in his long, dark neck. It seemed that he could not breathe, that his body could not contain this passion, that he would be, before their eyes, dispersed into the waiting air.[159]

It is not clear whether Elisha is still performing or whether he is possessed by the Holy Spirit; whatever the case may be, he suffers a kind of epileptic seizure here, wracked by convulsions, and the only explanation we get is that "his body could not contain this passion." Instead of spontaneously combusting, as though "dispersed into the waiting air," Elisha begins to dance:

> His hands, rigid to the very fingertips, moved outward and back against his hips, his sightless eyes looked upward, and he began to dance ... and the rhythm of all the others quickened to match Elisha's rhythm; his thighs moved terribly against the cloth of his suit, his heals beat on the floor, and his fists moved beside his body as though he were beating his own drum. And so, for a while, in the center of the dancers,

head down, fists beating, on, on, unbearably, until it seemed the walls of the church would fall for very sound; and then, in a moment, with a cry, head up, arms high in the air, sweat pouring from his forehead, and all his body dancing as though it would never stop.[160]

The passage is unmistakably erotic, emphasizing that the rhythm of the music, combined with dancing and singing, can lead to physical abandon. This kind of worship affords sheer pleasure, but it also offers something deeper, for as the narrator concludes: "Their singing caused him to believe in the presence of the Lord; indeed, it was no longer a question of belief, because they made that presence real. He did not feel it himself, the joy they felt, yet he could not doubt that it was, for them, the very bread of life—could not doubt it, that is, until it was too late to doubt."[161] Whatever doubts John may still have about committing himself to his faith at this point, the passage leaves little doubt about the power of Pentecostal worship services like this one. The whole point of the tarry service is to praise God continuously until the Holy Spirit intervenes:

> While John watched, the Power struck someone, a man or woman; they cried out, a long, wordless crying, and, arms outstretched like wings, they began the Shout. Someone moved a chair a little to give them room, the rhythm paused, the singing stopped, only the pounding feet and the clapping hands were heard; then another cry, another dancer; then the tambourines began again, and the voices rose again, and the music swept on again, like fire, or flood, or judgment. Then the church seemed to swell with the Power it held, and, like a planet rocking in space, the temple rocked with the Power of God.[162]

Baldwin invites readers to give credence to the transformative and spiritual power at work here, whether they believe in God or not. He represents this worship service as an experience of the most joyful kind, and, moreover, he holds open the possibility that the spirit is truly present.

In *Go Tell It on the Mountain*, Baldwin offers a balanced portrait of storefront churches. On one hand, they provide a sense of community, spiritual renewal, and the promise of salvation, but on the other hand they demand conformity to strict moral standards, which tends to produce guilt and shame. Some critics have insisted that the novel presents a negative view of the church. Lynch claims, for instance, that "Baldwin indicts the black fundamentalist church for its image of a vengeful, unforgiving God and for the consequent devouring effects on its members, whose entrapment in guilt and fear prevents them from loving themselves and others."[163] Baldwin does indeed offer a scathing critique of religious hypocrisy and doctrinal rigidity in this novel, yet it is balanced by a more positive view of the salvific role that religion plays in the souls of black folk. In light of the historical context of the Great Migration, Baldwin represents how some migrants sought refuge in the storefront churches as a kind of safe haven from the streets. He writes: "A black boy born in New York's Harlem in 1924 was born of southerners who had but lately been driven from the land," but if storefront churches helped smooth the difficult transition to the city, "the black family had moved onto yet another sector of a vast and endless battlefield."[164] Thus, *Go Tell It on the Mountain* allows us to assess how urbanization and secularization transformed African American religious cultures in the twentieth century, a process that presages not decline so much as diversification and change, for religion would soon become one of the major factors behind the successes of the Civil Rights movement.[165]

The Souls of Black Folk

In his controversial essay "Everybody's Protest Novel" (1955), Baldwin declared that the novelist should always strive to keep in mind the complexity of individual identity. A character, in other words, must never be reduced to being only a member of this or that "Society or Group," as he puts it.[166] The problem with anti-slavery novels like *Uncle Tom's Cabin* (1852) and protest novels like *Native Son* (1940), according to Baldwin, is that their characters are not fully human:

In overlooking, denying, evading his complexity—which is nothing more than the disquieting complexity of ourselves—we are diminished and we perish; only within this web of ambiguity, paradox, this hunger, danger, darkness, can we find at once ourselves and the power that will free us from ourselves. It is this power of revelation which is the business of the novelist.[167]

Writing *Go Tell It on the Mountain* gave Baldwin an opportunity to flesh out the full humanity of his characters in all their "beauty, dread, power," for better and for worse.[168] Given the marked autobiographical nature of the novel, the author was clearly engaging in an act of self-revelation, or perhaps even confession, and as Sanders intriguingly suggests, "Once he had given voice to his sanctified conversion experience, he underwent a further conversion or call to the literary task of 'witnessing.'"[169] Baldwin certainly felt gratified, but also strangely relieved, to finish the book: "The morning I typed *the* end to my manuscript, I knew that I had come through something."[170]

The subject matter of *Go Tell It on the Mountain* was indeed close to his own experience, yet Baldwin went beyond mere autobiography. Consider the crucial differences in how Baldwin represents his own conversion experience in his nonfiction and John's conversion experience in the novel. The author's own conversion experience occurred in the summer of 1938. He recalls that, during a Sunday morning worship service, he suddenly "fell to the ground before the altar," with "all the vertical saints above me."[171] There was a distinct lack of volition in what happened: "It was the strangest sensation I have ever had in my life. One moment I was on my feet, singing and clapping, … the next moment, with no transition, no sensation of falling, I was on my back."[172] The involuntary quality of conversion is a prominent feature of so-called spirit baptism in Pentecostal churches. In her book *Fits, Trances, and Visions* (1999), as Ann Taves points out, "Pentecostals, to differing degrees, believe that spirit baptism swept away all barriers between the believer and God and allowed the Spirit to take control of the person. The baptism of the Holy Spirit, evidenced by speaking or singing in tongues, stood as the sign that the Spirit, not the self, was in control."[173] Although Baldwin apparently did not speak in tongues at his conversion, he nonetheless describes it as a trance-like state: he is "filled with anguish" and "unspeakable pain," a feeling that subsides only "when they raised me" and "told me that I was 'saved.'"[174]

At some point during the three-year period in which he served as a Young Minister in the church, Baldwin started to wonder whether his conversion had been something of a "gimmick" rather than a genuine transformation.[175] He begins to suffer from a kind of imposter syndrome, like a puppet master pulling the strings. "Being in the pulpit was like being in the theater," he writes. "I was behind the scenes and knew how the illusion worked."[176] He worries especially that the promise of salvation might in fact be nothing more than an invitation to political apathy: "I felt that I was committing a crime in talking about the gentle Jesus, in telling them to reconcile themselves to their misery on earth in order to gain the crown of eternal life."[177] The biggest scandal of the church, at least according to Baldwin's nascent black liberation theology, could be that Christianity had largely been a devil's bargain for black people: "The transfiguring power of the Holy Ghost ended when the service ended, and salvation stopped at the church door."[178]

By his own account, Baldwin was living a double life. In his essay "Autobiographical Notes," from *Notes of a Native Son*, he describes this as a period of considerable ambivalence:

> I was in high school and had been doing a lot of writing. ... But I had also been a Young Minister and had been preaching from the pulpit. Lately, I had been taking fewer engagements and preached as rarely as possible. It was said in the church, quite truthfully, that I was "cooling off."[179]

His stepfather had once advised Baldwin to get a job after finishing junior high school. But on the advice of the poet Countee Cullen, he applied to and was admitted in the fall of 1938 to the prestigious De Witt Clinton High School in the Bronx, which brought him into contact with a more diverse group of friends. De Witt Clinton High School was predominantly Jewish, and according to what he was taught: "This meant that I was surrounded by people who were, by definition, beyond any hope of salvation, who laughed at the tracts and leaflets I brought to school, and who pointed out that the Gospels had been written long after the death of Christ."[180] Baldwin recalls: "This might not have been so distressing if it had not forced me to read the tracts and leaflets myself, for they were indeed, unless one believed their message already, impossible to believe. I remember feeling dimly that there was a kind of blackmail in it."[181]

Baldwin was wrestling with the problem of religious pluralism, a problem made all the more pressing by the fact that, as he tells us: "My best friend in high school was Jewish."[182] At one point, Jimmy brought his best friend Emile Capouya home for dinner, and afterward his stepfather demanded to know if the boy was Christian, to which he replied, "No. He's Jewish":

> My father slammed me across the face with his great palm, and in that moment everything flooded back—all the hatred and fear, and the depth of a merciless resolve to kill my father rather than allow my father to kill me—and I knew that all those sermons and tears and all that repentance and rejoicing had changed nothing.[183]

This little Oedipal drama involves not only the ongoing conflict between young Baldwin and his stepfather, but also a confrontation between Christianity and another monotheistic faith, Judaism. The recognition that Jews are exempt from Christianity, as it were, irreparably damages his faith, and the rather grim recognition is that "the Jews in another Christian nation, Germany," were "not so far from the fiery furnace after all, and my best friend might have been one of them. I told my father, 'He's a better Christian than you are,' and walked out of the house."[184]

Baldwin began spending more time with his Jewish friend and less time with his family. Once, they went to hear the famous preacher known as Daddy Grace in Harlem. An enormous man of some three hundred pounds, Daddy Grace dressed in splendid robes and was carried on a large palanquin down the aisles of his church as worshippers fastened dollar bills to his robes, chanting "Sweet Daddy Grace, save my soul; Sweet Daddy Grace, save my soul."[185] Capouya introduced the young

Baldwin, in turn, to the jazz clubs of Greenwich Village. Baldwin preached his last sermon in 1941 toward the end of his senior year, and with Capouya's encouragement, he abandoned the church altogether after receiving his high school diploma in January 1942.

This period in Baldwin's life would soon become the subject matter of his first novel. Critics are divided over whether the novel is "an ironic indictment of Christianity" or a "stirring vindication" of it, but if *Go Tell It on the Mountain* was meant as a critique of religion, then as Barbara Olson points out, "Baldwin's plan to lambast the faith is hoisted with its own petard."[186] Because the author told the story of his own conversion with much more ambivalence, critics have made the mistake of assuming that John Grimes will eventually leave the church as well. "John's conversion is not an end in itself," Griffin writes. "John is now prepared to enter a new phase of his life—one that might eventually lead him away from the church."[187] Lynch concurs, "Although at the conclusion of the novel John enters the church community as one of the saved, his serious doubts about the freedom to develop his identity and ambitions under the church's strict authority foreshadow his eventual departure."[188] These readings are speculative, to be sure, but still we must be careful not to conflate the character with the author. Even if John Grimes might end up becoming an apostate himself, speculating about his future is entirely hypothetical.

Go Tell It on the Mountain is not *On the Road* (1957), after all. The publisher had forced Jack Kerouac to change the names of all the real people in his roman à clef manuscript, making it not so much a novel but something closer to creative nonfiction. Baldwin's novel is obviously autobiographical, but it is not a roman à clef, strictly speaking. Baldwin once told an interviewer:

> *Go Tell It on the Mountain* was about my relationship to my father and the church, which is the same thing really. It was an attempt to exorcise something, to find out what happened to my father, what happened to all of us, what had happened to me—to John—and how we were to move from one place to another. Of course it seems rather personal, but the book is not *about* John, the book is not *about* me.[189]

Baldwin is in danger of conflating author and character here even as he tries to pry them apart: "the book is not *about* John, the book is not *about* me." What then is the book about? "The book was very hard to write because I was too young when I started," he admits, and because "it was really about me and my father. There were things I couldn't deal with technically at first. Most of all, I couldn't deal with *me*."[190] A technical breakthrough came when he discovered that third-person limited omniscient narration could help distinguish between his own experiences and his character's. Determined to avoid first person, Baldwin developed a third-person narrator that is primarily focalized through John but also roams freely inside the minds of his other characters, as in the flashback scenes that make up Part 2: "This is where the reading of Henry James helped me, with his whole idea about the center of consciousness and using a single intelligence to tell the story. He gave me the idea to make the novel happen on John's birthday."[191]

Through limited omniscience, occasional free-indirect discourse, and even some passages that seem closer to stream of consciousness, Baldwin allows readers to experience a Pentecostal Holy Spirit baptism on the threshing floor of the Temple of the Fire Baptized, the culminating event both in John's life and in the narrative. Baldwin sets the stage for John's conversion at the end of Part 1: The Seventh Day, as all the major characters convene at the church for an all-night tarry service, beginning Saturday evening until dawn on Sunday, the seventh day: "The Lord was riding on the wind tonight. What might that wind have spoken before the morning came?"[192]

The narrator comes back to the all-night tarry service at various points in the ensuing sections that make up Part 2: The Prayers of the Saints. For instance, in the very next section, "Florence's Prayer," readers may be slightly disoriented switching from flashbacks to Florence's childhood to the church and back again. Here, the narrator describes the early stages of John's conversion as a sort of dark night of the soul:

> All over the church there was only the sound, more awful than the deepest silence, of the prayers of the saints of God. Only the yellow, moaning light shone above them, making their faces gleam like muddy

gold. Their faces, and their attitudes, and their many voices rising as one voice made John think of the deepest valley, the longest night, of Peter and Paul in the dungeon cell, one praying while the other sang; or of endless, depthless, swelling water, and no dry land in sight, the true believer clinging to a spar.[193]

Parched and uncertain, John continues to wonder what might happen—what is happening: "Tonight, his mind was awash with visions: nothing remained. He was ill with doubt and searching. He longed for a light that would teach him, forever and forever, and beyond all question, the way to go; for a power that would bind him ... to the love of God. Or else he wished to stand up now, and leave this tabernacle and never see these people any more."[194] Clearly John is not just ambivalent about his faith and the church but torn between two possible outcomes: either he will discern a way forward and see the light or be consigned to the darkness and leave the church forever. The interplay between light and dark, between silence and singing, textures the entire scene: "There was an awful silence at the bottom of John's mind, a dreadful weight, a dreadful speculation. ... And this weight began to move at the bottom of John's mind, in a silence like the silence of the void before creation, and he began to feel a terror like he had never felt before."[195] Indeed, at the end of this passage, John begins to wonder whether there was any point to praying and worshiping, whether there was any validity to religion at all: "And why did they come here, night after night after night, calling out to a God who cared nothing for them—if, above this flaking ceiling, there was any God at all?"[196]

Such doubts heighten the dramatic tension of the scene, but they should not mislead us into thinking that because John wavers here his faith is necessarily compromised or jeopardized, for as I have argued all along, doubt is an inevitable component of belief. John immediately feels the weight of his decision and wavering: "Then he remembered that the fool has said in his heart, There is no God—and he dropped his eyes, seeing that ... Praying Mother Washington was looking at him."[197] Nor should we assume that his conversion is not genuine. "Salvation was real for these others," John considers, "and it might be real for him.

He had only to reach out and God would touch him; he had only to cry and God would hear."[198] From what happens next, it is clear that John has made a decision to reach out to God for help. At the end of the section, his mother is praying and thinking distractedly about John's birth when, suddenly, she hears her son cry out: "not the cry of a child, newborn, ... but the cry of the man-child, bestial."[199] This strange bestial cry awakens Elizabeth from her reveries about the past: "She opened her eyes and stood straight up; all of the saints surrounded her; Gabriel stood staring, struck rigid as a pillar in the temple. On the threshing floor, in the center of the crying, singing saints, John lay astonished beneath the power of the Lord."[200]

These descriptions of what is happening to John are focalized through the characters, of course, and they are informed by their understandings of spirit possession or pleading the blood. "There was a rite in our church," Baldwin later explained, "called *pleading the blood*," adding:

> When the sinner fell on his face before the altar, the soul of the sinner then found itself locked in battle with Satan; or, in the place of Jacob, wrestling with the angel. All of the forces of Hell rushed to claim the soul which had just been astonished by the light of the love of God. The soul in torment turned this way and that, yearning, equally, for the light and for the darkness: yearning, out of agony, for reconciliation. ... Only the saints who had passed through this fire—the incredible horror of the fainting of the spirit—had the power to intercede, to "plead the blood," to bring the embattled and mortally endangered soul "through." The pleading of the blood was a plea to whosoever had loved us enough to spill his blood for us, that he might sprinkle the soul with his love once more, to give us power over Satan, and the love and courage to live out our days.[201]

The final section of the novel, "The Threshing Floor," provides a remarkable account of that harrowing experience. John is not quite sure what is happening to him; he only knows that some otherworldly force has overtaken him. He is utterly helpless as God and Satan battle for his soul:

And something moved in John's body which was not John. He was invaded, set at naught, possessed. This power had had struck John, in the head or in the heart; and in a moment, wholly filling him with the anguish that he could not have imagined, that he surely could not endure, that even now he could not believe, had opened him up; ... had ripped him and felled him in a moment, so that John had not felt the wound, but only the agony, had not felt the fall, but only the fear; and lay there, now, helpless, screaming, at the very bottom of darkness.[202]

During his initial moments of agony and terror, John feels surrounded by darkness and silence, which at times threatens to engulf him, despite the fact that he is apparently possessed by the power of the Holy Spirit, for "the darkness began to murmur—a terrible sound."[203] As if coming from beyond the grave, "like a thousand wings beating on the air," the sound seems to represent a litany of traumatic events in John's life "from the moment he had first drawn breath," but it also gives voice to "rage and weeping from time set free, but bound now in eternity; rage that had no language, weeping with no voice—which yet spoke now, to John's startled soul."[204] The murmuring voices are those of African Americans who had suffered from the "cruel lash" and the "strongest chains" under slavery, or who had been lynched: "Yes, the darkness hummed with murder: the body in the water, the body in the fire, the body on the tree."[205]

We still cannot tell if he will embrace or renounce his faith at this point in the threshing-floor scene. Some of the saints in the church, afterward, will resort to clichés about conversion, as Sister McCandless does when she insists that nobody could have predicted "that little Johnny was going to jump up so soon, and get religion."[206] But for all his doubts, John at last makes a heartfelt plea for God's forgiveness and mercy: "Oh, Lord, have mercy on me. Have mercy on me."[207] What follows from this repentance is a genuine—and genuinely moving—epiphany:

Then John saw the Lord—for a moment only; and the darkness, for a moment only, was filled with a light he could not bear. Then, in a moment, he was set free; his tears sprang as from a fountain; his heart, like a fountain of waters, burst. Then he cried: "Oh, blessed Jesus! Oh, Lord Jesus! Take me through!"[208]

This conversion is clearly a powerful, miraculous event, and Baldwin leaves no doubt about whether John is saved, "For his drifting soul was anchored in the love of God; in the rock that endured forever. The light and the darkness had kissed each other, and were married now, forever, in the life and the vision of John's soul."[209] Little wonder, then, that the narrator describes him in the subsequent scene as speaking "in the new voice God had given him."[210] In the parlance of evangelical Protestant churches, this character has been born again: "in the silence something died in John, and something came alive."[211] Combining memories of his own conversion as a teenager with a more mature knowledge—and open-mindedness—to spirit baptism, Baldwin has employed limited omniscience and free-indirect discourse to create an extraordinary account of what such an experience *feels* like to someone going through it.[212]

To the extent that John understands that experience as a struggle between darkness and light for his soul, or between God and Satan, Baldwin has captured the way that ideas about the spiritual warfare hold sway in the minds of holiness-Pentecostal believers, even if they coexist with nagging doubts about those ideas, as the characters' nervous banter about what has just occurred perhaps suggests. Baldwin subtly reveals the many psychological subtexts of John's motivations even if his conversion is genuine: the way that his conversion is an act of defiance against his father, for instance, or the fact that it will bring him closer to Elisha, albeit through an approved form of intimacy sanctioned by the work they will do together in the church. No one is happier about John's conversion than Elisha. As the marvelous exchange on their way home from church suggests, Elisha is aware of John's infatuation with him and also knows that it cannot be acknowledged, much less reciprocated. Elisha is also aware of Gabriel's reluctance to accept John's conversion. That is why Elisha forces Gabriel's hand by blessing John himself:

> John looked at his father and moved from his path, stepping down into the street again. He put his hand on Elisha's arm, feeling himself trembling, and his father at his back.

"Elisha," he said, "no matter what happens to me, where I go, what folks say about me, no matter what *any*body says, you remember—please remember—I was saved. I was *there.*"

Elisha grinned, and looked up at his father.

"He come through," cried Elisha, "didn't he, Deacon Grimes? The Lord done laid him out, and turned him around and wrote his *new* name down in glory. Bless our God!"

And he kissed John on the forehead, a holy kiss.[213]

Buoyed by Elisha's holy kiss, "like a seal ineffaceable forever," and by a community of believers surrounding and sustaining him in his faith, perhaps young John Grimes will keep the faith after all.[214] Make no mistake: whatever happened to John cannot be explained away by questioning his ulterior motives. And, moreover, it is clear that his conversion brings him considerable joy: "And he was filled with a joy, a joy unspeakable, whose roots, though he would not trace them on this new day of his life, were nourished by the wellspring of a despair not yet discovered."[215] This last comment acts as a kind of prolepsis that does point forward to difficulties the character may yet face, yet for now John has begun a new chapter in his life: "For his drifting soul was anchored in the love of God; in the rock that endured forever."[216] This is not a description of conversion as a coping mechanism or gimmick; rather, the character seems likely to persist in the church and in his faith. Baldwin resists the impulse to critique such conversion experiences in the novel, at least, though he recognizes the precariousness of belief.

However unbidden the conversion experience might be, the newly converted Christian still faces the daunting task of discarding old habits and adopting new ones, with the ever-present possibility of backsliding or regressing—one step back for every two steps forward, as it were. This is why, as Baldwin recognizes elsewhere, "conversions are notoriously transitory: within days, the reformed—'saved'—whore, whoremonger, thief, drunkard, have ventilated their fears and dried their tears and returned to their former ways."[217] The somewhat facetious tone of this comment should not obscure the sober truth that conversion is the first step in a long journey. "He got the steep side of the mountain to climb," as one character remarks.[218] Or as David puts it at the end of Baldwin's novel *Giovanni's Room* (1956): "I must believe, I must believe, that the heavy grace of God, which has brought me to this place, is all that can carry me out of it."[219]

Steeped in the culture and language of the black storefront Pentecostal churches in which the author was raised, *Go Tell It on the Mountain* gives a stunning fictional account of one black boy's conversion—a "nightmarish experience," but one that also generates "spiritual rebirth."[220] Literary critic Darryl Pinckney has argued persuasively that John's "deep trance of prayer and emotion at the altar" during the all-night "tarry service" is presented without irony as an ecstatic religious experience, and there is little reason to doubt that he will remain in the church, given "the note of acceptance with which the novel ends."[221] The closing lines are almost beatifying: "'I'm ready,' John said, 'I'm coming. I'm on my way.'"[222]

The current religious turn in literary studies offers an opportunity for us to reconsider a novel like *Go Tell It on the Mountain* with greater sensitivity to the ways that religious language and ideas permeate John's self-understanding and the storefront Pentecostal church in which his conversion occurs. Indeed, virtually all the characters in the novel subscribe to the view that spiritual forces are very much at work in the world, and that salvation depends upon belief and grace. If Baldwin went out of "intellectual fashion" for a time after his death in 1987, according to one critic, the "primary reason" was "his unflagging concern with the possibility of salvation, a term nearly meaningless in the vocabularies of late-twentieth-century intellectual culture."[223] As Baldwin himself had once lamented, "the word 'belief' has nearly no meaning anymore."[224] If religion had once seemed outmoded or obsolete according to resolutely secular literary-critical paradigms, more recent studies bring renewed attention to religion throughout Baldwin work.[225]

My reading of *Go Tell It on the Mountain* has focused on the way literary fiction can imagine religious communities from the inside, as it were, allowing readers access, if only imaginatively, to the ways of seeing and understanding the world that distinguish such groups. "Baldwin's first novel is saturated with Scripture and the rhetoric of Judgment Day as a settling of earthly accounts that still has a special meaning for black congregations," writes Pinckney. "Baldwin assigns his characters a sharp theological awareness and liturgical fluency," a shared idiom of "gospel songs, spirituals, and hymns" that binds them together as a community of like-minded believers.[226] Moreover, the author takes us inside the minds of the believers themselves. By allowing us to experience John's conversion on the threshing floor, he gives readers access to the lived experience of what Pentecostal churches call pleading the blood. The author creates an imagined community of a Harlem storefront church and then interiorizes the experience of spirit baptism so central to such churches. In a sense, literary fiction overrides one of the problems of cultural analysis that has long plagued religious studies for, as Taves points out, the "experience of religion cannot be separated from the communities of discourse and practice that give rise to it *without becoming something else.*"[227] Tarry services and threshing floors, Holy Spirit baptism and conversion, saints and sinners: these are the terms that make Baldwin's representation of that religious milieu so authentic. "The rhetoric of the Protestant church, inspired by the poetry of the early seventeenth-century Bible," as Hortense Spillers writes, "was, at one time, common as dirt to the language of the everyday," and in many religious communities, of course, it still is.[228]

Perhaps no twentieth-century American writer was better equipped to represent this taken-for-granted quality of religious rhetoric in African American communities than James Baldwin. "It is axiomatic that the Negro is religious," he once wrote, "which is to say that he stands in fear of the God our ancestors gave us and before whom we all tremble yet."[229] Let me be clear that I have no wish to rescue Baldwin from his apostasy or to reclaim him as a believer. There is no question that he rejected orthodox Christian faith. Here is Baldwin speaking to an interviewer for the BBC who asked whether "the concept of God" still meant something to him: "I'm not a believer in any sense that would make sense to any church, and any church would obviously throw me out. I believe—what do I believe? I believe in. ... I believe in love—that sounds very corny."[230] Note the hesitation in his answer, as if to suggest that what he believes is finally unsayable, but when pressed, Baldwin goes further: "I believe we can save each other. In fact, I think we must save each other. I don't depend on anyone else to do it."[231] This perhaps comes closest to being an article of faith for him, for Baldwin consistently advocated a radical mutuality in which everyone must take responsibility for "saving" each other.

As these statements suggest, however, Baldwin was prone to using religious language and concepts even when he was professing unbelief. He knew better than to dismiss his past as irrelevant or blaspheme the God he once believed in as merely a delusion of his youth; after all, as he later admitted, "I can produce no documents proving that I am not what I was."[232] In his rather unfortunately titled late book *The Devil Finds Work* (1976), Baldwin writes that he could neither fully recover from the trauma of his past nor betray the sense of accountability he still felt:

> It was very important for me not to have pretended to have surmounted the pain and terror of that time in my life, very important not to pretend that it left no mark on me. It marked me forever. In some measure I encountered the abyss of my own soul, the labyrinth of my destiny: these could never be escaped, to challenge these imponderables being, precisely, the heavy, tattered glory of the gift of God.[233]

Again, we see how the author consistently returns to and renovates Christian language and ideas whenever he wishes to state his deepest beliefs, commit himself to some moral cause, or admonish his fellow Americans in the prophetic voice that, for better or worse, appeared to be second nature to Baldwin. Note how he accepts his prophetic calling in an earlier essay, "The American Dream and the American Negro" (1965), which opens, "I find myself, not for the first time, in the position of a kind of Jeremiah."[234] More insightful about the religious underpinnings of Baldwin's career as a writer and political activist than most, his biographer David Leeming places him squarely in the prophetic tradition:

> Like Ezekiel, Isaiah, Jeremiah, and Samuel, whose words and agonies he knew from his days as a child preacher in Harlem, he understood

that as a witness he must often stand alone in anger against a nation that seemed intent on not "keeping the faith." He knew that his childhood "salvation" on the threshing floor of his church was but the preface to a life searching on the universal threshing floor of personal and societal pain.[235]

This statement captures the virtuosic syncretism with which Baldwin blended together his literary aspirations, religious background, racial identity, and sexual preference into a powerful prophetic vision. He internalized religion and made it his own, and then directed it outward to encompass others in a reciprocal relationship.[236]

Consider the extraordinary benediction of sorts toward the end of *The Devil Finds Work*:

To encounter oneself is to encounter the other: and this is love. If I know that my soul trembles, I know that yours does, too: and, if I can respect this, both of us can live. Neither of us, truly, can live without the other: a statement which would not sound so banal if one were not endlessly compelled to repeat it, and, further, believe it, and act on that belief.[237]

Baldwin envisions here something like what Emmanuel Levinas termed "alterity."[238] Like Levinas, Baldwin more or less retains the religious underpinnings of this radical conception of otherness, which amounts to an ethical vision whereby loving others is essential to mutuality, toleration, and peaceful coexistence. Baldwin's nonfiction essays are, in effect, jeremiads, in which he explores ideas about belief, community, identity, and otherness that could help us overcome the apparently polarized situation of twenty-first-century America, in which the deepest beliefs and values of Christian conservatives, especially those with an evangelical or fundamentalist bent, are more or less anathema to liberal secularists whose beliefs and values, which are often just as deeply held, derive from a basically incompatible worldview.[239]

In his late essay "Open Letter to the Born Again" (1979), Baldwin weighs in on the evangelical movement that was about to put Ronald Reagan in the White House and complains that the "people who call themselves 'born again' today have simply become members of the richest, most exclusive private club in the world, a club that the man from Galilee could not possibly hope—or wish—to enter."[240] Citing the New Testament in his preferred translation, "Inasmuch as ye have done it unto one of the least of these my brethren, ye have done it unto me" (Matthew 25:40), he comments: "That is a hard saying. ... It is a merciless description of our responsibility for one another," and then calls on evangelicals to live up to this ideal.[241] For my purposes, what is most interesting about this essay is that Baldwin claims to be "speaking as an ex-minister of the Gospel, and, therefore, as one of the born again. I was instructed to feed the hungry, clothe the naked and visit those in prison. I am very far from my youth, and from my father's house, but I have not forgotten these instructions, and I pray upon my soul I never will."[242] Clearly, he never relinquished the task of ministering to others and taking responsibility.

Twenty years after Flannery O'Connor declined a request from her friend Maryat Lee to meet with Baldwin during his journey through the South, Baldwin took another trip to the South for an article he had agreed to write for *The New Yorker* about the Civil Rights movement and the New South. "His plan was to revisit places and people who had been important to him in the fifties and sixties," writes Leeming, "to explore the condition of 'civil rights' all these years after the great events of the movement."[243] When Baldwin arrived in the South to do research for the article in April 1980 (accompanied by documentary filmmakers), O'Connor was long dead—the two never met—but he did meet another famous writer on that trip. His first stop was the annual meeting of the African Literature Association in Gainesville, Florida, where he met the Nigerian writer Chinua Achebe, whose great novel *Things Fall Apart* (1958) appeared just five years after Baldwin's *Go Tell It on the Mountain* and six years after O'Connor's debut, *Wise Blood*. "Mr. Baldwin, I presume!" Achebe greeted him, impishly.[244] In his opening remarks the next day, Baldwin spoke warmly of "my brother whom I met yesterday—whom I have not seen in four hundred years."[245] Baldwin was alluding to their shared African ancestry, yet he concluded his remarks on a somewhat oblique note by saying, "it was never intended that we should meet."[246]

As if to confirm O'Connor's own ominous statement in her letter to Lee twenty years earlier that Baldwin's presence could stir up "trouble and disturbance and disunion," a heckler interrupted the dialogue between Achebe and Baldwin. "Halfway into our conversation," Achebe remembered:

> A mystery voice broke into the public-address system, and began to insult Mister Baldwin. The geniality vanished. Some of the stalwarts in the audience rushed out to guard the exits. For a fraction of a second, Baldwin seemed nervous. But he quickly recovered his composure, stood erect and defiant, and began to reply to the intruder. "But Mister Baldwin will have his say; white supremacy has had its day."[247]

For whatever reason, Baldwin never published the planned essay in *The New Yorker*. But he did publish an essay about his journey to the South, "Dark Days," in *Esquire* in October 1980:

> Recently I was back in the South, more than a quarter century after the Supreme Court decision that outlawed segregation in the Republic's schools, a decision to be implemented with "all deliberate speed." ... Dark days, for we know how much there is to be done and how unlikely it is that we will live another sixty years. We know, for that matter, how utterly improbable it is—indeed, miraculous—that we can still have a drink, or a pork chop, or laugh together.[248]

Obviously, there is still work to be done, yet he points to the possibility of racial reconciliation.

In a remarkable late essay titled "Every Good-bye Ain't Gone" (1977), Baldwin wrote:

> *Every good-bye ain't gone*: Human history reverberates with violent upheaval, uprooting, arrival and departure, hello and good-bye. Yet, I am not certain that anyone ever leaves home. ... I suspect, though I certainly cannot prove it, that every life moves full circle—towards revelation: You begin to see, and even rejoice to see, what you always saw.[249]

Toward the end of his life, Baldwin wrote similarly in his introduction to *The Price of the Ticket* (1985): "If I were still in the pulpit which some people (and they may be right) claim I never left, I would counsel my countrymen to the self-confrontation of prayer, the cleansing breaking of the heart which precedes atonement."[250] This is an astonishing statement; it suggests that he never really rejected his religious upbringing, nor the pastoral role that had so decisively shaped him, even if he clearly had no desire to relive what he called "my adolescent holy-roller terrors."[251]

Today we are in a position to follow Baldwin's own lead and explore the possibility that, in one sense, he never did leave the pulpit. Like Martin Luther King, Jr., Baldwin drew on the resources available to him from his early years in the pulpit and transformed them into literature and first-rate essays about politics and race.[252] When Baldwin writes, again in *The Price of the Ticket*, that he "abandoned the ministry in order not to betray myself by betraying the ministry," he articulates a central paradox: that only by leaving his faith behind could he remain true to it.[253] Indeed, he continued his ministry in his writing, which is full of religious language and content. In a moving tribute to James Baldwin's prophetic voice, the Nigerian playwright Wole Soyinka once praised his "near-evangelical commitment to the principle that rules all being—love sought, denied, waiting in the wings or hovering on the wing, a veritable *deus ex machina*, lacking only a landing permit from a blinkered humanity that hesitates at the door of salvation."[254]

3

Secular Theodicy: Saul Bellow, E.L. Doctorow, and Philip Roth

In *The Fire Next Time* (1963), James Baldwin recalls that when he began attending a predominantly Jewish high school in 1938, "the Jewish boys in high school were troubling because I could find no point of connection between them and the Jewish pawnbrokers and landlords and grocery-store owners in Harlem."[1] Besides Harlem, his only other reference point for Jews was the Hebrew Bible, but this too confused him: "It was bewildering to find them so many miles and centuries out of Egypt, and so far from the fiery furnace."[2] According to his strict Baptist upbringing, these Jewish kids were, "by definition, beyond any hope of salvation," and thus destined for the fiery furnace of Hell.[3] Yet Baldwin had doubts about such an exclusive soteriology: "My best friend in high school was Jewish. I wondered if I was expected to be glad that a friend of mind, or anyone, was to be tormented forever in Hell."[4] The thought of eternal damnation suddenly brought to mind another fiery furnace that was even more unsettling to him: "and I also thought, suddenly, of the Jews in another Christian nation, Germany. They were not so far from the fiery furnace after all, and my best friend might have been one of them."[5]

As his friendship with Emile Capouya deepened, and conflict with his father intensified, Baldwin's personal faith suffered. Not long before he finished high school in 1942, he preached his last sermon. He would soon leave the church for good. Baldwin's crisis of faith had been exacerbated not just by grappling with the problem of religious others, but also by the horrific news coming out of Germany. Baldwin could not help but wonder about the implications for Christianity "when a Christian nation surrenders to a foul and violent orgy, as it did during the Third Reich."⁶ "From my own point of view," he writes, "the fact of the Third Reich alone makes obsolete forever any question of Christian superiority, except in technological terms."⁷

Baldwin arrives independently at an insight most influentially articulated by Theodor Adorno and Max Horkheimer in *The Dialectic of Enlightenment* (1947).⁸ It was not difficult for Baldwin to understand genocide, alongside slavery itself, as the dark underside of civilization:

> White people were, and are, astounded by the holocaust in Germany. They did not know that they could act that way. But I doubt very much whether black people were astounded—at least, in the same way. For my part, the fate of the Jews, and the world's indifference to it, frightened me very much. I could not but feel, in those sorrowful years, that this human indifference, concerning which I knew so much already, would be my portion on the day that the United States decided to murder its Negroes systematically instead of little by little and catch-as-catch can.⁹

Arthur Koestler likewise noted the appalling indifference to the Holocaust in his essay "On Disbelieving Atrocities" (1944), in which he excoriated those who doubted or ignored mounting evidence of genocide: "It is the greatest mass-killing in recorded history; and it goes on daily, hourly, as regularly as the ticking of your watch."¹⁰ Disbelief was a common reaction to the sheer magnitude of mass murder being perpetrated by the Nazis. As Baldwin himself attests, "The German experiment during the war … was a horror not to be believed."¹¹

For many American Jewish writers, of course, the personal connection to the Holocaust was even closer, and the crisis of faith it engendered more pronounced. In a compelling memoir, *New York Jew* (1978), literary critic Alfred Kazin writes about his experience growing up as part of a Jewish immigrant family during the war—the same years that Baldwin was in high school. This was a time when, as Kazin vividly recalls, "I took down every morsel of fact and rumor relating to the murder of my people."¹² He continues:

And I, too, could personalize History. The line-up was always before my eyes. I could imagine my father and mother, my sister and myself, our original tenement family of "small Jews," all too clearly—fuel for the flames, dying by a single flame that burned us all up at once.[13]

Although like Baldwin he witnessed the "systematic murder of Europe's Jews" from afar, his relationship to it was obviously closer, for he could picture his own family all too clearly in the fiery furnace.[14] In February 1945, Kazin sailed for England and spent the next seven months in Europe. Indeed, he was in London on May 8, 1945, when the war officially ended and then went to Paris in July to give a series of lectures sponsored by the Guggenheim Foundation, where he also attended an exhibition at the Grand Palais called "Hitler's Crimes in France." There he contemplated a large photograph of a corpse at a German concentration camp: "his skeletal arm outstretched, like Christ on the cross."[15] The analogy between a victim of the Nazis and the crucified Christ is striking. Just as the Holocaust had challenged Baldwin's already precarious faith, it also challenged Kazin's relationship to Judaism. He recalls: "Now began the nightmare that would bring everything else into question, that will haunt me to my last breath."[16] Indeed, there would be no waking up from the nightmare; to go on living after such knowledge was like being "at the edge of the abyss created in modern culture, in all our cultured minds, by the extermination of the Jews."[17] In fact, Kazin did have relatives who were victims of the Shoah. Recounting the story of his aunt's death at the hands of the Nazis, he suggests that her religious faith was naive at best, and at worst delusional in the face of such evil: "Years after the war, from her children in Israel, I heard in detail of how my aunt had refused to flee with everyone else into the forest. 'Maybe it is God's will?' she had wondered. She was shot on her doorstep."[18]

Such cynicism about religion became the defining feature of a brand of secularism shared by many Jewish intellectuals and writers in the late twentieth century. We may be tempted to call this attitude post-religious insofar as it presumes God's absence from and absolute irrelevance to modernity, but of course like most secularisms its true antagonist, or counterpoint, is still God. The question asked by many Jewish intellectuals is not, "How could God have stood by and let the Holocaust happen?" but rather, "How could anyone possibly still believe in such a God after the Shoah?" Call it a secular theodicy. Now this phrase might have an oxymoronic ring, since theodicy is generally understood as a branch of theology concerned with reconciling a just God with the prevalence of evil in the world. What distinguishes this secular theodicy from traditional theodicy is that these writers have largely abandoned the project of reconciling *any* idea of God with the existence of evil on such a scale, which renders the whole project of traditional theodicy moot. To borrow the title of a book by the Jewish intellectual Richard Crossman, any deity who could permit such a catastrophe as the Holocaust can only be called *The God That Failed* (1950), eclipsed by what Koestler in his contribution to the book calls "the shadow of barbed wire."[19]

The American Jewish literary renaissance of the 1950s and 1960s was fraught with such quasi-theological speculation about the God that failed. Like O'Connor's failed apostates, Jewish writers embraced a version of secularism that remained tied to the religion they had abandoned. Adopting secular beliefs and attitudes, they espoused a form of unbelief as fervent in its way as fundamentalism, fueled as it was by a kind of rage at the God who simply no longer obtains in the modern world. Critics have long recognized that the Holocaust gave a new sense of urgency to US Jewish writers, who revised their view of Jewish identity in the aftermath of genocide, as did many American Jews.[20] As Kazin himself once observed, "The Jews were once held together by God [but they] are now held together, or should I say scared together by the Holocaust."[21]

Saul Bellow, E.L. Doctorow, and Philip Roth are among the most prominent Jewish writers who sought to account for how the Holocaust affected Jewish identity and community in their fiction, and in doing so, they kept coming back to the question of why religion could still matter to Jews after the Holocaust. Judging by how persistent this question was in their writings, these authors were obviously perplexed by how much religion evidently did matter to many American Jews—and even more so, it seemed, to American gentiles. We will see that their continuing obsession with religion was prompted at least in part by the religious revivals of the late twentieth century that I discussed in previous chapters, especially the growing Protestant evangelical movement. Jewish writers watched the rise of conservative evangelicalism with a mixture of bemusement and fear, especially once it became a potent political force beginning in the 1980s. Given their longstanding commitment to the Constitutional separation of church and state as a safeguard for religious pluralism, Jewish writers were wary of this seemingly activist religious agenda in the political arena. In their fiction, such wariness found expression in a sort of running dialogue with America's dominant religion, Christianity.

These writers could have benefitted from a newer version of secularism now unfolding in the work of scholars who seek to reenvision secularism as a distinct project in its own right, not as religion's other, or as religion's dialectical partner, but as simply beyond reference to religion. Talal Asad and Jose Casanova, among others, helpfully distinguish between the secular as an epistemic category, secularization as the historical processes that gave rise to the secular, and secularism as a political ideology that considers religion to be potentially dangerous and worth contesting.[22] According to Michael Warner, secularism "refers to the idea that the complex set of social transformations called 'secularization' can be embraced as a good thing."[23] Note that even these newer "secularisms" still largely depend on the binary opposition religion/secular that has proven virtually impossible to do without.[24] In the introduction to *Rethinking Secularism* (2011), Craig Calhoun, Mark Juergensmeyer, and Jonathan VanAntwerpen invoke the binary without really figuring out how to go beyond the current impasse, other than to think about it some more:

> The very use of the term "secular" signifies that we are buying into a secular/religious distinction that in some way defines not only the secular sphere itself but also the realm of the religious. ... Whether

it is seen as an ideology, a worldview, a stance toward religion, a constitutional framework, or simply an aspect of some other project—of science or a particular philosophical system—secularism is, rather than merely the absence of religion, something we need to think through.[25]

Secularism is often conceived as a state of maturity, objectivity, and reason that can be achieved only by abandoning the supposed irrationality of religion. Yet the root meaning of the "secular" stood in opposition to eternity, not religion, and we will see that US Jewish writers emphasized a secular, historical time as opposed to the messianic conception of time so central to Judaism. These writers elaborated a version of secularism that, like most secularisms then as now, predictably relied on an opposition between secularism and religion—the very thing, in short, they thought they had jettisoned. Even so, this distinctly Jewish version of secular theodicy contributed a rich, heretofore unrecognized dimension to contemporary US literary fiction.

By examining the work of three major Jewish writers through the lens of secular theodicy, this chapter will take up two dominant critical terms in the study of American Jewish literature, assimilation and ethnicity, and ask what difference it makes to bring a third, relatively neglected term into the discussion, namely religion.[26] Unsurprisingly, it makes a big difference. For while Jews are by and large more secular than other Americans, and Jewish writers more so, it turns out that American Jewish writers cannot so easily jettison Judaism from their fiction.[27] Bellow, Roth, and Doctorow are fascinated with religious beliefs and practices, whether as a rich resource to draw from in their fiction, or as the source of guilt about their ignorance of Judaism, or as the target of critique and satire. Their secularism remains inextricable from a great deal of God talk in their work, a consequence less of sympathetic identification than of confrontational antipathy. Far from banishing God from their fiction, these writers can't stop talking about him, as if taking up the challenge posed by Dietrich Bonhoeffer in his book *Prisoner for God* (1959): "How do we speak in a secular fashion of God?"[28]

The Death of God

The exploration of the Holocaust in American Jewish fiction coincided with another phenomenon that captured public attention in the 1960s, the so-called "death of God" theology, prominently featured in a "God Is Dead" cover story in *Time* magazine in 1966, which entered the popular lexicon through bumper stickers and graffiti (e.g., "God is dead," signed Nietzsche).[29] This death of God movement was no joke for many Jewish thinkers, however. Whereas much discourse about the Holocaust focused on the psychology and responsibility of the perpetrators, these thinkers broached the idea that God himself bore a major responsibility, or more radically, that one could not go on believing in God, much less in the ancient covenant between God and his chosen people. "For Jews," writes Kathryn Lofton, "the theological labor needed to be done after the Holocaust seemed insurmountable," and many thinkers believed that "Jews must now enter an age without God, since the Holocaust had decimated the viability of Jewish theism."[30]

The problem of theodicy was a major impetus for the death-of-God theology movement. Protestant theologians were key figures in the movement, which began with Gabriel Vahanian's *The Death of God* (1961) and culminated in *Radical Theology and the Death of God* (1966), by Thomas J.J. Altizer and William Hamilton. Yet Jewish theologians also figured prominently, most notably Richard Rubenstein. "Unlike his Protestant brothers," observes historian John K. Roth, "Rubenstein put the Holocaust at the center of his contributions to radical theology in the 1960s."[31] In his book *After Auschwitz: Radical Theology and Contemporary Judaism* (1966), Rubenstein outlined his argument that God's sovereignty was untenable and that God's covenant with Jews was therefore ruptured:

> How can Jews believe in an omnipotent, beneficent God after Auschwitz? Traditional Jewish theology maintains that God is the ultimate, omnipotent actor in the historical drama. It has interpreted every major catastrophe in Jewish history as God's punishment for a sinful Israel. I fail to see how this position can be maintained without

regarding Hitler and the SS as instruments of God's will. ... To see any purpose in the death camps, the traditional believer is forced to regard the most demonic, antihuman explosion in all history as a meaningful expression of God's purposes. The idea is simply too obscene for me to accept.[32]

This book became as much a lightning rod in the Jewish community as Philip Roth's early fiction, earning Rubenstein what one critic calls "an unprecedented torrent of personal abuse."[33]

The firestorm surrounding the book generated a number of intriguing responses. The editors of *Commentary* magazine sent out a survey of Jewish rabbis asking about the significance of the "death of God" in their thinking, subsequently published as "The State of Jewish Belief" (1966). One of only two contributors (out of thirty-eight) to mention the Holocaust in their responses was Rabbi Emile L. Fackenheim, who writes that "the generation of Auschwitz" must do "what Jews have always done in times of darkness—contend with the silent God."[34] In a follow-up essay, "On the Self-exposure of Faith to the Modern-secular World" (1967), he writes: "The events that are associated with the dread name of Auschwitz still pass human comprehension. ... They call everything into question: for the believing Jew, for the unbelieving Jew, for the Jew who is neither believer nor unbeliever but merely asks unanswered or unanswerable questions."[35]

A year later the magazine *Judaism* sponsored a symposium at which Fackenheim was one of the participants, along with Elie Wiesel and George Steiner, whose book *Language and Silence* (1967) had just been published. All were asked to speak on the theme of "Jewish Values in the Post-Holocaust Future." Wiesel calls into question the viability of the covenant for Jewish theology: "Well, it seems that for the first time in our history, this very covenant is broken. This is why the Holocaust has terrifying theological implications. ... It can be explained neither with God nor without him."[36] Yet other Jewish thinkers felt compelled to defend covenantal theology, not least Emil L. Fackenheim himself, whose subsequent book *God's Presence in History* (1970) has been hailed as "the most compelling affirmation of the covenant in the post-Holocaust era."³⁷ For Rubenstein, though, the traditional Jewish understanding of a God who acted in history to punish or redeem his people must be abandoned. In a new chapter included in the second edition of *After Auschwitz*, with the curious (not to say tautological) title "God after the Death of God," Rubenstein writes, "Belief in the sovereign God of covenant and election requires interpreting events such as the extermination of European Jewry," but many Jews "find this idea too great a strain on their credulity. Their experience of the death of God rests upon their loss of faith in the transcendent God of History, but not necessarily upon the loss of the sense of the sacred."³⁸

Even if the "death of God" movement was relatively short-lived, the broken covenant controversy continued. An important intervention into the debate was David G. Roskies's book *Against the Apocalypse: Responses to Catastrophe in Modern Jewish Culture* (1983), which posed the seemingly paradoxical question of whether the Holocaust was merely "an event" like other previous catastrophes that "signaled a breach of covenantal promise," such as the burning of the Temple in Jerusalem, or whether it must be considered "the Event itself," which is to say "the cataclysmic end of history."³⁹ In his provocative book *Why Should the Jews Survive? Looking Past the Holocaust toward a Jewish Future* (1995), Michael Goldberg forcefully argues against substituting the Holocaust for the Exodus story as the defining event in Jewish history:

> But if we view Jewish existence through the perspectives of a Holocaust-shaped narrative, neither God nor covenant worked to save the Jewish people from Hitler: If Jews survived, it was simply because the gas chambers failed to work quickly enough to kill them all. ... The challenge to Jews today is not outliving Hitler and the Nazis but overcoming the life-threatening story created in their aftermath.⁴⁰

To the question why should Jews survive, Goldberg answers: because they are a chosen people.

American Jewish writers share many concerns with radical theology, yet, on the whole, they seem somewhat less invested in questions about the existence of God or a broken covenant. Their fiction tends to pluralize points of view on these questions, strenuously avoiding anything that resembles advocacy. Writers may well have strong positions of their own about these issues, but in keeping with the modernist legacy of eschewing didacticism, their fiction is more dialogic than didactic. As Philip Roth contends in his book *Reading Myself and Others* (1975): "Fiction is not written to affirm principles and beliefs that everybody seems to hold, nor does it seek to guarantee the appropriateness of our feelings. The world of fiction, in fact, frees us from the circumscriptions that society places upon feeling."[41]

Consider Chaim Potok's novel *The Chosen* (1967), which represents very different if equally anguished responses to the Holocaust but does not valorize any one response over others. The first-person narrator, a thoughtful teenager named Reuven Malter, tells us that when his father David, a Reformed Jew and high school teacher, learns about the concentration camps, he "seemed unable to believe what he was reading."[42] But once this terrible knowledge sinks in, two consequences follow: first, he questions his belief in God; and second, he embraces Zionism. Even though David Malter remains somewhat theistic—he does not go so far as to claim that God is dead—he articulates something close to what I am calling secular theodicy. Whether or not God exists, the character explains, Jews can no longer rely on God's protection: "We cannot wait for God. If there is an answer, we must make it ourselves. ... We cannot wait for God."[43] Like Richard Rubenstein in *After Auschwitz*, he insists that history unfolds in secular time, not according to some providential plan. Potok's novel indicates why, as David puts it, the "Jewish world is changed" forever by the Holocaust, because it irrevocably alters a covenantal view of Jewish history and thus gives new meaning, a tragic one, to what it means to be Jewish.[44] David channels his anger about genocide into the Zionist movement, asserting that the "slaughter of six million Jews would have meaning only on the day a Jewish state was established. Only then would their sacrifice begin to make some sense; only then would the songs of faith they had sung on their way to the gas chambers take on meaning."[45] Potok juxtaposes David's response to the Holocaust with that of Reb Saunders, a rabbi and the father of Reuven's friend Danny Saunders. Echoing defenders of covenant theology like Fackenheim and Goldberg, the fictional rabbi Reb Saunders is unwilling to give up on God. "Master of the Universe," he beseeches, "how do you permit such a thing to happen?" to which David pointedly asks, "And did God answer him?"[46]

The Holocaust provided the impetus for an important body of literature about religion in postwar and contemporary US fiction, albeit written by writers who were moving away from any religious affiliation or practice themselves. This secular trend among Jewish writers did not mean that their fiction ignored important questions about God, Judaism, and theodicy raised by the Holocaust, questions that were also hotly debated in the radical theology of the same period. On the contrary, such questions were precisely what prompted the secular turn to begin with. Indeed, one could argue the rejection of Judaism created the need for redefining Jewishness on some other basis. Out of this void, a more ethnic and cultural understanding of Jewishness emerged. Andrew Hoberek contends that during "the classic era of Jewish assimilation" in the postwar era, when "Jews enter the American mainstream by entering the white-collar workforce," Jewish fiction emerged as a "distinct, ethnically defined genre. ... In fact, Jewish fiction provided a concrete instance of Jewish visibility and the emergence of Jewishness as a form of identity."[47]

The very title of Herberg's *Protestant-Catholic-Jew* indicates the prominent place that Jews once held in the national imaginary at mid-century, yet the book was written at a time when religion was becoming less reliable as an indicator of cultural difference. In fact, religion was in the process of being replaced by what David Hollinger has labeled the "ethno-racial pentagon" of white, black, brown, yellow, and red.[48] In the new calculus of identity, Jews were no longer the religious others they had once been for Protestants—not just because pluralism was more inclusive, but also because Jews were, and are, less religious. With "the demise of religion as a central feature of differentiation in America," many Jews felt the need to accommodate more racially inflected notions of identity into their understandings of what it meant to be Jewish.[49]

While the Jewish literary renaissance of the 1950s and 1960s was more ethnically marked, it was decidedly less religious. By and large it was "a secular literature," as Murray Baumgarten has argued, "defining itself in part in response to the Holocaust by declaring God irrelevant."[50] Ambivalent about their ethnicity and heritage, Jewish writers navigated the shifting waters of identity and cultural value. According to Morris Dickstein, the American Jewish writer of the postwar period was "cut off from his own uprooted parents" and in a sense "doubly alienated, from the prevailing national culture and from his own traditional culture."[51] Almost a rite of passage for Jewish writers, the disavowal of Judaism raised the possibility of a sort of diluted Jewishness, if not deracination. Leslie Fiedler worried, for instance, that as an assimilated Jew who wanted "to escape the limitations of my ancestral religion," he cannot "lay claim to being really Jewish."[52] Cynthia Ozick goes further: "When a Jew becomes a secular person he is no longer a Jew. This is especially true for makers of literature."[53] Ozick is being deliberately provocative, yet she points to the peculiarity, or problem, of the secular Jew, which likewise puzzled Alfred Kazin: "The problem, as always, is how to be a 'Jew' without 'Judaism.'"[54]

Bellow wrestled with this problem in a two-part lecture, "A Jewish Writer in America," which was first delivered in 1988 but not published until 2011 in *The New York Review of Books*: "I try to understand what it may signify to be a Jew who cannot live by the rules of conduct set down over centuries and millennia."[55] Since he cannot "be reconciled with Jewish orthodoxy," Bellow concedes "that my ancestors, if they were able to see and judge for themselves, would find me a very strange creature indeed, no less strange than my Catholic, Protestant, or atheistic countrymen. Yet their scandalously weird descendant insists that he is a Jew."[56] For Bellow, one simply had to accept that a secular Jew, however weird, was a Jew: "And of course he is one."[57]

Philip Roth is much less perturbed by the weirdness of the secular Jew. "Like Bellow and Malamud," Roth once wrote, "I was born to Jewish parents and raised self-consciously as a Jew. I don't mean that I was raised according to Jewish traditions or raised to be an observant Jew but that I was born into the situation of being a Jew, and it did not take me long to be aware of its ramifications."⁵⁸ Growing up in "an ethnic or cultural enclave" like Newark, New Jersey, which was "predominantly Jewish," he tells us, "wasn't unusual for an urban American child of my generation."⁵⁹ Yet even as Roth extols the assimilationist Jewish community of postwar Newark, there are still notable tensions in his fiction between modern secular Jews and traditional Jews, as perceptive critics of his work have argued. "I once reminded Philip Roth that the Jews were born in the desert, not in Newark," Kazin wrote in his *Journals*. "His intense, afflicted, sometimes screaming sense of his own Jewishness comes down, ritually, to a kind of shell game."⁶⁰

Suffice it to say that with the rise of identity politics in the postwar period, Jewish writers participated in the process of redefining and reimagining Jewish identity. In his essay "Imagining Jews" (1974), Roth himself observes in his inimitably breathless style:

> In an era which has seen the avid and, as it were, brilliant Americanization of millions of uprooted Jewish immigrants and refugees, the annihilation as human trash of millions of Europeanized Jews, and the establishment and survival in the ancient holy land of a spirited, defiant modern Jewish state, it can safely be said that imagining what Jews are and ought to be has been anything but the marginal activity of a few American-Jewish novelists.⁶¹

American Jewish novelists did not presume to tell Jews what they are or ought to be. Instead, they set out to represent Jews in all their complexity and multiplicity, which "might be described as imagining Jews *being* imagined, by themselves and others."⁶² I turn now to these imaginings.

Bellow's Blasphemies

"I can't remember going out of my way to be heterodox," Saul Bellow once said in an interview. "But I was born into an orthodox family, and I detested orthodoxy from the first."⁶³ Rejecting orthodoxy from an early age, Bellow hoped to transcend his own Jewish immigrant childhood by becoming a writer. The rejection of religion among aspiring Jewish writers was no doubt motivated in part by the fact that acceptance into the US literary canon would increasingly be predicated, not on religious, but on ethnic difference. Yet Bellow was notably resistant to the notion that his election to the canon had anything to do with Jewishness, just as he was resistant to thinking of Jewishness as an ethnic identity within a multicultural framework in the first place. "Can it be that we are tired of whatever it is that we in fact are—black, white, brown, yellow, male, female, large, small, Greek, German, English, Jew, Yankee, Southerner, Westerner, etc.—that what we now want is to rise above all these tiresome differences?" he asked.[64] Even when it came to what he in fact was—an American Jewish writer—Bellow could be notoriously prickly, as if the very idea of being an ethnic writer was somehow anathema to his humanist sensibility. When an interviewer asked him, "Would you consider yourself specifically a Jewish writer?" he responded, "I have never consciously written as a Jew. I have just written as Saul Bellow."[65] He repeatedly rejected labels: "This whole Jewish writer business is a sheer invention, by the media, by critics and by 'scholars.'"[66] Bellow declared again and again that he was under no obligation to represent Jews in his writing, making what amounts to a declaration of independence from his Jewish roots: "I don't have any sense of ethnic responsibility. That is not my primary obligation. My primary obligation is to my trade and not to any particular ethnic group."[67]

By the time he gave a two-part lecture mentioned earlier, "A Jewish Writer in America," whose very title signals acceptance of the label, Bellow seems to have reconsidered his position somewhat. Here, Bellow admits that he often wondered "how to position himself, and how to combine being a Jew with being an American and a writer. Not everyone thinks well of such a project."[68] Unlike some of his "Jewish contemporaries" who resorted to "evasions, dodges, ruses, and disguises," Bellow claims that for his part: "I had little patience with that kind of thing."[69] He now recognizes how much his religious upbringing must have influenced him: "This was my 'given' and it would be idle to quarrel with it, to try to revise or efface it."[70] Nonetheless, Bellow cannot help but move on from his Orthodox roots to embrace a modern secular Jewish identity:

> A millennial belief in a Holy God may have the effect of deepening the soul, but it is also obviously archaic, and modern influences would presently bring me up to date and reveal how antiquated my origins were. To turn away from those origins, however, has always seemed to me an utter impossibility. It would be a treason to my first consciousness to un-Jew myself.[71]

In the second part of the lecture, as if having it both ways, Bellow declares that he tried to find some middle ground between "Judaic mystical humanism" and "American secular humanism."[72] This accords with Tony Tanner's description of Bellow as someone who was both "in touch with immigrant experience" and "deeply immersed in the vast urban complexes of modern America," such that identity was "continually to be discovered and defined, never inherited and assumed."[73]

Bellow's fiction embodies this negotiation, or détente, between a religious inheritance and a secular sensibility. From his early novels *The Victim* (1947) and *The Adventures of Augie March* (1953), to later novels such as *Herzog* (1961) and *Mr. Sammler's Planet* (1970), Bellow explores the recurring themes of Jewish identity, religious pluralism, secularism, and theodicy. These novels can be read as part of a sustained meditation on secular theodicy throughout his career, especially insofar as Bellow grapples with the problem of theodicy after the Holocaust.

Looking back on the period just after the war, the author recalls that his "real revelation" about the Holocaust came in 1946, "more than a year after the German surrender, when I took my mother to a motion picture and we saw in a newsreel some details of the entrance of the American army into the concentration camp at Buchenwald."[74] He writes: "We witnessed the discovery of the mounds of dead bodies, the emaciated, wasted, but still living prisoners who were now being liberated, and of the various means of extermination in the camp, the various gallows, and also the buildings where gas was employed to kill the Nazis' victims en masse."[75] He felt moral outrage, of course, but he also felt "a deeply troubling sense of disgrace or human demotion, as if by such afflictions the Jews had lost the respect of the rest of humankind."[76]

A year later, Bellow published *The Victim* (1947), which includes a conversation about the origin of evil and the cause of human suffering—a dialogue, in other words, about theodicy. Kirby Allbee, a descendant of New England Protestant ministers, insists that from a "Jewish point of view," when a "man suffers, he's being punished."[77] "You'll find it all over the Bible," he declares. "God doesn't make mistakes. He's the department of weights and measures."[78] His interlocutor Asa Leventhal does not defend the Jewish point of view so much as he invokes the Holocaust to disqualify Allbee's view: "I don't see how you can talk that way. That's just talk. Millions of us have been killed. What about that?"[79] Leventhal avers that such suffering cannot be attributed to God; otherwise, millions of Jews were killed as some sort of divine punishment. Written only two years after the war, *The Victim* anticipates the argument of radical theologians: theodicy becomes virtually impossible to take seriously in the wake of the Holocaust.

In his early masterpiece of dialect literature, *The Adventures of Augie March*, Bellow again directs attention to the problem of theodicy. Early in the novel, we meet a character whose faith is shattered by the war. "What had made him an atheist was a massacre of Jews in his town," the narrator explains: "From the cellar where he was hidden he saw a laborer pissing on the body of his wife's younger brother, just killed. 'So don't talk to me about God,' he said."[80] Mr. Anticol considers himself an atheist, but ironically "he talked about God, all the time," and "his idea of grand apostasy" was that he attended the synagogue only on high holidays.[81] While denying God's existence, then, this character is still more or less committed to religious practice. Such residual religiosity after disavowing religion is another recurring theme in Bellow's fiction.

In Bellow's philosophical novel *Herzog* (1961), the protagonist Moses Elkanah Herzog suffers a midlife crisis and suddenly finds himself "desperate with longing for reality, for God."[82] A religious studies scholar,

Herzog is writing a book about religious revivals in "post-Christian America," *The Re-enchantment of the West in Modern Believing*.[83] Bellow was critical of the therapeutic ethos that dominated so many expressions of religion and spirituality in the 1960s, yet as Louis Menand has shown, he once owned an "energy accumulator," a specially designed box "in which the patient sits and absorbs potency-enhancing cosmic rays."[84] Herzog, too, is a spiritual seeker, and Bellow is self-aware enough to see the comedic potential of such seeking. At one point, he is "greatly stirred by the open horizon," which makes him think that there must be a Creator: "Herzog sighed and said to himself, 'Praise God—praise God.'"[85] At another point, he riffs on the Lord's Prayer: "*O Lord! He concluded, forgive all these trespasses. Lead me not into Penn Station.*"[86] Secular by both temperament and training, he is surprised by these spiritual stirrings late in life: "Evidently I continue to believe in God."[87] By the end of the novel, Herzog does little but copy the psalms in a frenzy of devotional writing, "putting into words what he had often thought but, for the sake of form, or something of the sort, had always suppressed."[88]

Herzog is much more than a semiautobiographical novel of religious longing, though. The eponymous protagonist's visit to Poland provides an occasion for serious engagement with theodicy in the novel. When he visits the "ruins of the ghetto" in Warsaw, for instance, Herzog believes that "he scented blood," as if the "stones" were "still smelling of wartime murders."[89] He decides that no "*theology of suffering*" can fully explain "*the making of corpses*" in what historian Timothy Snyder calls the bloodlands, where "Europe's most murderous regimes did their most murderous work."[90] "What is the philosophy of this generation?" Herzog wonders. "Not God is dead, that point was passed long ago. Perhaps it should be stated Death is God. This generation thinks—and this is the thought of thoughts—that nothing faithful, vulnerable, fragile can be durable or have any true power ... Herzog heard this as if it were being spoken slowly inside his head."[91] The passage calls attention to the novel's interiority; indeed, much of the narrative consists of Herzog's letters to God and others, including Kierkegaard, Nietzsche, Spinoza, and Whitehead. Here is another interior monologue:

> You think history is the history of loving hearts? You fool! Look at these millions dead. Can you pity them, feel them? You can nothing! There were too many. We burned them to ashes, we buried them with bulldozers. History is the history of cruelty, not love, as soft men think.... If the old God exists he must be a murderer.[92]

The "unbearable intensity of these ideas," the narrator tells us, makes Herzog faintly nauseous.[93] *Herzog* is surely the author's most searching rumination on the problem of theodicy to date.

The most explicit engagement with theodicy in Bellow's work is *Mr. Sammler's Planet*, arguably his only Holocaust novel. Just as he resisted the label Jewish writer, Bellow does not presume any special connection to the Holocaust as an American Jew, and although the novel's protagonist is a Holocaust survivor, Bellow does not "produce a valorized Jewish identity," as Amy Hungerford puts it, nor is he especially "committed to the Holocaust as a unique event or a uniquely Jewish event. Rather, Bellow consistently undermines such ideas of uniqueness and ethnic particularity within the novel."[94] The protagonist himself is reticent about relating his experiences during the war. "Why speak of it?" Artur Sammler declares.[95] When he finally does, however, it is predictably horrific.

Sammler had barely escaped death at the hands of the Nazis. Now blind in one eye and suffering from survivor's guilt, he describes himself as "an old Jew whom they had hacked at, shot at, but missed killing somehow, murdering everyone else with their blasts."[96] Primo Levi describes survivor's guilt as a sense of "shame" from being "alive in the place of another, at the expense of another."[97] Recounting the details of his near-death experience, Sammler emphasizes that his survival depended not on courage or strength but on mere chance: "he and sixty or seventy others, all stripped naked and having dug their own grave, were fired upon and fell in. Bodies upon his own body. Crushing. His dead wife nearby somewhere. Struggling out much later from the weight of corpses, crawling out of the loose soil."[98] The sentence fragments suggest that this is a repressed memory almost too painful to recall, but they lend psychological depth, plausibility, and weight to the scene, which is at once grammatically and psychologically fractured. Despite its staccato verbal rhythm, the scene is extraordinarily vivid and even visual. Later, Sammler again recalls how he and his wife had been thrown into a mass grave, which the soldiers began to fill with dirt. However, he insists that almost being buried alive was in no way exceptional or worse than what happened to others: "Certainly Sammler had not experienced things denied to everyone else. Others had gone through the like. Before and after."[99] Indeed, Sammler is quite matter of fact—stoic, even—about what happened to him: "Thing that happen, happen."[100] What happened that day was not a matter of fate; Sammler does not believe in fate. Nor did his survival depend on any sort of divine intervention; he does not believe in God either. He had simply "clawed his way out" of the grave, his survival a mere coincidence owing to the fact that he had been near the top: "If he had been at the bottom, he would have suffocated."[101]

Revisiting his well-known statement "To write a poem after Auschwitz is barbaric" in his subsequent book *Prisms* (1981), Theodor W. Adorno admits that "it may have been wrong to say that after Auschwitz you could no longer write poems," because "suffering has as much right to expression as a tortured man has to scream."[102] Adorno goes on to characterize survivor's guilt in a way that resonates with *Mr. Sammler's Planet*:

> But it is not wrong to raise the less cultural question whether after Auschwitz you can go on living—especially whether one who escaped by accident, one who by rights should have been killed, may go on living ... this is the drastic guilt of him who was spared. By way of atonement he will be plagued by dreams such as that he is no longer living at all, that he was sent to the ovens in 1944 and his whole existence since has been imaginary, an emanation of the insane wish of a man killed twenty years earlier.[103]

Bellow's protagonist could be described in much the same terms as a man who had been killed years earlier but who, cruelly resurrected from the grave, had to find some way to go on living.

A master of interiority, Bellow represents Artur Sammler's psychic and spiritual wounds through third-person limited omniscient narration focalized through the character's restless mind. Like Moses Herzog, Artur Sammler is an intellectual. He has translated Augustine, read Adorno. He is now working on a book about H.G. Wells, whom he met in Bloomsbury in the 1930s. Mr. Sammler also resembles Herzog insofar as he, too, is an atheist who retains a spiritual longing. "During the war I had no belief," he recalls. "I saw that God was not impressed by death."[104] Unable to explain why God remained silent, Sammler is not quite ready to put the last nail in God's coffin: "Not as long as the sense of God persists. I could wish that it did not persist. The contradictions are so painful. ... But very often, and almost daily, I have strong impressions of eternity. This may be due to my strange experiences, or to old age."[105] He calls these impressions "God adumbrations," and they are persistent enough to make him have doubts about his doubt.[106]

By the end of the novel, Sammler's mysticism has evolved into something closer to Pascal's wager, a tentative leap of faith. In the final scene, Sammler offers the "mental whisper" of a prayer over his nephew Dr. Arnold Elya Gruner's dead body, commending his soul to God:

> Remember, God, the soul of Elya Gruner, who, as willingly as possible and as well as he was able, ... was eager ... to do what was required of him. ... He was aware that he must meet, and he did meet—through all the confusion and degraded clowning of this life through which we are speeding—he did meet the terms of his contract. The terms which, in his inmost heart, each man knows. As I know mine. As we all know. For that is the truth of it—that we all know, God, that we know, that we know, we know, we know.[107]

Alan L. Berger has called this prayer "a secular *kaddish*," referring to the ancient Jewish prayer, and the novel's ending does indeed seem "hopeful about the possibility of redemption."[108] In Hungerford's reading, Bellow offers "a glimmer of redemptive power" at the end of the novel.[109]

Bellow's postwar fiction found a way to dramatize the inner life of highly self-conscious Jewish Americans, all of them haunted by genocide. In an extraordinary letter to Cynthia Ozick in 1987, Bellow castigated himself for not reckoning with the Holocaust earlier in his career:

I was too busy becoming a novelist to take note of what was happening in the Forties. I was involved with "literature" and given over to preoccupations with art, with language, with my struggle on the American scene, with claims for recognition of my talent or, like my pals of the Partisan Review, with modernism, Marxism, New Criticism, with Eliot, Yeats, Proust, etc.—with anything except the terrible events in Poland. Growing slowly aware of this unspeakable evasion I didn't even know how to begin to admit it into my inner life. Not a particle of this can be denied. And can I really say—can anyone say—what was to be done, how this "thing" ought to have been met? ... I can't even begin to say what responsibility any of us may bear in such a matter, in a crime so vast that it brings all Being into Judgment.[110]

Bellow's guilt, which might be seen as analogous to survivor's guilt, obscures what he did do in his fiction, for as Morris Dickstein observes: "In some sense they were all Holocaust novels, starting with *The Victim*, though the murder of Europe's Jews is scarcely mentioned in them."[111]

What I find compelling about Bellow's fiction is that, far from embracing a thoroughly secularized view of the cosmos, it contains remnants of a discarded Judaism that makes it open to mystery and wonder. Bellow attests that he was unwilling to "set aside as unimportant the age-long inclination of connecting the spiritual order in the universe with our own lives," combining a "pragmatic approach toward the social order" with a moral seriousness that he believed was not possible "without maintaining some connection to ancient religious notions such as the soul."[112] For a writer who also took a pragmatic approach toward the social order yet was highly skeptical about any religious notions such as the soul, we now turn to Bellow's heir apparent, Philip Roth.

Roth's Counter-pastoral

"I have no argument with God, because I don't believe in God," Roth once declared.[113] And in a documentary film, the writer all but gloats: "There's not a religious bone in my body."[114] No wonder Hungerford calls him a "post-religious writer" committed to a "secular vision."[115]

But if he is post-religious in his sensibility, then why is there so much religious content in his fiction? And why did he originally conceive of his vocation as a writer in quasi-religious terms? "At that time, still in my twenties, I imagined fiction to be something like a religious calling, and literature a kind of sacrament, a sense of things I have had reason to modify since."[116]

One answer to these questions can be found in his obvious indebtedness to Saul Bellow. Roth dedicated his early book of essays, *Reading Myself and Others* (1975), to Bellow, whom "I have read from the beginning with deepest pleasure and admiration."[117] From his predecessor, he learned that supposedly sacrosanct subjects such as religion need not be treated with reverence. In a 1966 interview, Roth owned that Bellow was

> important to me personally, [because] he laid claim upon certain areas of experience that no Jewish writer had before, and also took a certain attitude towards this experience. That is, he really knocked off the reverence and the piety, and that was a great relief, that you could really examine this material and treat it like a novelist, rather than a public relations man.[118]

Literature allowed him to "be funny in certain ways, and funny about certain things," even irreverent if necessary.[119] The controversy surrounding Roth's early fiction, and the fact that some of the most virulent attacks came from other Jews, was instructive as well, "I became aware of enormous differences of *sensibility* between my Jewish adversaries and myself—a good deal of the disagreement, I realized, had to do with somewhat antithetical systems of aversion and tolerance."[120] It was important for Roth to be "as loyal to one's doubts and uncertainties as to one's convictions. ... In this sense, the genre is the message, and the message is agnostic."[121] Bellow and Roth both understood that religion should not be treated "too piously, really," which is not to say that they didn't take the subject seriously.[122]

For examples of this refreshingly irreverent approach to religion, we need look no further than Roth's first book of fiction, *Goodbye,*

Columbus (1959). In the short story "The Conversion of the Jews," for example, Oscar "Ozzie" Freedman becomes convinced that if God can create the world in six days, as Genesis holds, then why is he not also be capable of a Virgin Birth?[123] Clearly provoking his teachers, Ozzie cannot help but blurt out to Rabbi Marvin Binder, "You don't know anything about God!"[124] The Rabbi punches Ozzie in the nose and bloodies it, whereupon Ozzie proceeds to the roof of the building and threatens to jump off unless everyone, the Rabbi included, get down on their knees "in the Gentile posture of prayer."[125] "Rabbi Binder, do you believe in God," Ozzie shouts from the rooftop. "Tell me you believe God can make a child without intercourse."[126] All of twenty-three years old when he wrote this story, Roth once said in an interview that he wanted to parody the kind of "religious exclusiveness" that can lead religious people to affirm some miracles while denying others, but according to the writer, "the comedy" derives less from "any satire directed at the characters" than from "the bizarre nature" of the plot, in which "a little Jewish boy finds himself playing God on a synagogue roof."[127]

Much of the humor also derives from what we might call religious syncretism, Roth's relentless blurring of boundaries between Christianity and Judaism, which is also evident in the title story "Goodbye, Columbus." After dropping off his girlfriend Brenda Patimkin in a doctor's office to be fitted for a diaphragm, the Jewish protagonist Neil Klugman then ventures into St. Patrick's Cathedral, of all places, and sits down in one of the pews at the back of the church:

> I took a seat at the rear and while I couldn't bring myself to kneel, I did lean forward onto the back of the bench before me, and held my hands together and closed my eyes. I wondered if I looked like a Catholic, and in my wonderment I began to make a little speech to myself. Can I call the self-conscious words I spoke prayer? At any rate, I called my audience God. God, I said, I am twenty-three years old. I want to make the best of things. Now the doctor is about to wed Brenda to me, and I am not entirely certain this is all for the best.[128]

Along with a promiscuous mixing of Christian and Jewish traditions, Roth's early fiction also prominently features agnosticism insofar as the characters are uncertain about what they believe. We know that Neil is not observant from an earlier scene at Brenda's house in the leafy suburbs of Short Hills, New Jersey. When Mrs. Patimkin asks him what synagogue his family belongs to, Neil offers a "rueful confession" that he stopped going when his parents moved to Arizona.[129] He finds himself wondering "whether Mrs. Patimkin caught the false tone in my voice, … especially when I recalled the decade of paganism prior to my parents' departure."[130] When Neil Klugman prays to a God he doesn't believe in, readers may wonder if there is any genuine contrition in his mimicry of Catholic prayer or whether his performance is merely a sort of youthful insouciance. "My work does not offer answers," Roth often asserted. "I am trying to represent the experience, the confusion and toughness of certain moral problems. People always ask what's the message. I think the worst books are the ones with messages. My fiction is about people in trouble."[131] Neil certainly looks to be in trouble in Mrs. Patimkin's Short Hills mansion, as she refuses to drop the subject, demanding to know whether he is orthodox or conservative. Neil answers evasively: "I'm just Jewish."[132] This answer is not likely to appease Mrs. Patimkin, but suddenly, the phone rings, thereby ending her little interrogation about his faith. "I spoke a silent orthodox prayer to the Lord," Neil tells us, implying that God has actually saved him from her prying questions.[133]

Both the prayer in the cathedral and this silent orthodox prayer suggest that Neil is only pretending, though what occurs partway through the earlier prayer begins to look like something more earnest and authentic when Neil begins to question how humans can approach God at all:

> If we meet You at all, God, it's that we're carnal, and acquisitive, and thereby partake of You. … It was an ingenious meditation, and suddenly I felt ashamed. I got up and walked outside, and the noise of Fifth Avenue met me what an answer:
>
> Which prize do you think, *schmuck*? Gold dinnerware, sporting-goods trees, nectarines, garbage disposals, bumpless noses, Patimkin Sink, Bonwit Teller—

But damn it, God, that *is* You!
And God only laughed, that clown.[134]

Neil's imagined conversation with God flirts with blasphemy ("But damn it, God, that *is* You!") only to come back to a kind of belief, or leap of faith, a provisional assumption that God exists. What prompts Neil's self-conscious posturing in St. Patrick's Cathedral is not an underlying cynicism about Judaism (or Christianity for that matter), but a willful suspension of disbelief. Does Neil really imagine that he is praying to the Jewish God in a Catholic church? For that matter, does Neil believe that his prayer is heard? "At any rate, I called my audience God."[135]

This churchgoing episode anticipates what will become a signature motif in Roth's work: namely, a residual religiosity that haunts his mostly secular and sex-obsessed male protagonists. His characters tend to be as unbelieving as the author himself, yet they betray a fascination with religion and evince a playful attitude toward the sacred that borders on nostalgia even as they disavow any personal connection to Judaism. When Brenda invites Neil to visit her at Radcliffe for the Jewish holidays, and he tells her he can't take time off his work at a local Newark library, she tells him to say he's had a conversion. Neil likes the idea: "I'm an orthodox Jew, for God's sake, I ought to take advantage of it."[136] He proves willing to play the religion card, as it were.

The most controversial story in *Goodbye, Columbus*, "Defender of the Faith," whose very title invokes the honorific that Pope Leo X bestowed on British monarch Henry VIII, features a manipulative Jewish solider Sheldon Grossbart who similarly persuades sergeant Nathan Marx, also Jewish, to issue him a weekend pass for what he claims will be a Seder meal at his aunt's house. It turns out to be takeout Chinese food, the implication being that Grossbart, too, is being disingenuous. Both characters obtain special privileges for rituals they do not actually observe.

Roth's best-selling novel *Portnoy's Complaint* (1969) shows how disputes about religion sowed divisions in Jewish families, driving a wedge between the younger and older generations.

During a heated exchange with his father on the Sabbath, Alexander Portnoy announces that he refuses to go to synagogue: "Look, I don't believe in God and I don't believe in the Jewish religion—or in any religion. They're all lies."[137] This dispute predictably exacerbates a growing and somewhat Oedipal rivalry with his father: "I will not pretend to be anything that I am not!" Portnoy exclaims. "I don't care how lonely and needy my father is, the truth about me is the truth about me, and I'm sorry but he'll just have to swallow my apostasy whole!"[138]

The eponymous Everyman of Roth's late novel *Everyman* (2006) shares a striking resemblance to Portnoy in his adolescent rebellion against Judaism. In *Everyman*, the character brags that he "stopped taking Judaism seriously at thirteen—the Sunday after the Saturday of his bar mitzvah—and had not set foot since then in a synagogue."[139] Like Portnoy, Everyman is not reticent about sharing his contempt for religion: "Religion was a lie that he had recognized early in life, and he found all religions offensive. ... No hocus-pocus about death and God or obsolete fantasies of heaven for him."[140] Similarly, Portnoy throws a tantrum on the morning of his bar mitzvah, admonishing his father for sucking, as he puts it, on "that sour grape of a religion."[141]

Taking advantage of "all manner of dwindling prohibitions" in the postwar period, the first generation of Jews born to immigrant parents often found themselves disconcerted by their "surprisingly goylike Jewish children."[142] These "breakaway young," as Roth calls them in *Operation Shylock* (1993), refused to be constrained by the old prohibitions and rules; indeed, somehow they "had it in their heads to be Jews in a way no one had ever dared to be Jews in our three-thousand-year history: speaking and thinking American English, *only* American English, with all the apostasy that was bound to beget."[143] As the word "apostasy" obviously suggests, this grand experiment in reinventing Jewish identity often involved disavowing religious observance. In the first volume of his critically acclaimed American trilogy, *American Pastoral* (1997), Roth returns to Newark at "the historical moment in postwar American life" that had "the greatest impact on my generation."[144] "Let's remember the energy," recalls Roth's fictional alter ego Nathan Zuckerman at the start of his speech given at Weequahic High School for a class of 1950 reunion, notably the same high school and year as the author.[145] In a paean to postwar prosperity, Nathan tells his classmates that in spite of "a generalized mistrust of the Gentile" world and "an undercurrent of anxiety" following the war, "ours was not a neighborhood steeped in darkness. The place was bright with industriousness. There was a big belief in life and we were steered relentlessly in the direction of success: a better existence was going to be ours."[146]

But instead of the "anticipated American future that was simply to have unrolled out of … each generation's breaking away from the parochialism a little further," what happens in *American Pastoral* is a cautionary tale in which Seymour "the Swede" Levov's optimism and complacency are "disrupted" by the countercultural upheavals of the 1960s.[147] Seymour had tried to be "rid of the traditional Jewish habits and attitudes," freeing himself from the "constraining obsessions" of religion "so as to live unapologetically as an equal among equals."[148] His parents objected to him marrying a Catholic, but he ignores them, marries a former beauty queen, and buys a farmhouse in Old Rimrock, New Jersey, where "differences of religion" meant nothing.[149] Seymour's seemingly perfect life unravels, however, when his daughter Merry becomes a violent revolutionary and then a religious fanatic: "They raised a child who was neither Catholic nor Jew, who instead was first a stutterer, then a killer, then a Jain."[150] She planted a bomb in Hamlin's General Store that killed a local citizen, Dr. Fred Conlon. "That bomb detonated his life," the narrator Nathan Zukerman writes. "His perfect life was over."[151] In a remarkable passage, the narrator describes how the bomb completely shatters the Swede's pastoral idyll,

> initiating the Swede into the displacement of another America entirely, the daughter and the decade blasting to smithereens his particular form of utopian thinking, the plague America infiltrating the Swede's castle and there infecting everyone. The daughter who transports him out of the longed-for American pastoral and into everything that is its antithesis and its enemy, into the fury, the violence, and the desperation of the counterpastoral—into the indigenous American berserk.[152]

In a sense, Merry was only enacting a more radical form of her parents' earlier rebellion, during a tumultuous time when "traditional family cohesion was under attack from many directions."[153]

The Plot Against America (2004), Roth's extraordinary counterfactual novel and the final volume of the American trilogy, again turns back the clock to a period of optimism in the 1940s, when American Jews defined themselves more or less on their own terms. "It was work that identified and distinguished our neighbors far more than religion," Roth writes. "Nobody in the neighborhood had a beard or dressed in the antiquated Old World style or wore a skullcap."[154] Even if they were observant, they "were no longer observant in the outward, recognizable ways," and their Jewish identity "didn't issue from the rabbinate or the synagogue or from their few formal religious practices."[155] Rather, being Jewish was simply another way of being American:

> These were Jews who needed no large terms of reference, no profession of faith or doctrinal creed, in order to be Jews, and they certainly needed no other language—they had one, their native tongue, whose vernacular expressiveness they wielded effortlessly and, whether at the card table or while making a sales pitch, with the easygoing command of the indigenous population. Neither was their being Jews a mishap or a misfortune or an achievement to be "proud" of. What they were was what they couldn't get rid of. Their being Jews issued from their being themselves, as did their being American. It was as it was, in the nature of things, as fundamental as having arteries and veins, and they never manifested the slightest desire to change it or deny it, regardless of the consequences.[156]

That American Jewish identity was the product of a particular moment. In 1940, there were about four and a half million American Jews. It was a period of relative freedom and optimism. "Israel didn't yet exist, six million European Jews hadn't yet ceased to exist," Roth points out.[157] After the Holocaust, "everything changed."[158]

If the burdens of ethnicity and religion were being sloughed off by younger generations of American Jews, the Holocaust turns out to be one burden that could not be easily dismissed, whether or not one had any direct connection to the Nazi genocide. *The Ghost Writer* (1979), Roth's first Nathan Zuckerman novel, is a frankly iconoclastic attempt to reckon with the Shoah. Zuckerman, an aspiring young writer based on Roth, is "at odds with his family over a story they find anti-Semitic," so he decides to get back at his family by writing an even more controversial short story.[159] In this story, titled "Femme Fatale" and included as a chapter in *The Ghost Writer*, Zuckerman imagines that the young woman he met while spending the night at the home of his mentor E.I. Lonoff (probably based on Bernard Malamud) is none other than Anne Frank. Contrary to what everyone believes, she actually survived the Holocaust and lives under an assumed name: "After the war she had become Amy Bellette."[160] The popular identification with Anne Frank as a representative Jewish victim of the Holocaust, a sort of surrogate for the six million, is surely one of Roth's satirical targets. In defending her decision to take an alias and go into hiding, Amy Bellette explains: "I was the incarnation of the millions of unlived years robbed from the murdered Jews. It was too late to be alive now. I was a saint."[161] According to Roth, the sanctification of Anne Frank amounts to something like a "new religion, Holocaustomania."[162]

The term comes from *Operation Shylock*, which Michael Rothberg calls Roth's "most sustained and direct engagement with the Nazi genocide and its implications."[163] What is most interesting about the novel for my purposes is its engagement with the problem of theodicy. In this novel, the protagonist "Philip Roth" confronts yet another authorial double, Moishe Pipik, who is trying to garner support for a repatriation effort called Diasporism in hopes of reviving the "European Jewish life that Hitler all but annihilated between 1939 and 1945."[164] The fictional character Philip Roth (like the real one) travels to Israel to interview the Holocaust survivor and novelist Aharon Appelfeld for *The New York Times*. While in Jerusalem, the character and narrator Philip Roth decides "to face down my imposter" and find out once and for all whether "one or the other of us" is a "ghost."[165] And when he finally encounters his impersonator at the King David Hotel, Moishe Pipik is indeed ghost-like: "He was ridiculously light, as though the disease had eaten through his bones, as though there was nothing left of him."[166] Only then does Roth realize that he parts his hair on the opposite side, suggesting that he has "modeled himself on my photograph."[167] Facing his double, in other words, is like looking at himself in the mirror. No sooner has Moishe Pipik been ejected from the hotel room during the ensuing scuffle than the phone rings, and Roth picks up the receiver. A raspy voice then asks him the following question:

> "Philip Roth, where was God between 1939 and 1945? I'm sure he was at Creation. I'm sure He was at Mount Sinai with Moses. My problem is where He was between 1939 and 1945. That was a dereliction of duty for which even He, *especially* He, cannot ever be forgiven."
>
> I was being addressed in a thick, grave Old Country accent, a hoarse, rough, emphysemic voice that sounded as though it originated in something massively debilitated.
>
> Meanwhile someone had struck up a light, rhythmic knuckle rapping on my door. ... Could it be Pipik on the phone if it was also Pipik at the door? How many of him were there?
>
> "Who is this?" I asked into the phone.
>
> "I spit on this God who was on vacation from 1939 to 1945!"
>
> I hung up.[168]

This character recalls debates about the covenant in Jewish theology insofar as he cannot believe God could have abandoned his chosen people, much less punished them through the Holocaust. The caller still believes in God, apparently, yet he cannot forgive God for this dereliction of duty. The dismissiveness of Roth's response ("I hung up") hints that the author, or at least his persona, cannot really be bothered to consider such matters, since he doesn't believe in God to begin with. "I could almost believe I was smart enough not to be asking" such questions, Roth ambiguously declares, but then again, perhaps "it was my own voice that I had heard and mistaken for his."[169]

This fictional meditation on theodicy is doubly mediated, of course, since it issues from a disembodied voice on the telephone that may or may not be Moishe Pipik. In a 1986 obituary of Bernard Malamud in *The New York Times Book Review*, Roth noted "the freedom conferred by masks," which affords writers "a weirdly exhilarating sort of masochistic relief from the weight of sobriety and dignified inhibition."[170] Roth takes obvious pleasure in using fictional alter egos and other characters to voice controversial ideas. Consider a scene in *Operation Shylock* when the character George Ziad offers an account of how American Jews reacted to the Holocaust while driving from Jerusalem to Ramallah, which a fictional Roth redacts as follows:

> First—according to George's historical breakdown of the cycle of Jewish corruption—were the pre-Holocaust, postimmigration years of 1900 to 1939: a period of renouncing the Old Country for the New ... the feverish period of toiling to construct in America, and in English, a new life and identity as Jews. After this, the period of calculated amnesia, 1939 to 1945, the years of immeasurable catastrophe, when, with lightning speed, those families and communities from which the newly, incompletely Americanized Jews had voluntarily severed their strongest ties were quite literally obliterated by Hitler. The destruction of the European Jewry registered as a cataclysmic shock on American Jews, not only because of its sheer horror but also because this horror, viewed irrationally through the prism of their grief, seemed to them in some indefinable way *ignited* by them—yes, instigated by the wish to put an end to Jewish life in Europe that their massive emigration had embodied.[171]

There is much to say about this often-cited passage, but the first thing we can say is that the character Philip Roth provides "a condensation of his argument, a good deal more cogent for being summarized."[172] George Ziad is also described as an unbridled and inexhaustible talker. Clearly, Roth means to distance himself from this peroration on the meanings of the Holocaust. The narrator imagines that his many semiautobiographical characters—Zuckerman, Kepesh, Tarnapol, Pipik, and Ziad—have "broken free of print and mockingly reconstituted as a single satirical facsimile of me."[173] Yet he also assures us that "there is no collusion here, no secret machinations between Moishe Pipik and me or between George Ziad and me, that I have not put anyone up to anything for any personal, political, or propagandistic reason whatsoever."[174] When asked whether "we should read your books as confession, as autobiography barely disguised," an exasperated Roth replied: "You should read my books as fiction, demanding the pleasures that fiction can yield," and then adds: "These words *confessional* and *autobiographical* constitute yet another obstacle between the reader and the work—in this case, by strengthening the temptation, all too strong in a distracted audience anyway, to trivialize fiction by turning it into gossip."[175]

In his last novel *Nemesis* (2010), Roth offers another profound meditation on the problem of theodicy. Set during a devastating polio outbreak in the summer of 1943, the novel describes this tragedy through the perspective of an earnest playground director named Bucky Cantor, age twenty-three, whose poor eyesight prevents him from fighting in the war. No sooner had he begun work as playground director for the summer than one of his charges, Herbie Steinmark, gets ill and dies, followed by another victim, Alan Avram Michaels. The death of one so young, not least a boy in his care, makes Bucky think long and hard about religion. "*Nemesis* is notable among Roth's books for containing a Hebrew prayer," Claudia Roth Pierpont points out, one altogether "more serious" than the pseudo-prayers of Neil Klugman and Alexander Portnoy mentioned earlier.[176] The prayer reads in part: "May His great Name be blessed forever and ever."[177] When the rabbi recites the "God-glorifying Kaddish," Bucky cannot bring himself to join in reciting the prayer, not because he doesn't know the words but rather because he does not wish to glorify God.[178]

While it had never occurred to him to question God when his grandfather died, Bucky now finds himself enraged at God for a boy whose life was cut short in the prime of his youth: "How could there be forgiveness—let alone hallelujahs—in the face of such lunatic cruelty?"[179] In a masterful passage of free indirect discourse, Roth goes off on an extended riff in this vein:

> They all joined the rabbi in reciting the mourner's prayer, praising God's almightiness, praising extravagantly, unstintingly, the very God who allowed everything, including children, to be destroyed by

death. ... It would have seemed far less an affront to Mr. Cantor for the group gathered in mourning to declare themselves the celebrants of solar majesty, the children of an ever-constant solar deity, and, in the fervent way of our hemisphere's ancient heathen civilizations, to abandon themselves in a ritual sun dance around the dead boy's grave—better that ... than to swallow the official lie that God is good and truckle before a cold-blooded murderer of children.[180]

All this comes directly before Roth reproduces the actual prayer, in both Hebrew and in English, which stacks the deck against any defense of God. However, the reason he is so angry with God is because he accepts that God is all-powerful and sovereign. If God lies behind everything in existence, including the polo virus, then blame for the epidemic's victims can be placed at the foot of "the creator ... who made the virus."[181] Bucky's reasoning here involves him in the branch of theology known as theodicy. Theologians have worked out a number of responses, not to say solutions, to the problem of evil, all of which attempt to redirect the cause and origin of evil. Augustine argued that God is ultimately not the source of evil; in fact, evil does not exist except as a corruption or what Augustine calls the privation of goodness. Whatever solution one might devise, however, the problem of evil still remains as a fundamental challenge to theodicy.

Does evil originate in our free will to disobey God, as in the biblical account of Cain's first crime? One of the typical moves theodicy makes is to drive a wedge between God and evil. When Bucky joins his girlfriend Marcia at a summer camp in the Poconos after his program in Newark is shut down because of the virus, she tries to assuage his feeling of guilt by letting God off the hook for what happened, because, after all "God didn't create polio."[182] By this point, Bucky is on the verge of renouncing his faith and attributing human suffering to mere chance:

> He was struck by how lives diverse and by how powerless each of us is up against the force of circumstance. And where does God figure in this? Why does He set one person down in Nazi-occupied Europe with a rifle in his hands and the other in the Indian Hill dining lodge in front of a plate of macaroni and cheese? Why does He place one

Weequahic child in polio-ridden Newark for the summer and another in the splendid sanctuary of the Poconos?[183]

If God is omnipotent, then He must be held responsible for whatever happens in the world. If there is no God, then everything that happens in the world is more or less a matter of chance. What are readers to make of the fact that Bucky is the one who had carried the virus all along? It turns out that he is the one responsible for the outbreak in Newark, and when he joins Marcia at summer camp in the Poconos, he brings the virus there as well. We know this because Bucky ultimately contracts polio and becomes paralyzed from the waist down. While this doesn't let God off the hook, exactly, it does provide epidemiological evidence for how the polio virus was introduced to the Jewish neighborhood in Newark and then spread to the Poconos summer camp.

At the end of the novel, Bucky encounters one of his old students, Arnie Mesnikoff, who has in fact been the narrator all along. Unlike Bucky, Arnie had gotten married and had children. He started a business retrofitting old buildings, making them accessible to those with disabilities. "You speak of God," Arnie remarks, but do you "still believe in this God you disparage?"[184] Bucky somewhat surprisingly answers yes, which leads Arnie to reflect on his friend's belief:

> Bucky's conception of God, as I thought I understood it, was of an omnipotent being whose nature and purpose was to be adduced not from doubtful biblical evidence but from irrefutable historical proof, gleaned during a lifetime passed on this planet in the middle of the twentieth century. His conception of God was of an omnipotent being who was a union not of three persons in one Godhead, as in Christianity, but of two—a sick fuck and an evil genius.[185]

Yet Roth's narrator goes on to develop a counterargument to this version of theodicy that seems to me to stand at the heart of Roth's secular enterprise. What Arnie objects to in Bucky's conception of God is not the blatant blasphemy of declaring Him a sick fuck and an evil genius, but the "stupid hubris" of imagining that his own or anyone's suffering is anything more than "pointless, contingent, preposterous, and tragic."[186]

Insisting on being the tragic scapegoat, Bucky believes that he was God's "invisible arrow" that caused the polio outbreak in 1944.[187] The truth is that we cannot know, just as Marcia had insisted all along. "You have no idea what God is! No one does or can!"[188] Roth admits that it is impossible to prove that God does not exist, much less that He does exist. The best we can hope for is mystery and uncertainty.[189]

The cultural historian Susan Jacoby attributes her own atheism "to my first encounter ... with the scourge of polio" at age seven.[190] When a nine-year-old friend contracted the disease in 1952, Jacoby visited him in the hospital. "Why would God do that to a little boy?" she asked her mother, whose response hints of a divergence between the official religious response and that of laypeople like her mother: "She sighed in a way that telegraphed her lack of conviction and said: 'I don't know. The priest would say God must have his reasons, but I don't know what they could be.'"[191] Jonas Salk's polio vaccine became available three years later, in 1955, though not in time to save Jacoby's friend or Jacoby's faith. Her friend died of the disease shortly after her hospital visit, "by which time," she adds, "I was a committed atheist."[192] In this anecdote, Jacoby portrays her atheism as a consequence of her encounter with the ravages of the polio epidemic, couching it as a kind of conversion experience, or "how I came to believe what I believe."[193] For Jacoby, atheism frees her from theodicy: "I do not have to ask, as all people of faith must, why an all-powerful, all-good God allows such things to happen."[194] And she views her freedom from "what is known as the theodicy problem" as "a positive blessing, not a negation of belief."[195]

But does atheism really free Jacoby from the theodicy problem? While they may not share the burden of asking why God allows bad things to happen, atheists very often rely on that very question to explain why they don't believe in God. "The atheist is free to concentrate on the fate of this world," Jacoby claims, "without trying to square things with an unseen overlord in the next. Atheists do not want to deny religious believers the comfort of their faith. We do want our fellow citizens to respect our deeply held conviction that the absence of an afterlife lends a greater, not a lesser, moral importance to our actions on earth."[196] Like

Jacoby, Roth remains somewhat surprisingly dependent on the very religious grounds that he, too, presumably rejects.

Consider Nathan Zuckerman's endorsement of Dionysian paganism in *The Human Stain* (2000). Ostensibly reporting Faunia Farley's personal beliefs following her affair with a much-older man, Coleman Silk, Zuckerman (through Silk's mistress) asserts that the human stain has

> nothing to do with disobedience. Nothing to do with grace or salvation or redemption. It's in everyone. ... All she was saying about the stain is that it's inescapable. That, naturally, would be Faunia's take on it: the inevitably stained creatures that we are. Reconciled to the horrible, elemental imperfection. She's like the Greeks, like Coleman's Greeks. Like their gods. ... Not the Hebrew God, elementally alone, elementally obscure, monomaniacally the only god there is, was, and always will be, with nothing better to do than worry about Jews. And not the perfectly desexualized Christian man-god and his uncontaminated mother and all the guilt and shame that an exquisite unearthliness inspires. Instead the Greek Zeus, entangled in adventure, vividly expressive, capricious, sensual, exuberantly wedded to his own rich existence, anything but alone and anything but hidden. Instead the *divine* stain. A great reality-reflecting religion for Faunia Farley if, thought Coleman, she'd known anything about it. As the hubristic fantasy has it, made in the image of God, all right, but not ours—*theirs*. God debauched. God corrupted. A god of life if ever there was one. God in the image of man.[197]

Once again, Roth insulates himself from the charge that he himself espouses such a view, which is multiply mediated here as Zuckerman's interpretation of Faunia Farley's paganism. Roth has never been in the business of justifying his own beliefs. "I don't write about my convictions," he insists. "I write about the comic and tragic consequences of holding convictions."[198] Fiction allows him to think his way into convictions, be they Christian or Jewish, pagan or secular. Readers may find themselves disoriented, if not offended, by the almost vertiginous cacophony of ideas and voices bouncing off one another in his fiction, yet comedy has the salutary effect of disarming whatever personal offense they might take from Roth's irreverent secular sensibility.

Saint Doctorow

Although he was raised in the Bronx by lower-middle-class American Jewish parents, E.L. Doctorow is "routinely omitted from the canon of Jewish literature."[199] Like both Bellow and Roth, Doctorow thinks religion "need not play a critical role in defining oneself as a Jew."[200] Still, Doctorow describes himself as the product of "an irresolvable religious conflict" in his family: the men tended to be skeptics going back many generations, while the women remained "to one degree or another observant," and the author has had a lifelong fascination with religion:

> As the son of my fathers I am nonobservant, a celebrant of the humanism that has no patience for a religious imagination that asks me to abandon my intellect. But as the son of my mothers, I am unable to discard reverence, however unattached to an object, in recognition that a spontaneously felt sense of the sacred engages the whole human being as the intellect alone cannot.[201]

This openness to mystery and reverence makes Doctorow an astute observer of the US religious landscape. Delivering the William E. Massey Lectures in the History of American Civilization at Harvard University in 2003, Doctorow pointed to an interesting paradox, suggesting that while "our mainstream religious traditions" have "liberalized themselves," this secularizing process "has, in turn, provoked the rise of evangelical and fundamentalist movements that are defiantly orthodox."[202] Both the liberalization of mainline churches and the emergence of fundamentalism are part of the same historical processes—two sides of the same coin, as it were—which help us understand that religion and the secular are not in opposition but in a dialectical relationship. To be sure, Doctorow does not have much patience with fundamentalism. "It's very hard to discuss faith with militantly faithful people," he observes elsewhere. "Faith is closure."[203] Although he is highly critical of dogmatism, Doctorow is an advocate of religious pluralism, which compels him to recognize that secularists cannot bar religious conservatives from our deliberative democracy.

In his ambitious postmodern novel *City of God* (2000), a fictional reworking of Saint Augustine's classic work with the same title, Doctorow delves into a number of events and themes we have been tracing in the novels of Bellow and Roth: in particular, the problem of theodicy in relation to the Holocaust. In *City of God*, Augustine assured early Christians that whatever the fate of Rome might be (the city had just been sacked by the Visigoths in 410), those who keep their eyes on the heavenly city of New Jerusalem, or the City of God, will ultimately prevail. Doctorow's earthly city is New York, not Rome, and his secularism makes him question the binary between the heavenly city and the earthly one. "You wonder how much God had to do with this," he writes, "how much the splendor and insolence of the modern city creatively built from the disparate intentions of generations of men comes of the inspiration of God."[204] This is Doctorow's version of Tertullian's famous question: what has Manhattan to do with Jerusalem?

City of God begins with a remarkable fictional account of the Big Bang, as if to suggest that the greatest challenge to our anthropocentric understandings of God is not how to explain the origins of evil but how to reconcile our idea of God with a potentially infinite universe. For Doctorow, the mere contemplation of a universe that has "expanded exponentially from a single point," with "everything flying away from everything else for the last fifteen or so billion years" is enough to make us question everything about God, for the idea that the universe "would come into being by some fluke happenstance ... is even more absurd than the idea of a Creator."[205] Given what we know about the vastness of the universe, such a Creator must be "so fearsome as to be beyond any human entreaty for our solace, or comfort, or the redemption that would come of our being brought into His secret."[206] Implicitly challenging the comforting notion of a God who has already counted every strand of hair on our heads, Doctorow's theology is at odds with the intimate, personal God promoted by many evangelical churches today.[207] Doctorow suggests, persuasively I think, that we simply cannot assume our ideas about God correspond to God.

One character in the novel articulates similar ideas about the unfathomable nature of God. This character is none other than Albert Einstein. Although Einstein was skeptical of traditional theological understandings of God, he actually "lived quite easily with the concept of a Creator," whom he often referred to as "the Old One," according to the narrator.[208] This is a fairly accurate take on Einstein's views about God, as evidenced by the often-quoted statement from Einstein: "I believe in Spinoza's God who reveals himself in the harmony of all that exists, but not in a God who concerns himself with the fate and actions of human beings."[209] While not abandoning theism altogether, Einstein certainly rejected the idea of a God who intervened in human affairs, or more pointedly, a God who chose not to intervene in human affairs. Einstein declared in 1932: "I cannot imagine a God who rewards and punishes the objects of his creation, whose purposes are modeled after our own—a God, in short, who is but a reflection of human frailty."[210]

Doctorow's narrator, Reverend Thomas Pemberton, is rector of St. Timothy's Episcopal Church in New York, a congregation that has all but died out, dwindling to no more than "five parishioners" on any given Sunday.[211] At one stroke, the novel registers the decline of mainline denominations like the Episcopal Church. Tom Pemberton's heterodox sermons have gotten him in trouble with the archdiocese, and the bishop eventually asks him to give up his episcopacy. Apart from raising questions about the Trinity, however, Pemberton's true struggle is theodicy. In one sermon, he challenged his poor parishioners (all five of them) to consider how Christians can go on believing in God after the Holocaust: "I merely asked the congregation what they thought the engineered slaughter of the Jews in Europe had done to Christianity. To our story of Christ Jesus. I mean, given the meager response of our guys, is the Holocaust a problem only for Jewish theologians?"[212] The answer is already implicit in the way he frames the question: the Holocaust is a problem for theologians, period, and there has been no "commensurate Christian response to the disaster."[213] Theodicy is a genuine stumbling block for Pemberton, as it was for the "death of God" theologians in the 1960s. Elsewhere,

Doctorow observes that we still haven't come to terms with the fact that the Nazis "sprang from the heart of Western civilization."[214]

In a series of flashbacks to the Holocaust, Doctorow investigates a similar sort of theological debate among Jews in Lithuania during the war. These scenes make *City of God* something of a Holocaust novel as well. Through a series of bizarre circumstances in the novel—the cross at his church is stolen and somehow shows up at a synagogue across town—Thomas Pemberton falls in love with a young rabbi, Sarah Blumenthal, whose father became a runner for the resistance fighters in the Jewish ghetto, smuggling meticulous records of all those killed by the Nazis compiled by Dr. Josef Barbanel: "Of course his doing so was illegal. The Germans were quite aware of their culpability and forbade unauthorized writings or photographs. They had confiscated all cameras."[215] Yet Dr. Barbanel keeps a record of Nazi atrocities all the same, and Yehoshua Mendelssohn smuggles these documents across the border "through an abandoned viaduct" to a small Catholic church called the Church of St. Theresa in Vilna, Lithuania, which is run by Father Petrauskas.[216] These riveting, suspenseful scenes are the best part of *City of God*, and they burnish Doctorow's reputation as a master of historical fiction. They are relevant for my purposes because they engage in the kind of secular theodicy I have been tracing in this chapter. At one point, a Jewish resistance fighter offers them a chance to escape the ghetto by fleeing into the forest. Rabbi Pomeranz objects to the plan, mostly on the grounds that they will not survive in the forest, but when he promises that he will pray for their continued safety in the ghetto, he provokes the resistance fighter's scorn: "Since your prayers are so effective and have already done so much good, you, I expect, will choose to remain and pray to the Lord your God to save your people."[217] In response, the Rabbi puts on his "battered homburg" and mutters, "That is not why I pray to the Lord, blessed be His name, he said to no one in particular. I pray to bring Him into being."[218] This is a beautiful passage: like his battered homburg, all that remains of the rabbi's threadbare faith is a sliver of hope that God exists, despite all evidence to the contrary.

That slender hope in God's existence also finds expression in contemporary New York, where the Holocaust is a distant memory that must be kept alive by the survivors' descendants.[219] One major subplot in *City of God* involves Tom Pemberton's and Sarah Blumenthal's efforts to recover Dr. Barbanel's records from the church in Lithuania. Sarah Blumenthal is a rabbi at the Synagogue of Evolutionary Judaism, an "errant little synagogue" on the Upper West Side.[220] When Tom begins to fall in love with Sarah, he assures her of his own ecumenism, "I'm on the Committee for Ecumenical Theology of the Trans-Religious Fellowship."[221] Their subsequent marriage joins two major Abrahamic religions. At their wedding, Tom prays that his faith might survive "the relentless and unimaginable genocidal cruelties shuddering across the world."[222] A scholar on interreligious dialogue and religious pluralism, Sarah gives a keynote address to the Conference of American Studies in Religion in Washington, in which she proposes that far from being a stumbling block to faith, doubt is something that should be prized, along with humility, as powerful antidotes to religious fundamentalism and religious violence:

> In the twentieth century about to end, the great civilizer on earth seems to have been doubt. Doubt, the constantly debated and flexible inner condition of theological uncertainty, the wish to believe in balance with rueful or nervous or grieving skepticism, seems to have held people in thrall to ethical behavior, while the true believers, of whatever stamp, religious or religious-statist, have done the murdering. The impulse to excommunicate, to satanize, to eradicate, to ethnically cleanse, is a religious impulse. In the practice and politics of religion, God has always been a license to kill.[223]

We are ill-advised to infer an author's beliefs from a character's, of course, yet all this sounds like something Doctorow would surely agree with. As it turns out, much of this fictional speech to the Conference of American Studies in Religion in Washington appears almost verbatim in Doctorow's Massey lectures at Harvard, mentioned earlier, which were subsequently published in his book *Reporting the Universe* (2003). Commenting on the irony that a religious person is no more likely to "live a moral life than an irreligious person," Doctorow echoes Sarah's speech when he writes, "the great civilizer on earth seems to have been doubt," and he then continues:

> Doubt, the constantly debated and flexible inner condition of theological uncertainty, the wish to believe in balance with rueful or nervous or grieving skepticism, seems to have held people in thrall to ethical behavior, while the true believers of whatever stamp, religious or religious statist, have done the murdering. The impulse to exclude, satanize, eradicate, is a religious impulse. But to hold in abeyance and irresolution any firm convictions of God, or of an afterlife with him, warrants walking in his spirit, somehow.[224]

This passage is lifted directly from *City of God*. Recall the passage in which Rabbi Pomeranz prays, not because he believes in God, but because by praying he might bring God into existence. Doctorow borrows from that passage in his lectures, which include strikingly similar language:

> When I am moved by religious worship, it is by its innocence and trust. That innocence and trust always seems to carry with it the idea of promise, ... a prayerful waiting, as if, given our knowledge of the unthinkable horrors brought down upon our forebears, and the ordinary suffering to which we are all subject, we seek the finally effective prayer, the hymn that will be heard, and hold ourselves to the resolute belief in God that may someday actually bring him into being.[225]

These echoes of *City of God* are not instances of plagiarism, if only because Doctorow is quoting himself. Nonetheless, the fact that he pilfers these ideas about religion from his novel does raise the possibility that literary fiction might be especially useful for thinking about religion in our time. For it is clear that the ideas about religion that Doctorow lays out in the Massey lectures had already been fleshed out in his fiction. As in Roth's fiction, such ideas are not necessarily the author's own ideas when they appear in the novel, but when Doctorow adapts them for a lecture, they become his ideas. Doctorow may not share Sarah Blumenthal's "secular disdain for faith," but evidently, he does share her views about doubt as an antidote to dogmatism.[226] In the novel, the very fact that her ideas are juxtaposed to other, competing ideas seems apposite to the kind of religious pluralism that Doctorow himself advocates. By allowing space for opposing views and voices, fiction may have some advantages over nonfiction. Sarah's critique of dogmatism is itself a form of dogmatism; the novel makes clear that her unselfconscious liberalism is not altogether worthy of admiration. Some readers will no doubt nod their heads in agreement at the notion that religion has caused more violence throughout history than irreligion, but others might well want to quibble with it. The dialogism of literary fiction makes room for disagreements. In one sense, literature frequently embodies the very pluralism and syncretism that is so often represented in it.

Less than a year after Doctorow borrowed a character's words for his own lecture at Harvard, we find him thinking his way into something like the fundamentalist mindset that she (and he) both denounced as the source of so much murdering, as if he were trying to imagine, and perhaps better understand, the impulse to demonize or exclude others. In Doctorow's short story "Walter John Harmon," from *Sweet Land Stories* (2004), the author investigates the appeal of fundamentalist sects in an ostensibly secular culture. The main character is a cult leader named Walter John Harmon who, in the narrator's words, "has in his effortless way drawn so many of us to his prophecy."[227] The story is told in the first person from the point of view of a cult member who first learned about Walter John Harmon on the internet. He now serves as a lawyer for the community, which is fighting a lawsuit about whether "using only the Book of Revelation to teach our children to read and write" violates mandatory education laws for school-age children.[228] The narrator is defensive about the suggestion that he is deluded or brainwashed:

> We are not idiots. We are not cult victims. In many quarters we are laughed at for following as God's prophet a garage mechanic who in his teens was imprisoned for car theft. But this blessed man has revolutionized our lives. From the first moment I was in his presence

> I felt resolved in my soul. Everything was suddenly right. I was who I was. It is hard to explain. I saw the outside world darkened, as in a film negative. But I was in the light.[229]

Giving us an insider's perspective, Doctorow shows how religious communities can train their members to think differently. Literary fiction offers access to something ineffable about spiritual things; in this case, the author captures the mysterious appeal of belonging and transcendence. They remain no less committed to the community even when it becomes clear that Walter John Harmon is exploiting them. They drive run-of-the-mill SUVs, while he drives a Hummer. They give up all their possessions and wealth, while he maintains a secret bank account. Scandalously, wives and daughters undergo a ritual known as Purification: "Walter is at a level beyond lust. This is apparent, since all the wives, even the plainest, partake of his communion. His ministry annuls the fornications of a secular society."[230] His ministry prohibits sex for everyone but him.

The first major crisis occurs when their leader runs off with the narrator's wife. Upon deliberation, the Elders determine that "by running off with one of the purified wives," Walter had merely done what was required of him, "foreordained by the nature of his prophecy."[231] The contorted logic of this justification is obvious: they believe they are being "confronted with the beautiful paradox of a prophecy fulfilling itself by means of its negation."[232] Assembling the members of the community, the Elders explain in apocalyptic language drawn from the Book of Revelation—their favored text—that when "the four horsemen come riding over the land and the plagues rise like a miasma from the earth and the sun turns black and the moon blood-red, and when firestorms engulf whole cities and the nuclear warriors of the world consume one another" then Walter John Harmon will return to them and they will "reside there forever."[233] Even the cuckolded narrator finds their arguments convincing and remains committed to the cult. Indeed, he becomes a kind of surrogate prophet for the group: "Walter John Harmon has come to live through me and will speak in my voice."[234] They begin to stockpile weapons and build a wall around the compound from designs left by Walter John Harmon before he absconded with the narrator's wife. Doctorow hints of a possible assault on the compound like the one on David Koresh and his followers in Waco, Texas, in 1993. In the event of such an assault, the narrator tells us, ominously, "We are assured of a clear and unimpeded field of fire."[235]

Like John Updike's *In the Beauty of the Lilies* (1996), Doctorow's short story allows readers to imagine themselves as part of a cult, to identify at least for the duration of the story with the point of view of a cult member who thinks in terms of apocalyptic rhetoric and teaching. As Doctorow well knows, such teaching gripped the imaginations of an astonishing number of Americans during what one historian has called the Age of Evangelicalism, which began in the aftermath of Watergate and lasted into the twenty-first century.[236] This new evangelicalism was distinct from the holiness-Pentecostal movement that Baldwin had described in *Go Tell It on the Mountain* (1953), but it was sometimes called "neo-Pentecostalism" because it placed a similar emphasis on piety and charismatic practices like Holy Spirit Baptism and speaking in tongues. Along with charismatic elements, evangelicalism was distinguished by a prevalent eschatology, also known as premillennial dispensationalism, which posits that the Second Coming of Christ would inaugurate a thousand-year period of Christ's reign on earth, hence the term "premillennial" to describe the current era, when certain "dispensations" could be read as signs of Christ's return. Like other prophets of premillennial dispensationalism, Walter John Harmon believes that the imminent apocalypse will divide the saved from the damned. The narrator calls it an "Unfolding Revelation" that will ultimately leave behind "the denizens of the dark ages of secular life" who "refuse to abjure the false values of the world and rise from its filth."[237] They will be left behind.

Hal Lindsey's *The Late Great Planet Earth* (1970), which sold 10 million copies by the end of the 1970s, making it by far the biggest best seller of the decade, was the book that first popularized such an invidious eschatology, but the astonishing success of Timothy LaHaye and Jerry B. Jenkins's *Left Behind: A Novel of the Earth's Last Days*

(1995) and its many sequels has been a publishing phenomenon—more than 50 million copies sold and counting—that speaks to the enduring fascination with premillennial dispensationalism. Whereas American Jewish writers looked to the Holocaust as a rupture in human history that stood as a major challenge to theism, evangelical writers prognosticated on the basis of current events that, in Hal Lindsey's phrase, were said to "herald the imminent return of Christ."[238] And whereas American Jews looked to the founding of the state of Israel not as the fulfillment of a prophesied return to their homeland but as the most militant and ultimately secular means to prevent further persecution, Lindsey believed that the founding of Israel was a "prophetic sign" that the "end-times" had begun.[239] The 1967 Six-Day War only confirmed what the Book of Revelations, read properly, had already predicted.[240] In Lindsey's audacious if improbable reworking of Jewish Messianic traditions, "a seven-year period climaxed by the visible return of Jesus Christ" could not "begin until the Jewish people re-established their nation in their ancient homeland of Palestine," but now that Israel exists, the world now stands "on the brink" of "the final Great War" called Armageddon, "which is to be triggered by an invasion of the new state of Israel."[241] Such was the power of this theory that it reached even into the Oval Office of the White House, informing Ronald Reagan's characterization of Russia as an "evil empire." Reagan's first use of the phrase was in a 1982 speech to the National Association of Evangelicals, and by associating the Soviet Union with a possible nuclear apocalypse he was at once revealing his own personal interest in prophecy and appealing to the kinds of apocalyptic scenarios that he knew would resonate with evangelicals.[242]

"The religious fundamentalists and the political right have made explosive contact," Doctorow declared at the time, "and in the light of their conjunction it says Armageddon."[243] A keen cultural observer, he puts his finger on a nexus of politics and religion that is still with us.[244] A year after Reagan's speech, Larry McAffrey asked Doctorow what he thought about Philip Roth's contention that writers were finding it more difficult than ever to write in a realistic mode because "reality" itself was now so improbable: "Do you share this sense of a world outstripping your ability as an artist to produce wonders?" to which Doctorow responded: "Fortunately, he keeps trying. Whatever the difficulties are, the obstacles, that's the nature of the game."[245]

Saul Bellow, Philip Roth, and E.L. Doctorow have been among the most prolific writers in American fiction since 1950. Together, these writers help us understand how religion persists in a secular age yet persists in a dialectical relationship with both secularization and secularism. Their work also sheds light on a broader, more inclusive pluralism that developed in the postwar period. American Jews played a major role in the development of this more inclusive pluralism, not least because they occupied such influential roles in the professions and culture industries.[246] But if American Jews played an important role in securing this stronger form of pluralism, they often gave up much of their religious heritage in the process. Pluralism ideally serves as a bridge between the religious and the secular, by placing demands on those who are religious to tolerate others, while also compelling secularists to make space for religious others. In practice, however, pluralism all too often meant downplaying one's religious identity.[247]

Bellow, Roth, and Doctorow began their careers at a time when the Protestant consensus was starting to crumble, yet they kept writing through a number of important developments in religious history, including the emergence of a politically engaged Christian evangelicalism.[248] Since the 1960s and 1970s, Protestant Christians have by and large become more conservative, whereas Jews have become ever more secular. Low levels of synagogue affiliation combined with high rates of intermarriage—more than half of American Jews were married to non-Jews by 1990, according to the National Jewish Population Survey (NJPS)—signal a shift toward less religious affiliation. By 2000 the NJPS showed that two out of five Jewish adults did not claim Judaism as their religion, and the fact that a majority of those who identified as secular or as Christian Jews are products of mixed marriages confirms that increasing rates of intermarriage is one of the most important factors transforming Judaism.[249] Based on current trends, Bruce Phillips predicts that the "number of adherents to Judaism will decline as the twenty-first century progresses."²⁵⁰

Of course, such generalizations tend to appear somewhat more complicated when seen from up close—that is, in the context of lived religion—as we have observed in the work of these three writers. The secular vision of Bellow, Roth, and Doctorow, as elaborated in their fiction, anticipates some of what sociologists of religion tell us about the decline of religious affiliation and practice, the secularizing effects of intermarriage, and so on, yet at the same time, these writers also complicate such matters at every turn. Because they are writing fiction and not history or sociology, their perspectives tend to be intuitive, provisional, and speculative. In an often-quoted passage in *The Counterlife*, for instance, Roth favors a version of Jewish identity that does not require a false choice between mutually exclusive alternatives:

> I don't have to act like a Jew—I am one. ... The burden isn't either/or, consciously choosing from possibilities equally difficult and regrettable—it's and/and/and/and/and as well. Life *is* and: the accidental and the immutable, the elusive and the graspable, the bizarre and the predictable, the actual and the potential, all the multiplying realities, entangled, overlapping, colliding, conjoined—plus the multiplying illusions!²⁵¹

Roth envisions Jewish identity here on a model of ethnic hybridity, or perhaps multiculturalism, about as far from a traditional understanding of Jews as a chosen people as one could imagine.²⁵²

We have seen that while Bellow, Roth, and Doctorow are decidedly post-religious in their sensibilities, they were fascinated, if not obsessed, with religion. The sacred and profane intermingle in their fiction, often with uproarious results. Working from inside out, rather than outside in, they focus our attention on characters in plausibly rendered situations and settings, and then let the chips fall where they may, allowing us to decide on the implications for ourselves. When Doctorow was once asked to reveal the magic tricks of this alchemy of literary creation, he deflected the question back to the interviewer:

What is experience and what is imagination? The imagination obviously imposes itself on the world, composes a world which, in turn, affects what is imagined. ... But I also know that books can affect consciousness—affect the way people think and therefore the way they act. Books create constituencies that have their own effect on history, and that's been proven time and again.[253]

In short, fiction is one way to engage in this reciprocal process, training readers in the kind of pluralism that a diverse culture demands of us.

4

Apocalypse Then: Eschatology in Don DeLillo's America

"You're a product of your geography," the Jewish comedian Lenny Bruce tells his audience in Don DeLillo's novel *Underworld* (1997). "If you're a Catholic from New York, you're a Jew. If you're a Jew from Butte, Montana, you're a totally goyish concoction. You're like instant mashed potatoes."[1] An iconoclastic comic who was once arrested for impersonating a priest, Lenny Bruce could always count on jokes about religion to offend polite sensibilities. Like a priest or shaman figure, he was given to making pronouncements such as the following: "Nobody knows the day or the hour," indulging in what he calls "some vintage Christian shit."[2] He then launches into a not-so-funny monologue about a young girl "hiding in the empty lots, down the maze of back alleys, because her mother's gone again and she thinks the landlord will have her arrested. Let's make her human. Let's give her a name."[3] He does not give her a name, but DeLillo does, for the girl he describes turns out to be none other than Esmeralda, the young woman from the projects whose effigy appears on a billboard in a sort of miraculous resurrection after her death. The revelation makes Lenny Bruce nothing short of prophetic, suggesting that the role of the prophet in late twentieth-century America has been taken up by our stand-up comics. When the biographer Claudia Roth Pierpont asked Philip Roth about two of his contemporaries, Cormac McCarthy (the same age as Roth) and Don DeLillo (three years his junior), he answered: "These guys are interested in extremes. They make me look ordinary."[4] One might quibble with this statement, for Roth is an extremist himself, but he has a point about DeLillo, who gravitates to extreme forms, as befits a writer who once declared that fiction is a kind of fanaticism: "At its root, fiction is a kind of religious fanaticism, with elements of obsession, superstition and awe."[5]

The novel *Mao II* (1991) opens at a mass wedding ceremony at Yankee stadium for members of the Unification Church, often called "Moonies" for short, after their leader, the late Reverend Sung Myung Moon. Up in the stands, Rodge Janney looks through his binoculars, trying to get a glimpse of his estranged daughter Karen, who has joined the Moonies. "When the Old God leaves the world," he muses, "what happens to all the unexpended faith?"[6] By posing the question in this way, the character invokes the proverbial death of God—the notion most often attributed to Nietzsche but popularized in the mid-twentieth century by magazines like *Time*, which ran a 1966 cover story asking a similar question, "Is God Dead?"[7] As her parents try to spot their daughter among the sea of brides and grooms on the field below, they also struggle to understand her allegiance to a religious zealot. "When the Old God goes," Rodge laments, "they pray to flies and bottletops."[8] Predictions of God's demise have been greatly exaggerated, for many of the world's religions have proven to be quite resilient, yet Rodge's offhand remark here about praying to flies and bottle caps may not be so far off the mark, after all, because at least some of all that unexpended faith was transmuted into new religious forms and practices.

While the remarkable resurgence of religion in many parts of the world during the late twentieth century caught many cultural commentators and some scholars of religion off guard, DeLillo's novels have taken note of some of the more extravagant forms of unexpended faith. The growth of conservative, evangelical Christianity; the rise of fundamentalist and Islamist groups; the popularization of quasi-religious practices such as apocalyptic environmentalism and yoga: all these phenomena and more have come under the author's capacious fictional purview. With his finger on the spiritual pulse of contemporary America, DeLillo has been representing not just "the increasingly complex hybridity of religious forms" but also a "flood of unorthodox spiritualities" often grouped under New Age religions, which "like the more traditional forms, are often inflected with the rhetoric and values of consumer capitalism, but they tend, at the same time, to appeal to people dissatisfied with secular strategies of fulfillment."[9] Bestselling books like *The Secret* (2006) exemplify this new therapeutic sensibility, as does the talk-show host Oprah Winfrey, who often couches her self-help message in salvific language.[10] With his trademark mixture of satire and sympathy, DeLillo captures how such forms have proliferated in the late twentieth century, especially in the United States, which according to historian Richard Wightman Fox remains "by far the most religious of advanced industrial societies."[11]

His fiction also raises questions about how religion and spirituality have been reshaped by various secularizing forces that, while they failed to stamp out religious beliefs altogether, have nevertheless altered the context in which beliefs are held, if not their actual content. For even traditional forms of religion have arguably become at once more varied and less orthodox. As Charles Taylor points out in *A Secular Age* (2007), belief in God is not quite the same thing today as it was five hundred years ago, since we have gone "from a society where belief in God is unchallenged and indeed, unproblematic, to one in which it is understood to be one option among others, and frequently not the easiest to embrace."[12] As if anticipating Taylor's insights, DeLillo illuminates one of the central paradoxes about religion today: wherever there is belief, there is likely to be some measure of doubt: "We cannot help looking over our shoulder from time to time, looking sideways, living our faith also in a condition of doubt and uncertainty."[13] Especially in his mid-career novels like *The Names* (1982), *White Noise* (1985), *Mao II* (1991), and *Underworld* (1997), but also in more recent ones like *Falling Man* (2007), DeLillo shows how fragile and precarious belief can be when it is attenuated by doubt. His characters tend to be seekers and spiritual wanderers rather than fanatics, though there are plenty of both. These novels disclose "a sense of something extraordinary hovering just beyond our touch and just beyond our vision," intimations of the sacred that the author calls "a kind of radiance in dailiness."[14] This radiance can be found in unexpected places, such as when Murray Jay Suskind marvels in *White Noise* about a supermarket: "This place recharges us spiritually."[15]

Perhaps the "central religious intuition" of DeLillo's work, according to John McClure, is that there is something "beyond the quotidian," and by creating a literary form of "sacramental materialism" that "emphasizes the immanence of divine grace and the holiness of this world," the author's fiction in effect "resacralizes the world."[16] Amy Hungerford also contends that his "insistence on something like the immanence of transcendent meaning in the material of daily life" arguably makes him more of a Catholic writer than we thought; like so many disaffected Catholics, "he skirts doctrine while maintaining a Catholic understanding of ... transcendence."[17] Educated at Cardinal Hayes High School in the Bronx—"like a prison for Catholic boys," he quips—and a graduate of Fordham University, the author belongs to a fairly large demographic of non-practicing Catholics.[18] His characters are lapsed Catholics as well, and as such, similarly conflicted about religion. For example, one character in *Underworld* "hadn't been to church in forty years except for midnight mass at Christmas, which he attended, as they say, religiously," and another "shunned any form of organized worship and thought God was a mass delusion."[19]

Like Flannery O'Connor, a Catholic writer living in what she memorably called the Christ-haunted (and predominantly Protestant) South, DeLillo recognizes the superficial and indeed paradoxically secular nature of so many contemporary expressions of religion. Whereas O'Connor sustained her relationship to the church, however, DeLillo writes in an agnostic mode. He is primarily a post-secular writer, though residually Catholic in his religious inclinations and interests. For example, the writer's fascination with apocalyptic discourses and ideas surely owes something to the fact that he was raised Catholic. Anthony DeCurtis once asked him about this: "There's something of an apocalyptic feel in your books, an intimation that our world is moving toward greater randomness and dissolution, perhaps cataclysm."[20] DeLillo's response is telling:

> I don't have a political theory or doctrine that I'm espousing. I follow characters where they take me. ... I mean, what I sense is suspicion and distrust and fear, and so, of course, these things inform my books.

It's my idea of myself as a writer—perhaps mistaken—that I enter these worlds as a completely rational person who is simply taking what he sees all around him and using it as material.[21]

Although the secondary literature on the prevalence of apocalyptic themes in his fiction is vast, literary critics seldom mention that the subject might bear some relation to Christian eschatology, a branch of theology concerned with end times.[22] To be sure, DeLillo does not regard apocalypse as imminent so much as immanent, a symptom of our "difficult and sometimes chaotic world."[23] Still, his novels suggest that recent appropriations of apocalyptic ideas retain some of the darker implications of their scriptural sources. Once confined to the canonical genre of apocalyptic, especially the Book of Daniel in the Hebrew Bible and the Book of Revelation in the New Testament, the provenance of eschatology has long since expanded to include speculation about how current events predict the Second Coming of Christ, as evidenced in two best-selling books, Hal Lindsay's *The Late Great Planet Earth* (1970), and Timothy LaHaye and Jerry B. Jenkin's *Left Behind: A Novel of the Earth's Last Days* (1996). In part because of his Catholic upbringing, DeLillo grasps both the scriptural wellsprings and the geopolitical ramifications of apocalypse.

A careful observer of contemporary culture, DeLillo attests to the resiliency and vitality of religion and spirituality in our time. His novels register inchoate longings for transcendence. They track not just important trends in religious history, but also the felt experience of religion. He follows eruptions of unexpended faith, to recall Rodge's formulation, wherever they appear: in a mass wedding ceremony at Yankee stadium or a Pentecostal church service in the heartland; among pilgrims entering the Old City of Jerusalem through the Damascus Gate; or cult members living in caves on the outskirts of Athens, Greece; or frenzied mourners following the death of the Ayatollah Khomeini in Tehran, Iran. He finds them even in the most unlikely places, such as remote communes, supermarkets, tourist traps, temporary shelters, and so on. As this preview of such phenomena in his work suggests, DeLillo is among our most perceptive writers in mapping out the global circuits and networks that connect a new religious America to the larger world.[24]

Protestant Disrepair

To understand DeLillo's mapping of this new religious America, we first need to examine the historical roots of religious diversity. Far from bringing about the demise or eclipse of religion, secularization has in fact seen a proliferation of options, which Taylor memorably calls the nova effect.[25] This effect intensified in the postwar period, when economic expansion created more opportunities for social mobility and brought about dramatic changes in education, family life, leisure, and work. Amidst the generational conflict and social upheaval in the 1960s, baby boomers turned away from traditionally religious understandings of meaning and purpose toward a more psychological understanding of self-realization as the ultimate purpose of life. Not surprisingly, this new therapeutic sensibility crept into all but the most insular and sectarian religious communities, even as many people went in search of spiritual fulfillment elsewhere.[26] "America has always been given to spasms of religious enthusiasm," Morris Dickstein writes, but a new "spiritual fervor" took hold during what is now commonly called the Age of Aquarius: "This fervor also animated some of those who sought nirvana through sex, drugs, and rock 'n' roll, along with many others who simply looked for some new sense of purpose in their lives."[27]

Disparaging organized religion, baby boomers were drawn to new forms of spirituality—hence the common refrain (still often heard today): "I'm spiritual, but not religious." A Gallup poll in 1978 found that 80 percent of Americans felt that "an individual should arrive at his or her own religious beliefs independent of any churches or synagogues."[28] This meant decoupling religion and spirituality from institutions. Indeed, churchgoing declined from nearly 50 percent in the 1950s to about 40 percent in the early 1970s. During roughly the same period, the three mainline denominations (Episcopalian, Methodist,

Presbyterian) lost between 20 and 40 percent of their members, while Catholic churches experienced declines of between 71 percent to 55 percent in parish membership.[29] On the other hand, conservative evangelical churches were flourishing, especially those associated with Pentecostalism.[30] While "evangelical Christianity is the fastest-growing form of religious life," such growth has notably occurred against the backdrop of considerable religious diversification, and "nowhere is the sheer range of religious faith as wide as it is today in the United States."[31]

Meanwhile, the number of Americans who identify themselves as "unaffiliated" with any particular religion has also increased dramatically. In a 2008 US Religious Landscape Survey published by the Pew Forum on Religious and Public Life, more than one-quarter of all adults have left the faith tradition in which they were raised, and almost half of all adults have either changed their religious affiliation, joined a religious group after not having one, or dropped their previous affiliation to one. About 16 percent of Americans say they are currently unaffiliated with any religious tradition. Among these unaffiliated, nearly one-half were once Protestant (44 percent) and more than one-quarter were once Catholic (27 percent). The researchers conclude that Americans' religious affiliations can be described as "very diverse and extremely fluid."[32]

This short excursus into US religious history is relevant to DeLillo's novels, not least because they have indirectly tracked many of the changes I've just described, including the rapid growth of Pentecostalism and the related expansion of charismatic practices such as glossolalia. Consider his novel *The Names*, for instance, in which James Axton marvels at how widespread that particular charismatic practice has become:

> Many kinds of people knew the experience. Dallas executives spoke in tongues in gospel meetings in the shimmering tinfoil Hyatt. Catholics knew the experience, and middle-class blacks of the charismatic revival, and fellowships of Christian dentists. Imagine their surprise, these tax-paying people, he said, these veterans of patio barbecues, when they learned they were carriers of ecstasy.[33]

Scholars have shown how charismatic practices cut across denominations to influence a variety of religious traditions.[34] In DeLillo's novel, people engage in ecstatic religious worship even in Hyatt hotels. The final chapter of *The Names* portrays another Pentecostal church, in which a young boy, Orville Benton, despite exhortations to yield to the power of the Holy Spirit, cannot bring himself to speak in tongues. No matter how much "he wished to do so," the words do not come: "Why couldn't he understand and speak? There was no answer that the living could give. Tongue tied! His faith was signed. He ran into the rainy distance, smaller and smaller. This was worse than a retched nightmare. It was the nightmare of real things, the fallen wonder of the world."[35] His aphasia is reminiscent of the all-night tarry service in James Baldwin's *Go Tell It on the Mountain* (1953), in which young John Grimes has a similar experience on the threshing floor of a Pentecostal church in Harlem, but while John Grimes embraces the freedom offered by spirit baptism, Orville chooses to flee from the church: "There was nowhere to run but he ran."[36]

This turns out to be a fictional account of Owen Brademas's childhood experience written by a precocious would-be writer, Tap, who is himself the son of the writer James Axton and his estranged wife Kathryn. Like a Mobius loop narrative that circles back on itself, the novel ends with a manuscript written by a fledgling writer about another "character in a story" who recalls going to a small church "fifteen miles outside of town," where the young preacher struggles "to get these people right with God."[37] Owen Brademas's "early memories" of going to church "were a fiction in the sense that he could separate himself from the character" and hence distance himself from those memories; indeed, "Owen believed that memory was the faculty of absolution."[38] As if to highlight the power of fiction to render lived religious experience, Tap fictionalizes Owen Brademas's childhood memories of his family church in the following scene:

> The boy is spellbound by the young man's intensity and vigor. It is startling, compelling. He listens to the clear voice, watches the man roll up his shirt-sleeves and shoot a hand in this and that direction,

touching people, squeezing their flesh, shaking them hard. Owen's mother is saying Jesus Jesus Jesus, softly, in her seat, in awe, exalted. There is a stirring up front, an arm flying into the air. The preacher turns, walking toward the altar, talking along with the man, exhorting. He does not rush, he does raise his voice. The noise and hurry are in Owen's mind. The preacher turns again to face the congregation, watches the man in the front row get to his feet. Owen's father gets to his feet.[39]

With its clipped sentences and omitted quotation marks around dialogue, the passage sets the stage for a dramatic conversation experience, bringing a Pentecostal church alive on the page. The preacher invites Owen to speak in tongues: "Be free in the Spirit. Let the Spirit knock you free. You start, the Spirit takes over. ... The sense of expectation is tremendous. The boy is chilled. Time seems to pause whenever the preacher does. When he speaks, everything starts again, everything moves and jumps and lives. Only his voice can drive the meeting forward."[40] For whatever reason, Owen resists this exhortation to spirit baptism, and he is stubbornly silent.

Given his boyhood crisis of faith, we expect Owen to reject Pentecostalism and religion altogether. At any rate, we would not expect him to join a cult, yet this is precisely what happens. An expert in ancient languages, Owen Brademas is in charge of an archeological dig in Greece where Kathryn, James Axton's former wife, has been working. During his travels, he encounters an obscure cult that practices a bizarre form of ritual human sacrifice, killing individuals whose initials match the name of the place where they are killed—hence *The Names* of the novel's title. "The cult lived in two caves above the village," the narrator tells us. "They were elusive men, rarely seen, except for one of them who occasionally came down into the streets and talked to the children."[41] Hiding out with them in a remote area as they search for their next sacrificial victim, Owen Brademas rather surprisingly becomes for all intents and purposes a member of the cult.

Shocked by their friend's apparent susceptibility to indoctrination, Axton and Kathryn now wonder whether Owen's childhood experience among Pentecostals might have predisposed him to intense religious experience. "We were doubters, skeptics of the slightly superior type," Axton tells us, yet he is discomfited by "the polyglot surge" of pilgrims he saw at the Damascus Gate: "their streams of belief made me uneasy. It was all a reproach to my ardent skepticism."[42] "If there is *God*," he declares at one point, then "how could we fail to submit completely?"[43] In DeLillo's fiction, even the most unbelieving characters like Axton are harried by faith. In short, they are part of the "Christian dispersion," which is to say former believers who are now secular, or they are searching for something besides religion to fill the void left by their discarded faith.[44]

As we have seen, the decline of mainline churches, the growth of evangelicalism, and a stronger form of religious pluralism unseated liberal Protestantism from its place of dominance at the center of American culture. Jack Gladney's spouses in *White Noise*—he has been married four times, albeit twice to the same woman—exemplify this weakened Protestant hegemony.[45] The narrator describes Tweedy Browner, Jack's third wife, as follows: "She wore a Shetland sweater, tweed skirt, knee socks and penny loafers. There was a sense of Protestant disrepair about her, a collapsed aura in which her body struggled to survive."[46] Tossed off with DeLillo's usual aplomb, the phrase Protestant disrepair nicely captures the shrinking of mainline Protestant denominations since the 1960s. But if Tweedy Browner exemplifies this Protestant disrepair, Jack's ex-wife Janet Savory points to an increasingly diverse religious landscape; she goes by the name "Mother Devi" and resides in a commune or "ashram" on the outskirts of Tubb, Montana, which is now called "Dharamsalapur."[47] Insofar as they have both gravitated away from mainline churches, these characters provide one index of the declining fortunes of liberal Protestantism.

These characters are seekers, of course, a phenomenon influentially described by Robert Wuthnow in which a "traditional spirituality of inhabiting sacred places has given way to a new spirituality of seeking."[48] Nowhere is the seeker phenomenon more evident than in Murray Jay Siskind, who advises Jack to sample the world's religions and simply "pick one you like": "Read up on reincarnation, transmigration, hyperspace, the resurrection of the dead and so on. ... Some gorgeous systems have evolved from these beliefs."[49] When Jack asks him if he actually believes "any of these things," Murray dodges the question: "Millions of people have believed for thousands of years. Throw in with them. Belief in a second birth, a second life, is practically universal. This must mean something."[50] The vast array of world religions is a kind of spiritual playground for Murray, who takes his cue in this respect from the late Elvis Presley, who believed in UFOs and dabbled in metempsychosis by reading from *The Tibetan Book of the Dead*, which Murray extols as nothing less than a practical "guide to dying and being reborn."[51] The closest Murray ever gets to having a genuine religious experience is while visiting a tourist attraction known as the most photographed barn in America: "Being here is a kind of spiritual surrender. A religious experience in a way, like all tourism."[52] As a scholar of American popular culture, Murray is nothing if not eclectic. Another character, the New York transplant Alfonse Stompanato, embraces popular culture itself as religion: "When he talked about popular culture, he exercised the closed logic of a religious zealot, one who kills for his beliefs."[53] By skewering academic fads and intellectual pretentiousness, DeLillo is having fun at his characters' expense. But the author also wants to suggest something about credulity and incredulity in US culture, the way that some beliefs have become diffuse and enervated, while others are no less virulent for being attached to objects of worship as ephemeral as celebrities and tourist attractions.[54]

Following Murray's advice to sample the world's religions and pick one you like, for example, Jack's current wife Babette (who has been married four times) embarks on an eclectic soul quest through basic lifestyle changes, exercise regimens, and psychopharmacology. To the divorcees and retirees of Blacksmith, Babette becomes a sort of self-help guru, giving lectures at a local Congregational Church on topics ranging from yoga to Sufi dervishes to correct posture, all presented as an alternative means to personal enlightenment than that offered, presumably, in the same building on Sundays, which suggests not only denominational decline but also the way many Christian churches have accommodated New Age beliefs and practices. Babette's disciples listen with rapt attention as she lectures about to them about the latest therapeutic New Age fads:

> We seem to believe it is possible to ward off death by following rules of good grooming. Sometimes I go with my wife to the church basement and watch her stand, turn, assume various heroic poses, gesture gracefully. She makes references to yoga, kendo, trance-walking. She talks of Sufi dervishes, Sherpa mountaineers. The old folks nod and listen. Nothing is foreign, nothing too remote to apply. I am always surprised by their acceptance and trust, the sweetness of their belief. Nothing is too doubtful to be of use to them as they seek to redeem their bodies from a lifetime of bad posture. It is the end of skepticism.[55]

This softening of belief is evident in an uncritical acceptance of tabloids in *White Noise*. Sitting in a temporary shelter with "a small and brightly colored stack of supermarket tabloids," Babette begins to read aloud from them about "documented cases of life after death," "transmigration of souls," and "personalized resurrection through stream-of-consciousness computer techniques."[56] The pseudo-journalistic discourse of the tabloids does not seem ridiculous or scandalous to her listeners; on the contrary, they accept even the most preposterous stories with a sort of "passive belief," as "a set of statements no less real than our daily quota of observable household fact."[57]

While such credulity is easy to ridicule, DeLillo underscores the extraordinary appeal of supermarket tabloids, which attract somewhere between 25 and 50 million readers per week.[58] Consider the scene in which Jack, standing in the checkout line at the supermarket, cannot help but notice the tabloids, with their glossy covers and attention-grabbing headlines: "Everything we need that is not food or love is here in the tabloid racks. The tales of the supernatural and the extraterrestrial. The miracle vitamins, the cures for cancer, the remedies for obesity. The cults of the famous and the dead."[59] In his memoir *Self-Consciousness* (1989), written four years after *White Noise*, John Updike commented that supermarket tabloids demonstrate, if nothing else:

"How remarkably fertile the religious imagination is, how fervid the appetite for significance; it sets gods to growing on every bush and rock. Astrology, UFO's, resurrections, mental metal-bending, visions in space, and voodoo flourish in the weekly tabloids we buy at the cash register along with our groceries."[60] Despite an "almost Pop Art atmosphere," as DeLillo once described their hyperbolic aesthetics, the tabloids nonetheless "ask profoundly important questions about death, the afterlife, God," and the author admits that they are "closest to the spirit of the book."[61] No less than in his humorous characterization of spiritual seekers, which is at once satirical and sympathetic, this comical treatment of tabloids seems to be written in the same generous spirit.

Miracles and End Times

At the heart of the postmodern condition lies a crisis of epistemology: virtually anything can be questioned. One symptom of this crisis is the uproarious debate in *White Noise* about whether it is raining. Heinrich refuses to admit that it is raining because the radio had reported no rain until evening. Jack points to rain on the windshield and says, "Just because it's on the radio doesn't mean we have suspend belief in the evidence of our senses," to which his son retorts, "Our senses? Our senses are wrong a lot more often than they're right. This has been proved in the laboratory."[62] According to scientific evidence, he claims, our senses are not to be trusted.

Such skepticism finds its counterpart in a radical openness to supernatural explanations, however, as DeLillo's characters find intimations of the sacred in the most unexpected places. The fictional world of the novel is re-enchanted: a bag of groceries offers a sense of well-being, a family dinner gives off "extrasensory flashes and floating nuances of being," a daughter's "ecstatic chant" strikes her father "with the impact of a moment of splendid transcendence," a child's crying evokes "a mingled reverence and wonder" in the rest of the family, and the simple act of watching his children sleep makes Jack Gladney feel "selfless and spiritually large."⁶³ The "colloquial density" of the domestic sphere awakens long dormant religious impulses in Jack and puts him in touch with the transcendent, which consequently "makes family life the one medium of sense knowledge in which an astonishment of heart is routinely contained."⁶⁴ Among many examples, perhaps the most touching one is when Jack watches his children sleep in a "random tumble of heads and dangled limbs," and he becomes contemplative: "There must be something, somewhere, large and grand and redoubtable enough to justify this shining reliance and implicit belief. A desperate piety swept over me. It was cosmic in nature, full of yearnings and reachings. It spoke of vast distances, awesome but subtle forces."⁶⁵ The passage suggests that outmoded, primitive forms of religion may survive in suburban domestic life, though in transmuted forms. This scene is a prelude to an extraordinary passage in which Steffie repeats an advertising jingle:

> Steffie turned slightly, then muttered something in her sleep. It seemed important that I know what it was. ... I sat there watching her. Moments later she spoke again. Distant syllables this time—but a language not quite of this world ... that seemed to have ritual meanings, part of a verbal spell or ecstatic chant.
> Toyota Celica.
> A long moment passed before I realized this was the name of an automobile. The truth only amazed me more. The utterance was beautiful and mysterious, gold-shot with looming wonder. It was like the name of an ancient power in the sky, tablet-carved in cuneiform. It made me feel that something hovered. But how could this be? A simple brand name, an ordinary car. How could these near-nonsense words, murmured in a child's restless sleep, make me sense a meaning, a presence?⁶⁶

The brand name is like a shamanistic chant. When Jack's youngest child Wilder's seven-hour bout of ululation finally ends, it seems "as though he'd just returned from a period of wandering in some remote and holy place."⁶⁷ Clearly no ordinary toddler, Wilder is also a shaman-like character despite his tender age, as if the family were practicing an archaic form of idol worship. Elsewhere, Jack's twelve-year-old son Heinrich is described as a "primitive clay figurine, some household idol of obscure and cultic derivation."[68] The sacred intrudes into their domestic life at regular intervals, making them seem more like a primitive tribe than a typical American family.

Although they perceive their world through a dominant secular materialism, DeLillo's characters often turn to religious concepts and language as a counterpoint to official discourse. Thus, Jack likens the thick black billowing cloud that forms over Blacksmith to the sublime: "Our fear was accompanied by a sense of awe that bordered on the religious. It is surely possible to be awed by the thing that threatens your life, to see it as a cosmic force, so much larger than yourself, more powerful, created by elemental and willful rhythms."[69] In the Romantic era, the sublime was said to invoke raw emotions of awe, terror, and wonder. The "airborne toxic event," in a euphemism designed to lessen public fear about the consequences of the industrial disaster, still carries a quasi-religious valence. From a freeway ramp outside Blacksmith, the characters gather night after night to gaze in wonder on a "postmodern sunset" caused by the toxic spill.[70] No doubt the vaguely religious notion of the sublime is being parodied here just as the official discourse of an "airborne toxic event" is, but the interweaving of scientific and religious registers suggests that the world of Blacksmith is not quite as disenchanted as Max Weber would have it.

In another scene near the end of *White Noise*, the youngest child Wilder performs what amounts to a small miracle by riding his tricycle across an expressway in rush-hour traffic and emerging unscathed at the other end. What we are supposed to make of this miraculous event is not entirely clear; since DeLillo goes out of his way to emphasize its utter incomprehensibility: "The women could only look, empty mouthed, each with an arm in the air. ... The drivers could not quite comprehend. In their knotted posture, belted in, they knew this picture did not belong to the hurtling consciousness of the highway, the broad-ribboned modernist stream. ... What did it mean, this little rotary blur?"[71] Invoking Sergei Eisenstein's famous Odessa steps sequence in *Battleship Potemkin* (1925), the scene is deliberately cinematic, an ironic comment on countless chase scenes in which the hero improbably dodges adversaries and bullets with nary a scratch.[72] Bystanders watching it can only hope "for the scene to reverse, the boy to pedal backwards ... like a cartoon figure on morning TV," yet the narrator applies a religious frame of reference for Wilder's wild ride; he is described as "mystically charged," as if protected by guardian angels.[73] By interpreting Wilder's miraculous survival as a "good omen," Jack "has indeed succumbed to superstition," according to Mark Conroy, but this argument relies on the disenchantment divide, whereas for DeLillo even the most resolutely secular characters are open to the realm of spirits.[74] These characters appear to be both buffered and porous simultaneously, following Taylor, which is to say they are autonomous and bounded yet "open" and "vulnerable" to supernatural forces.[75] For instance, when a cash machine confirms that Jack's bank balance roughly corresponds with what he had recorded in his checkbook, "waves of relief and gratitude flow through him," and an immense burden is lifted: "The system had blessed my life. I felt its support and approval."[76]

The longing for transcendence is inseparable from a fear of death in *White Noise*. Taylor explains: "in a world where the guarantee of meaning has gone, where all the traditional sources, theological, metaphysical, historical, can be cast in doubt," there would seem to be nothing left but "a definitive emptiness, the final dawning of the end of the last illusion of significance."[77] One of the key tenets of a secular worldview is that there is nothing beyond the here and now, leaving many with a "lurking suspicion that all our getting and spending amounts to nothing more than fidgeting while we wait for death," as Andrew Delbanco puts it, making it virtually impossible "to hold back the melancholy suspicion that we live in a world without meaning."[78] DeLillo's novels may seem at first glance to grow out of this largely secular worldview, but on closer examination, they grapple with big questions like the existence of God and what happens after death. "I think there is a sense of last things in my work that probably comes from a Catholic childhood," DeLillo writes. "For a Catholic, nothing is too important to discuss or think about, because he's raised with the idea that he will die any minute now and that if he doesn't live his life in a certain way this death is simply an introduction to an eternity of pain."[79] Without the benefit of older certainties, much less catechisms, DeLillo's characters are terrified of death: "I woke in the grip of a death sweat," Jack tells us. "Defenseless against my own racking fears. A pause at the center of my being."[80] Babette, too, is apprehensive about the "emptiness, the sense of cosmic darkness," having rejected any notion of an afterlife.[81] Murray Jay Suskind is somewhat less concerned about death, if only because he has adopted a Buddhist view of death as "a waiting period," a "transitional state between death and rebirth" when "the soul restores itself to some of the divinity lost at birth."[82] He assures Babette: "Once we stop denying death, we can proceed calmly to die and then go on to experience uterine rebirth or Judeo-Christian afterlife or out-of-body experience or a trip on a UFO or whatever we wish to call it."[83] Babette is not buying it. Unbeknownst to her family, she starts taking the experimental drug Dylar in the hope that it "could eliminate the fear of death."[84] Since death may simply be a form of oblivion, these characters are desperate to outwit death: "Don't let us die, I want to cry out to that fifth century sky ablaze with mystery and spiral light. Let us both live forever, in sickness and health, feeble-minded, doddering, toothless, liver-spotted, dim-sighted, hallucinating. Who decides these things? What is out there? Who are you?"[85] Their sense of foreboding is funny, but also poignant and serious; *White Noise* is a masterpiece of dark comedy. Interestingly enough, DeLillo claims that he felt a strange cloud hovering over his shoulder as he wrote *White Noise*: "all the time I was writing it, I felt a hovering sense of death in the air. ... It was like a cloud hanging over my right shoulder. As soon as I finished, the cloud lifted. I never had an experience like that since."[86]

If we recall that one working title for the novel was "The American Book of the Dead," the seriousness of DeLillo's satire comes into better focus. To be sure, the book's signature style is deadpan humor. After the airborne toxic event spreads panic throughout Blacksmith, however, the overall tone turns darker and more apocalyptic. The Gladney family encounters a "rangy man with sparse hair" in the disaster shelter who views it as a sign that "God's kingdom is coming."[87] Jack cannot help but wonder about the man's certainty that the Second Coming was at hand:

> I wondered about his eerie self-assurance, his freedom from doubt. Is this the point of Armageddon? No ambiguity, no more doubt? He was ready to run into the next world. ... I did not feel Armageddon in my bones but I worried about all those people who did, who were ready for it, wishing hard, making phone calls and bank withdrawals.[88]

DeLillo was writing at a time when growing numbers of Americans were convinced that the end was nigh. The popularity of Hal Lindsey's *The Late, Great Planet Earth* made premillennial dispensationalism familiar to many Americans, and Billy Graham made it a mainstay of his ministry.[89] By the 1980s, its influence reached even into the White House. In one major study of American evangelicalism, Matthew Avery Sutton shows that the oil crisis of the 1970s and the acid rain scare of the 1980s "inspired visions of disaster and doom among a new crop of evangelical writers," who intuited that after the social upheavals of the 1960s and 1970s, many anxious Americans "found solace" in "promises of salvation from the cataclysm that was to come."[90] Influenced by such apocalyptic thinking, Heinrich becomes "practically giddy … with some kind of end-of-the-world elation" at the prospect of unmitigated disaster in the wake of the airborne toxic event.[91] The author clearly understands the popular appeal and reach of eschatology in late-twentieth-century America. "Out of some persistent sense of large-scale ruin," the narrator observes, "we keep inventing hope."[92]

To explore religion and spirituality in these novels necessarily involves us in eschatology. His characters are obsessed with end times, even if their fascination is tinged with narcissism. As Nick Shay says of his son Jeff in *Underworld*: "It's the special skill of an adolescent to imagine the end of the world as an adjunct to his own discontent. But Jeff got older and lost interest and conviction."[93] This is the same boy who "believed, at thirteen, that the border between him and the world was thin and porous enough to allow him to affect the course of events."[94] Again, we see DeLillo suggesting that late modern selfhood may in fact be more porous than Taylor allows. At any rate, his characters may strike us as both buffered and porous, materialist and mystical, secular and religious. It's not always clear whether the characters actually believe that the world will end, for instance, or whether they are simply bemused by predictions of the world's demise. Flipping through a magazine in bed one night, Marian informs Nick in a matter-of-fact tone that the Rapture will occur on October 28: "Look at this. They give the exact date."[95] Evidently, Marian is unaware of the biblical admonition against setting a date. Elsewhere in *Underworld*, Cotter Martin and his mother stop to listen to a sidewalk preacher predicting the Second Coming. "No one knows the day or the hour," she tells her son. "I believe this is Matthew twenty-four."[96] But this does not prevent plenty of characters from prophesying in DeLillo's fiction. In a chilling passage, the Texas Highway Killer Richard Henry Gilkey remarks: "When the wind dies there's a suspense that falls across the land and makes you think of the hush before the Judgment."[97]

New Religious Movements and Conspiracy Theory

"Here they come, marching into American sunlight."[98] So begins the opening set piece of DeLillo's novel *Mao II*: a mass wedding ceremony at Yankee Stadium presided over by the Reverend Sung Myung Moon, head of the Unification Church, better known as the Moonies.[99] The narrator describes Moon as "a man of chunky build who saw Jesus on a mountainside, ... and now he is here, in American light, come to lead them to the end of human history."[100] What follows is surely the best of DeLillo's crowd scenes, as some 6,500 couples gather to be married: "The blessed couples move their lips in unison, matching the echo of his amplified voice. There is stark awareness in their faces, a near pain of rapt adoration. ... His voice leads them out past love and joy, past the beauty of their mission, out past miracles and surrendered self ... out past religion and history."[101] Reverend Moon promises to remove his followers from the cares of this world; in return, they agree to cease all contact with their families and give up their former lives and personal desires. John Duvall points out, "DeLillo has long been fascinated with crowds and people's collective urge to be part of something larger than themselves, to surrender to a power that would help explain the felt alienation of their lives and to protect them from a recognition of their own mortality."[102] One character in *The Names* associates crowds with religion: "The nightmarish force of people in groups, the power of religion—he connected the two. Masses of people suggested worship and delirium, obliteration of control, children trampled."[103] In an interview, DeLillo reveals that the opening crowd scene of *Mao II* originated in a photograph. "I saw a photograph of a wedding conducted by Reverend Moon of the Unification Church, and it was just lying around for months," he recalls. "And when I looked at it again, I realized I wanted to understand this event, and the only way to understand it was to write about it. For me, writing is a concentrated form of thinking."[104] To better understand new religious movements like the Unification Church, DeLillo turns to fiction, which allows him to enter the minds of its members.

At first, we mostly observe the scene from the point of view of Karen Janney's parents. Rodge and Maureen watch the ceremony anxiously from the stands, peering through binoculars in search of their estranged daughter. Looking out on the sea of faces, the father cannot help but think that the cult is "founded on the principle of easy belief. A unit fueled by credulousness."[105] Utilizing multiple points of view, DeLillo switches back and forth from an outsider's view of the organization to an insider's perspective. Although Karen herself is not aware that her parents are watching from the stands, she actually intuits her father's concern: "This is what frightens them. We really believe. They bring us up to believe but when we show them true belief they call out psychiatrists and police. We know who God is. This makes us crazy in the world."[106] To the outside world, Moonies are crazy to believe that Reverend Moon is actually a deity. According to Karen's friend Scott: "Karen thinks God is here. Like walkin' and talkin'."[107] He continues:

"If it's believers you want, Karen is your person. Unconditional belief. The messiah is here on earth."[108] To insiders, however, the reality is a bit more complicated. In their book *Acts of Faith: Exploring the Human Side of Religion* (2000), Rodney Stark and Roger Fink interview a young convert who admits that he has doubts about all this:

> You know, sometimes at night I wonder what if none of this is true. What if Rev. Moon is not inspired by God? Maybe all of this is for nothing. But then I say to myself, if it's true then I'm in on the ground floor of the greatest event in history. And if it isn't, so what? I was probably going to spend the rest of my life working in that plywood plant anyway.[109]

For Karen, the Unification Church similarly represents "a way out of weakness and confusion," much like the convert interviewed by Stark and Fink.[110] Disillusioned with what she calls "the strict plain shapes of churchly faith," Karen finds the Unification Church more compelling: "She believed deeply in Master and still thought of herself as a seeker, ready to receive what was vast and true."[111] Like other seekers in DeLillo's fiction, Karen seems "driven by homeless spiritual impulses and mesmerized by new religious movements."[112] Whereas Scott ridicules her belief, however, the photojournalist Brita Nilsson sympathizes with her will to believe: "I don't like not believing. I'm not at peace with it. I take comfort when others believe. ... I need these people to believe for me. I cling to believers. Many, everywhere. Without them, the planet goes cold."[113]

In the penultimate chapter of *White Noise*, Jack Gladney makes a similar observation when he encounters a nun who insists that she does not believe in God. Bleeding profusely from a bullet wound, Jack seeks help in "a three-story building that might have been a Pentecostal church, a day-care center, world headquarters for some movement of regimented youth."[114] What follows is a curious discussion about belief, the upshot of which, as Jack is astounded to learn, is that this particular nun does not believe in heaven. When Jack protests that nuns, of all people, have to keep the faith, she knowingly observes, "Nonbelievers need the believers. They are desperate to have someone believe."[115] "As belief shrinks from the world," she claims, "people find it more necessary than ever that *someone* believe. ... Those who have abandoned belief must still believe in us."[116] Recall Brita's comment in *Mao II* about "the enormous importance" of believers, like the men in Catania she saw "pulling a saint on a float through the streets," for instance, or people who "crawl for miles on their knees in Mexico City on the Day of the Virgin, leaving blood on the basilica steps and then joining the crowd inside," which reminds her, too, of the Day of Blood in Teheran: "I need these people to believe for me."[117] Here, we see a desire on the part of some unbelievers "to know that people out there believe in all the old verities, the old gods," as DeLillo puts it: "These things keep the planet warm."[118] This statement appears in an interview, but the fact that we see the same point in both *White Noise* and *Mao II* surely confirms its importance for the author: nonbelievers need to believe that there are believers. Ultimately, Jack Gladney resolves the apparent hypocrisy of this position by joining in with the believers: "White noise everywhere. ... I believed everything."[119] As Mark Osteen glosses this statement: "DeLillo is suggesting that the impulse to believe, a faith in the bare potential for sacredness or transcendence, will always endure."[120] One might go further: Jack's disavowal of skepticism, his exasperated decision to believe everything, makes belief and unbelief virtually indistinguishable.

A similar kind of credulity characterizes many forms of conspiracy theory, and DeLillo, who is nothing if not a connoisseur of conspiracy theory, has focused again and again on those aspects of American culture—espionage, paranoia, terrorism—associated with the Cold War. Dubbed "the chief shaman of the paranoid school of American fiction" by one critic, DeLillo's novels have demonstrated that conspiracy theories and paranoia abound in Cold War America.[121] As early as *Running Dog* (1978), DeLillo's narrator observes, "This is the age of conspiracy, the age of connections, links, secret relationships."[122] Twenty years later, in his novel *Underworld*, we find him still sounding the same paranoid credo: "everything is connected in the end."[123] For DeLillo, the postwar period was a time when "paranoia replaced history in American life," and the watershed moment for that process was undoubtedly the assassination of John F. Kennedy.[124]

In the novel *Libra* (1988), DeLillo describes JFK's assassination as "seven seconds that broke the back of the American century."[125] The assassination and the many conspiracy theories that followed it almost certainly tested the credulity of ordinary Americans about many things: the capacity of law enforcement agencies to uphold the rule of law, for example, or the possible involvement of organized crime. *Libra* brings readers into the mind of the world's most famous assassin, for the novel is told largely from Lee Harvey Oswald's point of view. In the "Author's Note" appended to the end of *Libra*, the author writes that as "a work of the imagination," the novel "makes no claim to the literal truth," offering readers "a way of thinking about the assassination without being constrained by half-facts or overwhelmed by possibilities, by the tide of speculation that widens with the years."[126] Notwithstanding the Warren Commission's conclusion that Lee Harvey Oswald acted alone, the Kennedy assassination has generated countless conspiracy theories, including most prominently Oliver Stone's film *JFK* (1992), which contends that Vice President Lyndon Johnson himself had authorized the assassination. Because JFK's assassination has been so contested, it is unsurprising that DeLillo returns to it once again in his quintessential conspiracy novel, *Underworld*. Watching a screening of the famous amateur footage of the assassination shot by Abraham Zapruder in a New York gallery, Klara and Miles notice "the same release of breath every time, like bursts of disbelief" as the fatal "headshot" appears onscreen.[127] Years after the event, viewers are still in a state of shock, yet while their bursts of disbelief are obviously meant to suggest surprise at the president's death, my sense is that DeLillo also wants to point to the way conspiracy theories have in effect created new forms of credulity: "The deeper the ambiguity, the more we believe, the more we trust."[128]

Conspiracy theories bear a striking resemblance to new religious movements insofar as they inspire an emotional and sometimes irrational devotion to widely discredited ideas. While visiting a clinic for victims of radiation exposure in Kazakhstan in *Underworld*, Nick

Shay and Biran Glassic meet a Russian named Viktor Maltsev, who tells them about "a woman in Ukraine who says she is second Christ. She is going to be crucified by followers and then rise from the dead. Very serious person. Fifteen thousand followers. You can believe this? Educated people, look very normal."[129] The implication here is that they are delusional: how can anyone believe this? Yet Viktor makes it clear that educated, rational people are among this woman's followers. According to DeLillo, paranoia hearkens back to presumably outmoded forms of religious belief:

> The important thing about paranoia in my characters is that it operates as a form of religious awe. It's something old, leftover from some forgotten part of the soul. And the intelligence agencies that create and service this paranoia are not interesting to me as spy handlers or masters of espionage. They represent old mysteries and fascinations, ineffable things. Central intelligence. They're like churches that hold the final secrets.[130]

Sister Alma Edgar is another obvious example of how conspiracy theory and religion are linked in the novel; she herself is characterized as "sinfully complicit with some process she only half understood," a process in which an "array of systems displaces religious faith with paranoia."[131] My interest in paranoia lies less in its political than in its religious implications, since paranoia also activates the kind of suspended disbelief that we see operating in so many forms of religion.

Conspiracy theories imagine that what goes on behind the scenes is more important than what is reported publicly about government officials, corporate leaders, and others in positions of power. Nick Shay has a word for this suspicious attitude toward authority figures, *Dietrologia*, which he describes as "the science of what is behind something."[132] DeLillo himself describes it this way: "In *Underworld*, there is a sense of larger forces at work, of a kind of overarching, technological mastery that makes people suspicious, distrustful, and even paranoid. That makes us prone to embrace a kind of halffaith. We half believe in everything, and we don't fully commit our faith to anything."[133] The novel includes many examples of what Peter Knight calls "low-level paranoia."[134] Here are a few of them: Graffiti artist Ismael Munoz, aka Moonman 157, wonders if the sudden interest in his work is really the result of a conspiracy by New York gallery owners; Jeremiah Sullivan, aka Jumpy Jerry because he is plagued by uncontrollable twitches, believes he is "being followed wherever he went, and they were recording his private thoughts"; a street preacher in Harlem believes the pyramid on the dollar bill is the means by which Freemasons "flash their Masonic codes to each other"; Nick's colleague Simeon Biggs believes the US government has altered census reports on the African American population; Sister Alma Edgar believes "Bobby Fischer had all the fillings removed from his teeth when he played Boris Spaasky in 1972" to prevent the KGB from controlling him during a chess match; a Park Avenue art collector, Carlo Strasser, believes US currency is itself some kind of conspiracy; Matt's coworker Eric Deming believes cancer rates among "downwinders" living near atomic tests sites were kept secret by the US government; Marvin Lundy believes the birthmark on Mikhail Gorbachev's forehead is actually map of Latvia and foretells the "total collapse of the Soviet system"; and finally, the narrator himself is clearly obsessed with the number thirteen.[135] Characters who traffic in such low-level paranoia are not especially interested in whether their pet theories are true. "You think these stories are true?" Matt asks his coworker Eric Deming, echoing Jack Gladney's question to his friend Murray about whether he actually believed in metempsychosis. Eric is forced to admit that he doesn't believe any of these theories; he just likes to spread rumors. Similarly, when Jesse Detwiler tries to persuade Nick that the CIA has smuggled heroin into the country, he bases his conspiracy theory not on any particular evidence but rather on the basic idea that "it's stupid not to believe it. Knowing what we know."[136] When in doubt, as Viktor Maltsev tells Nick in Kazakhstan: "Believe everything. Everything is true."[137]

No one looms larger in *Underworld*'s enormous cast of paranoid characters, of course, than FBI Director J. Edgar Hoover. Under his leadership, the FBI created dossiers on hundreds of individuals considered threats to national security. "The dossier was a deeper form of truth," Hoover believed, "transcending facts and actuality," and because the dossier was classified, "it was a truth without authority and therefore incontestable."[138] As the novel portrays him, anyway, J. Edgar Hoover took it upon himself to safeguard US national security by any means necessary: "Every official secret in the Bureau had its blood-birth in Edgar's own soul."[139] Although not particularly religious, Hoover is nonetheless a kind of "debased saint," according to DeLillo.[140] The author constantly associates this ultimate G-man with religion and even with eschatology. At one point, he describes J. Edgar Hoover as having "the sheen of Last Things in his eye."[141] Conspiracy theories at once appropriate from and infiltrate other belief systems in this novel.

As Richard Hofstadter argued in his classic essay, the paranoid style presumes a certain view of history in which the individual is largely powerless—a pawn in someone else's game. However, DeLillo seems to want to restore some degree of agency to individuals in *Underworld*, a novel Patrick O'Donnell has called "the most capacious fictionalization of human subjectivity in the postmodern era," in which fictional characters rub shoulders with historical figures.[142] "These people are all inventions issuing from the author's memory and imagination," DeLillo admits, but he also wants to reclaim his characters from a facile social determinism: "Against the force of history, so powerful, visible, and real, the novelist poses the idiosyncratic self. Here it is, sly, mazed, mercurial, scared half-crazy. It is also free and undivided, the only thing that can match the enormous dimensions of social reality."[143] The pronoun "it" unwittingly suggests that his characters are subject to social and historical factors beyond their control, yet he cannot quite bring himself to relinquish the dream of autonomy, the notion that we have some control over our destinies, or in Marx's formulation, that history is, finally, what we make of it: "Men make their own history, but they do not make it as they please; they do not make it under self-selected circumstances, but under circumstances existing already, given and transmitted from the past. The tradition of all the dead generations weighs like a nightmare on the brain of the living."[144] DeLillo shows us how conspiracy theories and new religious movements are among the social determinants that, like more orthodox religions, have often weighed on the brains of the living.

Material Christianity, Popular Culture, Revelation

The virtuoso opening section of *Underworld* is a stirring account of the October 3, 1951 baseball game between the New York Giants and the Brooklyn Dodgers, in which Bobby Thomson secured the National League pennant for the Giants by hitting a game-ending three-run home run in the bottom of the ninth inning. DeLillo gives the event subtle religious undertones, which seems appropriate given the role that baseball has played in the US national imaginary. With the Polo grounds as a sort of surrogate church, baseball fans gather to witness a miracle as the Giants improbably won the National League pennant, which perhaps seemed all the more miraculous as they had already overcome the Dodgers' double-digit lead in the standings leading up to the playoffs. DeLillo sets the stage for Thompson's game-winning home run expertly, capturing the unique aura of a baseball game at mid-century and the adrenaline rush of a magical moment in sports. Reproducing Russ Hodges's play-by-play of this famous "shot heard round the world," the novel registers the "disbelief and thrill" of that moment for New York Giants fans.[145]

The homerun baseball then becomes a kind of talismanic object, for as David Evans has argued, *Underworld* "is unified less by the actions of a single character than by the fate of a physical object, the Thomson homerun baseball, as it passes through the possession of a large range of individuals."[146] When a young black kid named Cotter Martin gains possession of the ball in the stands, he knows it has tremendous value even though he has no idea what it's worth. Cotter is not about to part with the ball, much less try to sell it, but his father, Manx Martin, immediately seized upon the baseball's potential value as a commodity rather than a keepsake. Manx Martin, in the process of trying to steal his son Cotter's baseball, "sees a woman standing under the Power of

Prayer sign, soliciting her trade," as if to underscore that everything is for sale in late capitalism.[147] But selling the ball proves to be more difficult than he imagined: even as he tries to convince a white man named Charlie that it is really the one Thomson hit to win the pennant, Manx realizes how crazy this claim sounds even to him. The seller can see immediately that Charlie suffers from buyer's remorse: "He sees that Charlie is feeling slightly down at the moment. Charlie is probably passing from the stage of half belief to the stage of disbelief."[148] Once Nick Shay comes into possession of the baseball, he treats it with the kind of reverence usually reserved for holy relics, calling to mind a material dimension to religious experience.[149]

At once the most personal and the most historical of his novels, *Underworld* marked a major achievement for the author: "In *Underworld*, DeLillo may have succeeded in wedding his cultural critique to characters with fully developed inner lives that recall an older novelistic sense of the human heart."[150] He represents the Italian-American Bronx neighborhood of his childhood as a vibrant ethnic community that would soon be transformed in ways few could have foreseen. Among "his warmest childhood memories" from the period is the Catholic Mass DeLillo once said: "It prompted feelings that art sometimes draws out of us."[151] Like his contemporary Philip Roth's fictional homages to the Jewish community of Newark, New Jersey, DeLillo pays tribute in *Underworld* to his Catholic upbringing in the Bronx.

If the novel is heartfelt and even nostalgic, though, it is also highly critical of that milieu. The author's portrait of the tyrannical Sister Alma Edgar, for instance, is a ferocious indictment of parochial education in the 1950s. An unlikely double of J. Edgar Hoover, not only does she share a name with the FBI director, she also views herself as a "junior G-man protecting laws," and she earns the nickname Sister Skelley Bone from her students at the Catholic high school.[152] She enforces the "grim recitation" of the Baltimore Catechism, "with its implicit argument that the world's mysteries can be tidily resolved into a black-and-white world of angels and devils, heaven and hell, God and Satan—no middle ground, no compromise."[153] Thus, when Sister Edgar asks, "What do we mean when we say that Christ will come from thence to judge the living and the dead?" the class responds in unison, "When we say that Christ will come from thence to judge the living and the dead, we mean that on the last day Our Lord will come to judge everyone who has ever lived in this world."[154] While Sister Edgar employs the Baltimore Catechism as a form of religious indoctrination, it still plays a significant role in spiritual formation.[155] Consider Nick's brother Matt, for instance: "Matty believed in the Baltimore Catechism. It had all the questions and all the answers and it had love, hate, damnation and washing other people's feet, it had whips, thorns and resurrections, it had angels, shepherds, thieves and Jews, it had hosanna in the highest."[156]

DeLillo does not need to downplay the aesthetic power of the Baltimore Catechism in order to lodge a litany of familiar complaints about Catholic education. With relative impunity, Sister Edgar subjects her students to much verbal and physical abuse, as when she bangs Michael Kalenka's head against the blackboard because he says Adam and Eve look like Tarzan and Jane, or when she treats Annette Esposito like "a freak of nature" in front of the whole class for having the audacity to grow breasts in the eighth grade, "which caused bulges under her blue jumper."[157] She takes sadistic pleasure in frightening students, announcing one day that they are under an "atomic attack," yelling "Duck and cover! Duck and cover! Duck and cover!" causing students cower under their desks and assume a "prayer posture" that makes them look as penitent as the "faithful of old Samarkand bending to their hojatollah," a comment that ironically displaces the students from the Bronx to Samarkand, in present-day Uzbekistan, an ancient city that was designated as a "crossroads of cultures" by UNESCO when it was added to its World Heritage List.[158] This throwaway line perhaps predicts the ethnic diversification of the Bronx to come.

By the 1980s, it has been utterly transformed by cultural, demographic, and religious changes. The Catholic Church itself has been transformed as a result of third-wave immigration. Accompanied by a younger nun, Sister Grace Fahey, who does not wear the habit,

Sister Edgar has become involved in urban ministry, attempting to help those living in the housing projects by distributing food and medicine to drug addicts, homeless people, and those afflicted with AIDS. Their approach to urban ministry stands in contrast to "a band of charismatics," or "shouters of the Spirit," whose idea of assistance is described as "treating knife wounds with a prayer."[159] We realize how much Sister Edgar has mellowed with age when she recalls visiting an underground chapel in Rome and "remembered thinking vindictively" that the buried dead would come out of the earth and punish the sins of the living: "But does she really want to believe that, still?"[160] Sister Edgar is no longer the strict disciplinarian who instilled the fear of damnation in her pupils. Instead, she is something of a realist. The contrast with her earlier self is striking.

When a young homeless girl she had been trying to help, Esmeralda, is brutally raped and murdered, Sister Edgar plunges into the depths of a crisis of faith. She had seen in the girl "a radiant grace" and "even a source of personal hope, a goad to the old rugged faith," but after Esmeralda dies, she suffers from a despondency that nearly deprives Sister Edgar of her faith.[161] Driving to the scene of the crime, she tries to quell her doubts by reciting the old Baltimore Catechism, which she describes as "the lucid music of her life."[162] Instead of reassuring her, though, it now seems only a "desperate prayer" to hold onto her crumbling faith:

> She believes she is falling into crisis, beginning to think it is possible that all creation is a spurt of blank matter that chances to make an emerald here, a dead star there, with random waste between. The serenity of immense design is missing from her life, authorship and moral form. ...
>
> It is not a question of disbelief. There is another kind of belief, a second force, insecure, untrusting, a faith that is spring fed by the things we fear in the night, and she thinks she is succumbing.[163]

On the verge of abandoning her faith, Sister Edgar does not succumb to atheism so much as she replaces her religious belief with another form of belief. She becomes deeply pessimistic about the essential depravity of human beings, making her more fearful, untrusting, and paranoid than ever before. Sister Edgar's loss of faith also has a lot to do with the familiar problem of theodicy, that is, the problem of how to reconcile a just, sovereign God with so much evil and suffering.[164]

But DeLillo does not leave Sister Edgar wallowing in despair. Toward the end of the novel, she receives what appears to be a sign of God's presence in the world, if not a miracle: namely a vision of the young Esmeralda on a billboard advertising Minute Maid orange juice, apparently put there by the graffiti artist Ismael Munoz. The image becomes visible when the headlights from the subway train shine on the back of the billboard, but it is understood by nearly everyone who sees it as a sign from God. People come from all over to witness the miracle.

In the ghostly image of Esmeralda on an ordinary billboard, DeLillo finds another instance of how the sacred and profane intersect in contemporary culture. To be sure, some are skeptical; Sister Grace regards the supposed image as "the worst kind of tabloid superstition."[165] Yet Sister Edgar insists on going to see what all the fuss is about. A huge crowd has gathered around the billboard, and when the girl's face appears, it engenders a kind of religious ecstasy:

> This is how a crowd brings things to single consciousness. Then she sees it, an ordinary commuter train, silver and blue, ungraffiti'd, moving smoothly toward the drawbridge. The headlights sweep the billboard and she hears a sound from the crowd, a gasp that shoots into sobs and moans and the cry of some unnamable painful elation. A blurted sort of whoop, the holler of unstoppered belief. Because when the train lights hit the dimmest part of the billboard a face appears above the misty lake and it belongs to the murdered girl. A dozen women clutch their heads, they whoop and sob, a spirit, a godsbreath passing through the crowd.
>
> Esmeralda.
> Esmeralda.
>
> Sister is in body shock. She has seen it but so fleetingly, too fast to absorb—she wants the girl to reappear.[166]

The crowd clearly believes they have witnessed a miracle, as evidenced by the women "holding babies up to the sign, to the glowing juice, let it bathe them in baptismal balsam and oil."[167] Sister Grace remains skeptical, but Sister Edgar is more inclined to believe that the image of the dead girl is indeed miraculous.[168] She waits for the next train. When it comes, and the lights hit the billboard at just the right angle, the vision reappears: "She sees Esmeralda's face take shape under the rainbow of bounteous juice and above the little suburban lake and there is a sense of someone living in the image, an animating spirit—less than a tender second of life, less than half a second and the spot is dark again."[169] According to DeLillo, the inspiration for this scene came from an event he had read about:

> It has happened in the U.S. that people see religious imagery on totally commonplace backgrounds. In Pittsburgh, people were seeing the face of Jesus in a fork full of spaghetti on a huge billboard, and cars would congregate, and people would congregate. I suppose that this was the sort of inspiration I had for Esmeralda's face being on the billboard, in an orange juice ad. I didn't mean it as some kind of mockery, I meant it as something that happens. Popular culture is inescapable in the U.S. Why not use it?[170]

In his reworking of this type of phenomena, DeLillo tries to maintain a studiously neutral tone. Although there is an element of satire here, Sister Edgar evidently experiences a profound sense of joy. Esmeralda's image is less a visible sign of divine intervention than a form of communal witness, or what the narrator describes as "a fellowship of deep belief."[171] In short, something like faith has been restored: "She feels something break upon her. An angelus of clearest joy."[172]

Despite the ironic denouement of the scene—the billboard is replaced several weeks later with the message, "*Space Available*, followed by a phone number in tasteful type"—DeLillo suggests that popular manifestations of spirituality and religion are everywhere in contemporary culture and that many people still hold all sorts of religious beliefs, sometimes quite fervently.[173] The narrative point of view momentarily switches to second person, as the narrator asks readers:

And what do you remember, finally, when everyone has gone home and the streets are empty of devotion and hope, swept by river wind? Is the memory thin and bitter and does it shame you with its fundamental untruth—all nuance and wishful silhouette? Or does the power of transcendence linger, the sense of an event that violates natural forces, something holy that throbs on the hot horizon, the vision that you crave because you need a sign to stand against your doubt?[174]

These are not rhetorical questions. If *Underworld* seems even more open to transcendence than previous novels, it may be because DeLillo manages to balance satire with measured sympathy. The miracle at the end of this novel again shows the dialectical interplay between belief and unbelief, sacred and profane, religion and secularism in contemporary culture, yet it does so without subjecting religion to the inherent skepticism of secular academic modes of thinking. DeLillo validates the religious impulses behind this miracle, even if he is silent about the cause.

Clearly interested in religious experiences outside of traditional worship spaces, the author takes popular religion seriously, showing how people are often quite invested in such experiences. In *Underworld*, for example, Louis T. Bakey, a crewmember of the B-52 bomber *Long Tall Sally*, recalls a mystical experience he had while flying through a mushroom cloud during a simulation in the Nevada desert: "A glow enters the body that's like the touch of God. ... I thought Lord God Jesus. I swear to Jesus I thought this was heaven. ... I thought I was flying right through Judgment Day."[175] This openness to mystical experiences and to heterodox forms of faith is present in other characters as well. However tenuous his own ties to the church have become, Nick found himself in his early forties longing "for a faith to embrace," and he found it in the field of waste management, which offers him a "comprehensive philosophy," a "whisper of mystical contemplation that seems totally appropriate to the subject of waste."[176] According to Duvall, garbage serves as a "figure" in the novel for "spiritually wasted lives," yet this argument does not accord with the religious language used to describe Nick's occupation.[177] "Waste is a religious thing," Nick tells us. "We entomb contaminated waste with a sense of reverence and dread."[178] As a waste management expert, he puts his faith in containing toxic waste, believing with religious conviction that radiation will not leak out of contaminated sites. Even when Nick takes his granddaughter Sunny to a recycling plant near the end of the novel, DeLillo describes the place as numinous and the process itself as sacred: "Brightness streams from skylights down to the floor of the shed, falling on the tall machines with a numinous glow. … The landfill across the road is closed now, jammed to capacity but gas keeps rising from the great earthen berm, methane, and produces a wavering across the land and sky that deepens the sacred work."[179] Nick has long since abandoned the philosophical and theological traditions of the Catholic Church, but while he cannot abide a simple, unproblematic faith, neither does he reject God altogether. Instead, like many lapsed Catholics, he remains spiritual but not religious. And his Catholic upbringing offers him a language and a way of understanding the world that is far from secular. Reading *The Cloud of Unknowing*, a book written in the fourteenth century as a guide to contemplative prayer, Nick resonates with the idea that God "withholds himself from us because this is the root of his power," adding: "Maybe we can know God through love or prayer or through visions or through LSD, but we can't know him through the intellect."[180]

At the end of *Underworld*, DeLillo explores new spiritual possibilities in the internet age. The narrator describes the World Wide Web as the apotheosis of the Enlightenment dream of containing all human knowledge in encyclopedias: "All human knowledge gathered and linked, hyperlinked, this site leading to that, this fact referenced to that, a keystroke, a mouse-click, a password—world without end, amen."[181] Indeed, the novel ends with a vision of the internet as eternity, as Sister Edgar is raptured into an electronic version of heaven. Floating around in cyberspace, "she sees God," but unlike her earlier epiphany, the narrator does not validate this one: "No, wait, sorry. It is a Soviet bomb she sees, the largest yield in history, a device exploded above the Arctic Ocean in 1961."[182] Another click and she encounters her doppelganger, J. Edgar Hoover, "hyperlinked at last to Sister Edgar—a single fluctuating impulse now, a piece of coded information."[183] As if to call into question Esmeralda's miraculous appearance on the billboard, when Nick's son Jeff types in "*dot com miraculum*" into his computer, he learns about "a miracle in the Bronx" that "took place earlier in the decade and is still a matter of some debate, at least on the web."[184] This is the same miracle, of course, that had earlier restored Sister Edgar's faith.

Nick observes that there is no "better place for the study of wonders" than on the internet; still, perhaps one reason the web seems enchanted is because it is so difficult to distinguish between information and misinformation; much of what appears on the internet is neither verifiable nor vetted: "The real miracle is the web," Nick remarks, "where everybody is everywhere at once."[185]

Although Nick remains ambivalent about religion, he comes to terms with his Catholic roots by arriving at a sort of compromise. Thus, when Big Sims asks him. "You believe in God?" Nick tentatively replies: "Yes, I think so."[186] Whatever one thinks about the surreal ending of *Underworld*, the novel surely evinces a greater openness to the consolations of religious faith, prompting more than one critic to contend that DeLillo has a soft spot for religion in the book. Tony Tanner suggests that *Underworld* "deliquesces into something close to sentimental piety," while John Leonard writes similarly of the "redemptive act of grace" at the end of the novel, where the author seems willing to run the risk of being mistaken for "a secret Holy Roller."[187]

DeLillo addresses the problem of theodicy in relation to the events of 9/11 in his brilliant novel *Falling Man* (2007). One character, Lianne Glenn, counsels a small group of Alzheimer patients at a local community center. She encourages her patients to write down their thoughts and memories in journals as part of the group therapy. Many of them write about grief and loss, such as the woman who knew a fireman who died in one of the towers. Others write about God. "How could God let this happen?" one patient writes. "He was glad he was not a man of faith because he would lose it after this."[188] One patient thinks 9/11 must be the devil's handiwork: "This is the devil. This is hell. All that fire and pain. Never mind God. This is hell"; another "wanted to know whether everything that happens to us has to be part of God's plan," while another asks: "If God let this happen, with the planes, then did God make me cut my finger when I was slicing bread this morning?"[189] In grappling with the age-old problem of theodicy, one patient insists on the impertinence of trying to do so: "It's not ours to ask. We don't ask."[190] In his book *Alone in America: The Stories That Matter* (2013), Robert A. Ferguson has suggested that since "DeLillo places all these questions in the faltering minds of his Alzheimer's patients," we can be sure "that God is no part of his own answer."[191] I find this unconvincing. At least one member of the focus group, a character named Rosellen S., discovers that she has in fact become "closer to God than ever."[192] Rosellen is losing her memory more quickly than other Alzheimer patients—at one point, she cannot even remember where she lives— and Lianne is haunted by the fate that awaits them: "the breathless moment when things fall away, streets, names, all sense of direction and location, every fixed grid of memory."[193] Rosellen finds consolation in the church.

Lianne's husband Keith Neudecker was a survivor of the 9/11 attacks. Covered in ash and carrying someone else's briefcase, he barely escapes from the World Trade Center towers. Lianne's mother Nina Bartos is enraged that the 9/11 attackers justified their actions on religious grounds: "How convenient it is to find a system of belief that justifies these feelings and these killings."[194] Lianne had been raised in a family that saw religion as infantilizing if not delusional, yet she is unsure about what she believes:

> Lianne struggled with the idea of God. She was taught to believe that religion makes people compliant. This is the purpose of religion, to return people to a childlike state. ... This is why religion speaks so powerfully in laws, rituals and punishments. And it speaks beautifully as well, inspiring music and art, elevating consciousness in some, reducing it in others. People fall into trances, people literally go to the ground, people crawl great distances or march in crowds stabbing themselves and whipping themselves. And other people, the rest of us, maybe we're rocked more gently, joined to something deep in the

soul ... We want to transcend, we want to pass beyond the limits of safe understanding, and what better way to do it than through make-believe."[195]

After 9/11, Lianne suddenly starts going to church, and her attitudes toward religion become less skeptical, softer: "She was stuck with her doubts but liked sitting in church. She went early, before mass began, to be alone for a while, to feel the calm that marks a presence outside the nonstop riffs of the waking mind. It was not something godlike she felt but only the sense of others. Others bring us closer. Church brings us closer."[196] Occasionally, she attends a storefront Pentecostal church called the Greater Highway Deliverance Temple, which she happened onto while coming out of the community center: "Here was the place, this temple whose name was a hallelujah shout, where she'd found refuge and assistance."[197] If nothing else, *Falling Man* shows how people deal with grief differently. Some are drawn to places of worship because they offer a sense of community. Thus, another survivor, Florence Givens, ventures into St. Paul's Chapel of Trinity Church Wall Street because, as she puts it, "I wanted to be with people, down there in particular. I knew there would be people there."[198] Although she rarely went to church before 9/11, Florence finds solace there, as it reawakens a long dormant spirituality: "I've always felt the presence of God. I talk to God sometimes. I don't have to be in church to talk to God."[199]

Such spiritual quests seem less quixotic than in DeLillo's earlier novels. For one thing, the stakes are much higher in *Falling Man*. Religion may motivate terrorists, but it can also offer a measure of comfort to the survivors. Lianne is more theologically sophisticated than any of the author's previous seeker characters: "God, she thought. What does it mean to say that word? ... Because once you believe such a thing, God is, then how can you escape, how survive the power of it, is and was and ever shall be."[200] Indeed, Lianne becomes something of a lay theologian in the novel, which demonstrates the author's willingness to probe into the mysteries of faith and to show, through his characters, how belief still matters to many people. A skeptical if sympathetic observer of our spiritual strivings, as W.E.B. DuBois called them, DeLillo recognizes along with Updike that for many people, belief is irrepressible. Lianne is amazed to discover, for example, that nothing can "snuff out the pulse of the shaky faith she'd held for much of her life."[201]

Contemporary novelists are highly attuned to the vicissitudes of religious belief in their fiction. As Hungerford points out, "The very idea of the internal disposition known as belief, and the centrality of that disposition to religion, is a Christian idea that comes to bear upon persons through the exercise of power within social structures."[202] Writers tend to emphasize belief over practice, yet even when characters struggle with doubts, they often understand their experience in religious terms. While arguably drawn more to heterodoxy and hybridity than to orthodoxy, contemporary US writers represent the varieties of religious experience with an ecumenical spirit. They raise questions that have long preoccupied scholars of religion, such as how to define religion as such, what constitutes religious experience, what is the fate of religion in modernity, and so on. By tracking the many different expressions of religion and spirituality in our times, contemporary US writers offer a compelling road map of the ever-evolving religious landscape.

One of the pitfalls of post-secular approaches to literature is a tendency to presume that secularization affects all religions in exactly the same ways, whereas in fact secularization affects them unevenly depending on the context. Similarly, we cannot comprehend all religions using a single explanatory framework or theory, as though all religions were more or less the same thing. If American literature is any indication, religion and spirituality are not likely to disappear any time soon. Far from predicting their demise, our writers all testify to the resilience of religions, which have adapted in remarkable ways to accommodate the immanent frame of our secular age. We cannot predict the future of all religions, but we "can expect changes in religion over time … New religions will be born. Most of them will die; some may survive. Established religions will mutate in various ways in response to social and cultural changes. Some will grow in numbers and influence, some will hold steady for periods of time, and some will weaken and decline."[203] Over the last century, we have witnessed the decline of mainline denominations, the global rise of Pentecostalism, the advent of New Age spirituality and other new religious movements, the emergence of the Christian Right, and so on. By considering American literature alongside such trends in US religious history, readers gain a deeper understanding of religion and its discontents.

Notes

Introduction

1. John Updike, *In the Beauty of the Lilies* (New York: Knopf, 1996), 5. Michiko Kakutani called it a "stunning" novel of "epic" scope that offers "a kaleidoscopic portrait of this country from its nervous entry into the 20th century to its stumbling approach to the millennium." Michiko Kakutani, "Intuitive and Precise, a Relentless Updike Mapped America's Mysteries," *The New York Times* January 28, 2009: A22.
2. Updike, *In the Beauty*, 18.
3. Ibid., 6–7.
4. Ibid., 10.
5. Ibid., 5.
6. Ibid., 15.
7. Noah Feldman, *Divided by God: America's Church-state Problem and What We Should Do about It* (New York: Farrar, Straus and Giroux, 2005), 125. See also Susan Jacoby, *The Great Agnostic: Robert Ingersoll and American Freethought* (New Haven: Yale University Press, 2013).
8. Updike, *In the Beauty*, 15–16. The relevant passage from Nietzsche, delivered in the voice of a madman, reads as follows: "God is dead. God remains dead. And we have killed him. … What after all are these churches now if they are not the tombs and sepulchers of God?" Friedrich Nietzsche, *The Gay Science*, trans. Walter Kaufman (New York: Vintage, 1974), 181–82.
9. Updike, *In the Beauty*, 18.
10. H.L. Mencken, *The Philosophy of Friedrich Nietzsche* (Boston: Luce and Company, 1908), 128.
11. John Updike, *Due Considerations: Essays and Criticism* (New York: Knopf, 2007), 27.
12. Updike, *In the Beauty*, 7, 42. The assumption that science "inexorably leads to corrosive skepticism would become central to the secularization of knowledge, and the related experience of 'losing one's faith' a virtual *rite de passage* among many nineteenth-century students and

intellectuals." Brad Gregory, *The Unintended Reformation: How a Religious Revolution Secularized Society* (Cambridge, MA: Harvard University Press, 2012), 33. For a different view, see Timothy Larsen, *Crisis of Doubt: Honest Faith in Nineteenth Century England* (Oxford: Oxford University Press, 2006).

13 Charles Taylor, *A Secular Age* (Cambridge: Belknap Press/Harvard University Press, 2007), 3, 256.

14 Ibid., 12–13.

15 Sarah Rivett, *The Science of the Soul in Colonial New England* (Chapel Hill: University of North Carolina Press, 2011), 7.

16 As A.N. Wilson has observed, "Even a fervent religious believer must, if honest, confront problems in relation to faith which were not necessarily present for those of earlier generations." A.N. Wilson, *God's Funeral* (New York: Norton, 1999), ix–x.

17 For the classic account of disenchantment, see Max Weber, "Science as Vocation," in *From Max Weber: Essays in Sociology*, ed. and trans. H.H. Gerth and C. Wright Mills (London: Routledge, 1948), 129–56. For critiques of this account, see Jane Bennett, *The Enchantment of Modern Life: Attachments, Crossings, and Ethics* (Princeton: Princeton University Press, 2001); Simon During, *Modern Enchantments: The Cultural Power of Secular Magic* (Cambridge: Harvard University Press, 2002); and Alex Owen, *The Place of Enchantment: British Occultism and the Culture of the Modern* (Chicago: University of Chicago Press, 2004). Pericles Lewis has argued that disenchantment bears a resemblance to what Michel Foucault called the repressive hypothesis: "If the modern age has so comfortably dispensed with the supernatural, why do we continue to produce so much discourse about the need to abandon it?" Pericles Lewis, *Religious Experience in the Modernist Novel* (Cambridge: Cambridge University Press, 2010), 27.

18 Talal Asad, *Formations of the Secular: Christianity, Islam, and Modernity* (Stanford: Stanford University Press, 2003), 200.

19 Charles LaPorte and Sebastian Lecourt, "Introduction: Nineteenth-century Literature, New Religious Movements, and Secularization," *Nineteenth-century Literature* Vol. 73, No. 2 (September 2018), 148. See also Peter L. Berger, ed., *The Desecularization of the World: Resurgent Religion and World Politics* (Grand Rapids: Eerdmans, 1999).

20 Gregory, *Unintended*, 370. See also Tomoko Masuzawa, *The Invention of World Religions: Or, How European Universalism Was Preserved in the Language of Pluralism* (Chicago: University of Chicago Press, 2005); and John Milbank, *Theology and Social Theory: Beyond Secular Reason*, 2nd edition (New York: Blackwell, 2006).

21 Taylor, *A Secular Age*, 41.

22 Ibid., 172. By social imaginary, Taylor means "the way ordinary people 'imagine' their social surroundings, ... the social imaginary is that common understanding which makes possible common practices, and a widely shared sense of legitimacy." Ibid., 171–72.

23 Wade Clark Roof, *Spiritual Marketplace: Baby Boomers and the Remaking of American Religion* (Princeton: Princeton University Press, 1999), 42.

24 See, for example, Vincent P. Pecora, *Secularization and Cultural Criticism: Religion, Nation, and Modernity* (Chicago: University of Chicago Press, 2006); Tracy Fessenden, *Culture and Redemption: Religion, the Secular, and American Literature* (Princeton: Princeton University Press, 2007); Janet R. Jakobsen and Ann Pellegrini, eds., *Secularisms* (Durham: Duke University Press, 2008); Michael Warner, Jonathan VanAntwerpen, and Craig Calhoun, eds., *Varieties of Secularism in a Secular Age* (Cambridge: Harvard University Press, 2010); Craig Calhoun, Mark Juergensmeyer, and Jonathan VanAntwerpen, eds., *Rethinking Secularism* (Oxford: Oxford University Press, 2011).

25 Michael Warner, "Secularism," *Keywords for American Cultural Studies*, eds. Bruce Burgett and Glenn Hendler (New York: New York University Press, 2007), 212.

26 Ibid., 210.

27 Reinhold Niebuhr, *Pious and Secular America* (New York: Scribner's, 1958), 1.

28 Wilfred Cantwell Smith, *Believing: An Historical Perspective* (Oxford: Oneworld, 1998), 44.

29 "We assume that belief is central because we assume that the person who is religious—we call that person a believer—must assent to a proposition, that divinity is real." T.M. Luhrmann, *When God Talks Back: Understanding the American Evangelical Relationship with God* (New York: Knopf, 2012), 319.

30 Updike, *In the Beauty*, 61, 65.

31 Ibid., 11.
32 John Updike, *Rabbit, Run* (New York: Random House, 1996), 133.
33 Taylor, *A Secular Age*, 13.
34 Updike, *Due Considerations*, 480.
35 "More recent work in cognitive science has given us a sharp awareness that humans, no matter how highly educated, reach for cognitive frames that are salient to the topic at hand: and those frames are not necessarily consistent with each other." Luhrmann, *When God Talks Back*, 385.
36 John Updike, "Religion and Literature," *The Religion Factor: An Introduction to How Religion Matters*, eds. William Scott Green and Jacob Neusner (Louisville: Westminster John Knox Press, 1996), 238.
37 Sanford Pinsker, "Restlessness in the 1950s: What Made Rabbit Run?" *New Essays on Rabbit, Run*, ed. Stanley Trachtenberg (Cambridge: Cambridge University Press, 1993), 58.
38 Updike, *In the Beauty*, 89.
39 Ibid., 350–51.
40 Ibid., 140.
41 Ibid., 417.
42 Robert Wuthnow, *After Heaven: Spirituality in America since the 1950s* (Berkeley: University of California Press, 1998); Robert C. Fuller, *Spiritual, but Not Religious: Understanding Unchurched America* (Oxford: Oxford University Press, 2001).
43 Christopher Lasch describes this therapeutic sensibility: "People today hunger not for personal salvation, let alone for the restoration of an earlier golden age, but for the feeling, the momentary illusion, of personal well-being, health, and psychic security. ... To live for the moment is the prevailing passion—to live for yourself, not for your predecessors or posterity." Christopher Lasch, *The Culture of Narcissism: American Life in an Age of Diminishing Expectations* (New York: Norton, 1979), 30, 33.
44 Updike, *In the Beauty*, 335.
45 Ibid., 354.
46 Robert Bellah, et al., *Habits of the Heart: Individualism and Commitment in American Life* (Berkeley: University of California Press, 1985, 2008), 220–21, 236.
47 Updike, *In the Beauty*, 354.
48 Ibid., 360.

49 Michael Barkun, *A Culture of Conspiracy: Apocalyptic Visions in Contemporary America* (Berkeley: University of California Press, 2006), 9.
50 Updike, *In the Beauty*, 398.
51 Ibid., 386, 396.
52 Ibid., 396.
53 Ibid., 398.
54 Amy Johnson Frykholm, *Rapture Culture: Left behind in Evangelical America* (Oxford: Oxford University Press, 2004), 25–26.
55 Updike, *In the Beauty*, 399.
56 Ibid.
57 Jon Butler, *Awash in a Sea of Faith: Christianizing the American People* (Cambridge: Harvard University Press, 1990), 1–2.
58 Lewis, *Religious Experience*, 25.
59 John Updike, "A Special Message for the First Edition," *In the Beauty of the Lilies* (Franklin Center, PA: Franklin Library, 1996), ii.
60 Updike, *In the Beauty*, 398.
61 Ibid., 486.
62 Ibid., 489.
63 Ibid., ii.
64 Ibid., 484.
65 Ibid., 5, 484. I am indebted to Jaji Hammer for pointing out this connection.
66 Updike, *In the Beauty*, 491.
67 Ibid., 484.
68 Sydney E. Ahlstrom, *A Religious History of the American People* (New Haven: Yale University Press, 1971), 12–13, 1079.
69 Robert D. Putnam and David E. Campbell, *American Grace: How Religion Divides and Unites Us* (New York: Simon and Schuster, 2010), 80–81. See also Daniel T. Rodgers, *Age of Fracture* (Cambridge: Belknap Press/Harvard University Press, 2011).
70 Marilynne Robinson, *Gilead* (New York: Farrar, Straus and Giroux, 2004), 19.
71 Ibid., 24, 235.
72 Ibid., 220.
73 Ibid., 114.
74 James Wood, "Acts of Devotion," *The New York Times* November 2, 2005. Accessed May 28, 2013.

75 Robinson, *Gilead*, 177.
76 Ibid., 179.
77 Ibid., 145.
78 Ibid., 143.
79 Marilynne Robinson, "Credo," *Harvard Divinity School Bulletin* Vol. 36, No. 2 (Spring 2008). Accessed May 6, 2019.
80 Robert W. Fogel, *The Fourth Great Awakening and the Future of Egalitarianism* (Chicago: University of Chicago Press, 2000).
81 Raymond Williams, *Marxism and Literature* (Oxford: Oxford University Press, 1977), 132.
82 Following the anthropologist Clifford Geertz, these writers understand that religion remains central to the "webs of significance" with which people make sense of themselves and their place in the world. Clifford Geertz, *The Interpretation of Cultures* (New York: Basic Books, 1973), 4–5. See also Christian Smith, *Religion: What It Is, How It Works, and Why It Matters* (Princeton: Princeton University Press, 2017).
83 During, *Modern Enchantments*, 50.
84 Joshua Landy argues that novels serve as "*formal models*, providing structures we may import into our own experience," and because our "deepest *beliefs* are not always fully present to us," they can become "simulation spaces" or "battlegrounds" in which "different ways of living, grounded in different belief systems, come into conflict, offering themselves for our selective appropriation." Joshua Landy, *How to Do Things with Fictions* (Oxford: Oxford University Press, 2012), 4–5.
85 Susan Mizruchi observes that "religious faith and practice distinguish themselves from other cultural practices by their insistence upon being *beyond* culture." Susan L. Mizruchi, "Introduction," *Religion and Cultural Studies* (Princeton: Princeton University Press, 2001), xii.
86 As Gauri Viswanathan has argued, "To engage in discussions about belief, conviction, or religious identity in a secular age of postmodern skepticism is already fraught with infinite hazards, not least of which is the absence of an adequate vocabulary or language." Gauri Viswanathan, *Outside the Fold: Conversion, Modernity, and Belief* (Princeton: Princeton University Press, 1998), xiv.
87 Robert A. Orsi, *The Madonna of 115th Street: Faith and Community in Italian Harlem, 1880–1950*, 2nd edition (New Haven: Yale University

Press, 2002), xiii–xiv. See also David L. Hall, ed., *Lived Religion in America: Toward a History of Practice* (Princeton: Princeton University Press, 1997).
88 James F. English, "Everywhere and Nowhere: The Sociology of Literature after 'The Sociology of Literature,'" *New Literary History* Vol. 41, No. 2 (Spring 2010): v–xxiii.
89 Caroline Levine, *Forms: Whole, Rhythm, Hierarchy, Network* (Princeton: Princeton University Press, 2015).
90 Updike, *Due Considerations*, 31.
91 Ibid., 31. The author attests to what Gregory calls "religious hyperpluralism," which he defines as "the widespread perception of religion per se as irreducibly subjective and arbitrary" and that "any adequate historical explanation of the present" religious landscape must account "for the full range of different worldviews, values, and commitments that people in fact hold, whether coherently or confusedly." Gregory, *Unintended*, 11, 175.
92 E.L. Doctorow, *Reporting the Universe* (Cambridge: Harvard University Press, 2003), 84–85.
93 Ibid., 84–85. Doctorow writes: "As the son of my fathers I am nonobservant, a celebrant of the humanism that has no patience for a religious imagination that asks me to abandon my intellect. But as the son of my mothers, I am unable to discard reverence, however unattached to an object, in recognition that a spontaneously felt sense of the sacred engages the whole human being as the intellect alone cannot." Doctorow, *Reporting*, 67.
94 Ibid., 93.

Chapter 1

1 Flannery O'Connor, *Mystery and Manners: Occasional Prose*, eds. Sally Fitzgerald and Robert Fitzgerald (New York: Farrar, Straus and Giroux, 1969), 162.
2 Ibid., 159–60.
3 Flannery O'Connor, *Collected Works* (New York: Library of America, 1983), 862.
4 Ibid., 862.

5   O'Connor, *Mystery*, 157.
6   Ibid., 163.
7   Flannery O'Connor, *The Habit of Being: Letters of Flannery O'Connor*, ed. Sally Fitzgerald (New York: Farrar, Straus and Giroux, 1979), 477.
8   O'Connor, *Mystery*, 154.
9   O'Connor, *Habit*, 510–11.
10 O'Connor, *Mystery*, 155.
11 Ibid.
12 The Judeo-Christian tradition concept dates back to the early 1930s, but it gained traction in the 1950s as a way of describing Judaism and Christianity as sister faiths sharing a common Abrahamic origin. See, for example, W. Lloyd Warner, *The Family of God* (New Haven: Yale University Press, 1961); and Stephen Prothero, *Religious Literacy: What Every American Needs to Know—and Doesn't* (San Francisco: HarperCollins, 2007), 112–13.
13 O'Connor, *Mystery*, 155.
14 Ibid.
15 O'Connor, *Habit*, 357. When the writer John Hawkes suggested that O'Connor's uncanny ability to ventriloquize the voice of the devil was due to the fact that she really was of the devil's party, O'Connor replied testily that "there is a difference in our two devils. My Devil has a name, a history and a definite plan. His name is Lucifer, he's a fallen angel, his sin is pride, and his aim is the destruction of the Divine plan. ... My Devil is objective and yours is subjective." Ibid., 456. See also John Hawkes, "Flannery O'Connor's Devil," *Sewanee Review* Vol. 70 (1962): 395–407.
16 Brad Gooch, *Flannery: A Life of Flannery O'Connor* (New York: Little, Brown, 2009), 156, 274.
17 O'Connor often complained in letters about being asked to defend her faith in public lectures. "I'm much more liable to try to get out of the way as fast as possible than to struggle to make my views plain," she wrote to Sister Mariella Gable after the lecture at Sweet Briar College. "When they ask you to make Christianity look desirable, ... ultimately what they are looking for is an apologetic fiction. The best of them think: make it look desirable because it is desirable. And the rest of them think: make it look desirable so I won't look like a fool for holding it. In a really Christian culture of real believers this wouldn't come up." O'Connor, *Habit*, 516.

18 O'Connor, *Habit*, 476.
19 Ibid.
20 Ibid.
21 Jay Watson, "Flannery O'Connor," *The Cambridge Companion to American Fiction after 1945*, ed. John N. Duvall (Cambridge: Cambridge University Press, 2012), 208.
22 Ibid.
23 John Desmond writes: "O'Connor saw her special problem as a writer to be rooted in the fact that the age speciously believed in its own capacity for achieving wholeness exclusive of the divine, a situation she found truly grotesque." John Desmond, *Risen Sons: Flannery O'Connor's Vision of History* (Athens, GA: University of Georgia Press, 1987), 57.
24 O'Connor, *Collected*, 863.
25 When a student wrote to inquire about "just what enlightenment" she should expect to get from her short stories, O'Connor shot back, "Forget about the enlightenment and just try to enjoy them." O'Connor, *Mystery*, 107.
26 O'Connor, *Collected*, 804.
27 Flannery O'Connor, *The Presence of Grace and Other Book Reviews* (Athens: University of Georgia Press, 1983), 16.
28 O'Connor, *Mystery*, 161–62.
29 O'Connor, *Collected*, 803–04.
30 Susan Srigley, *Flannery O'Connor's Sacramental Art* (South Bend: University of Notre Dame, 2004); Cristina Bieber Lake, *The Incarnational Art of Flannery O'Connor* (Macon: Mercer University Press, 2005).
31 O'Connor, *Collected*, 809–10.
32 Ibid., 808.
33 Ibid., 809.
34 Mark McGurl, *The Program Era: Postwar Fiction and the Rise of Creative Writing* (Cambridge: Harvard University Press, 2010), 133.
35 Ibid., 142–43.
36 Ibid., 143.
37 Flannery O'Connor, *A Prayer Journal* (New York: Farrar, Straus and Giroux, 2013), 5.
38 O'Connor confessed in her own inimitable fashion that she wanted to be read by the largest possible audience: "The writer, without softening his vision, is obliged to capture or conjure readers. And this means

any kind of reader. I used to think that it should be possible to write for some supposed elite, for the people who attend the universities and sometimes know how to read, but I have since found that, though you may publish your stories in the *Yale Review*, if they are any good at all you are eventually going to get a letter from some old lady in California, or some inmate of the Federal penitentiary, or the state insane asylum, or the local poorhouse, telling you where you have failed to meet his needs. And his need of course is to be lifted up." O'Connor, *Collected*, 863. The evangelical embrace of O'Connor is analogous to that of the Anglican writer C.S. Lewis. As T.M. Luhrmann has observed, "Many evangelicals still worry that secular intellectuals regard them as country bumpkins. Christians like Lewis have helped to keep that sense of cultural inferiority at bay." T.M. Luhrmann, "C.S. Lewis: Evangelical Rock Star," *The New York Times* June 26, 2013: A23.

39 O'Connor, *Habit*, 92.
40 O'Connor, *Collected*, 808.
41 Ibid., 803.
42 O'Connor, *Habit*, 229.
43 O'Connor, *Presence*, 19.
44 George A. Kilcourse, Jr. also observes that her "essays and letters repeatedly return to the identity of the Catholic fiction writer vis-à-vis the secularization process in the wider culture." George A. Kilcourse, Jr., *Flannery O'Connor's Religious Imagination: A World with Everything Off Balance* (New York: Paulist Press, 2001), 5–6. As Watson astutely points out, "Critics have given O'Connor an unusual amount of authority to dictate the terms according to which she is read. In occasional writings and her correspondence, she presented her artistic vision first and foremost as an expression of her Catholic worldview." Watson, "Flannery O'Connor," 208.
45 O'Connor, *Habit*, 90.
46 Farrell O'Gorman, *Peculiar Crossroads: Flannery O'Connor, Walker Percy, and Catholic Vision in Postwar Southern Fiction* (Baton Rouge: Louisiana State University Press, 2004), 6.
47 O'Connor, *Collected*, 811.
48 Romano Guardini, *The End of the Modern World: A Search for Orientation*, trans. Joseph Theman and Herbert Burke (New York: Sheed and Ward, 1956), 133.
49 O'Connor, *Collected*, 949.

50 O'Connor, *Habit*, 539.
51 O'Connor, *Collected*, 285.
52 Ibid., 285, 287.
53 O'Connor, *Mystery*, 134.
54 O'Connor, *Collected*, 1107. Compare Theodor Adorno's well-known assertion in 1949 that to write poetry after Auschwitz is barbaric. The relevant passage is from Adorno's 1949 essay "Cultural Criticism and Society": "The more total society becomes, the greater the reification of the mind and the more paradoxical its effort to escape reification on its own. Even the most extreme consciousness of doom threatens to degenerate into idle chatter. Cultural criticism finds itself faced with the final stage of the dialectic of culture and barbarism. To write poetry after Auschwitz is barbaric. And this corrodes even the knowledge of why it has become impossible to write poetry today. Absolute reification, which presupposed intellectual progress as one of its elements, is now preparing to absorb the mind entirely. Critical intelligence cannot be equal to this challenge as long as it confines itself to self-satisfied contemplation." Theodor Adorno, *Prisms*, trans. Shierry Weber Nicholsen and Samuel Weber (Cambridge: MIT Press, 1983), 34.
55 Will Herberg, *Protestant-Catholic-Jew: An Essay in American Religious Sociology* (Garden City, NJ: Doubleday Anchor, 1955, 1960), 59–60.
56 Ibid., 279–80.
57 Quoted in Noah Feldman, *Divided by God: America's Church-state Problem—and What We Should Do about It* (New York: Farrar, Straus and Giroux, 2005), 165. Amy Hungerford points out that Eisenhower immediately added a sentence that critics invariably do not include: "With us of course it is the Judeo-Christian concept but it must be a religion that all men are created equal." The quotation "has been reproduced, both at the time and subsequently by historians of religion, in an erroneous form that makes Eisenhower's notion of religion sound more vacuous than it was, even as he uttered something close to these words." Amy Hungerford, *Postmodern Belief: American Literature and Religion after 1960* (Princeton: Princeton University Press, 2010), 2.
58 Thomas Doherty, *Cold War, Cool Medium: Television, McCarthyism, and American Culture* (New York: Columbia University Press, 2003), 149.

59 Robert Wuthnow, *After Heaven: Spirituality in America since the 1950s* (Berkeley: University of California Press, 1998), 82.
60 Jon Lance Bacon, *Flannery O'Connor and Cold War Culture* (Cambridge: Cambridge University Press, 1993), 61.
61 Herberg, *Protestant-Catholic-Jew*, 61.
62 George Gallup, Jr., "Religion: In America: Will the Vitality of Churches Be the Surprise of the Next Century?" *U.S. Society and Values* Vol. 2, No. 1 (March 1997). Accessed April 27, 2005.
63 Quoted in Stephen J. Whitfield, *The Culture of the Cold War* (Baltimore: Johns Hopkins University Press, 1991), 77.
64 Quoted in James Davidson Hunter, *To Change the World: The Irony, Tragedy, and Possibility of Christianity in the Late Modern World* (Oxford: Oxford University Press, 2010), 11.
65 This pan-denominational American evangelicalism is reflected, for example, in the founding of the American Council of Christian Churches (ACCC) in 1941; the founding of the National Association of Evangelicals in 1942, a group that included Billy Graham; the founding of Fuller Theological Seminary in 1947; and the magazine *Christianity Today*, which appeared in 1956. Jan Blodgett, *Protestant Evangelical Literary Culture and Contemporary Society* (Westport: Greenwood Press, 1997), 34, 41.
66 Hugh B. Urban, *The Church of Scientology: A History of a New Religion* (Princeton: Princeton University Press, 2011), 19.
67 Anne Morrow Lindberg, *Gift from the Sea* (New York: Pantheon, 1955, 2005), 48.
68 Ibid.
69 Ibid., 50.
70 Nathan Hatch, *The Democratization of American Christianity* (New Haven: Yale University Press, 1989), 219. See also Molly Worthen, *Apostles of Reason: The Crisis of Authority in American Evangelicalism* (Oxford: Oxford University Press, 2013).
71 O'Connor, *Habit*, 479.
72 Ibid., 259.
73 O'Connor, *Mystery*, 147.
74 Herberg, *Protestant-Catholic-Jew*, 282. "The more citizens dutifully attended a church or synagogue, the less the traditional content of their

faith seemed to matter to them." Maurice Isserman and Michael Kazin, *America Divided: The Civil War of the 1960s*, 3rd edition (Oxford: Oxford University Press, 2008), 251.

75 Paul Tillich, *The Courage to Be* (New Haven: Yale University Press, 1952, 2000), 190.
76 Paul Tillich, *The Essential Tillich*, ed. R. Forrester Church (Chicago: University of Chicago Press, 1987), 1–2.
77 Gooch, *Flannery*, 288.
78 Ibid.
79 O'Connor, *Collected*, 805–06.
80 Alan Lloyd-Smith argues that O'Connor is best understood as a gothic writer, "although not in the conventional sense of working within a Gothic literary tradition; rather her Gothicism stems from the intensity and passion with which she works out the implications of what might be called a sort of fundamentalist, or even Puritan, Catholicism." Alan Lloyd-Smith, *American Gothic Fiction: An Introduction* (New York: Continuum, 2004), 122.
81 O'Connor, *Habit*, 105.
82 O'Connor, *Collected*, 805.
83 Flannery O'Connor, *Wise Blood* (New York: Farrar, Straus and Giroux, 1967), no page number.
84 O'Connor, *Collected*, 857.
85 O'Connor, *Mystery*, 44.
86 Reviewers didn't know what to make of *Wise Blood*. A reviewer in *Newsweek* described it as "a satire on the secularization of modern life," but another reviewer in *The New Yorker* groused: "Miss O'Connor tells her story in a dry, withered prose that suits her subject very well but makes the reader wonder if the struggle to get from one sentence to the next is worthwhile." Michael Kreyling, ed., *New Essays on Wise Blood* (Cambridge: Cambridge University Press, 1995), 41; R. Neil Scott and Irwin H. Streight, eds., *Flannery O'Connor: The Contemporary Reviews* (Cambridge: Cambridge University Press, 2009), 12.
87 O'Connor, *Wise*, 10–11.
88 Ibid., 31.
89 Ibid., 32.
90 Ibid.

91 Ibid., 31.
92 Ibid., 16.
93 Ibid.
94 According to Andrew Hoberek: "O'Connor's religious concerns enable her to relocate a Southern identity threatened by the postwar boom economy into the 'backwoods prophets and shouting fundamentalists' whose traditionalism paradoxically comes to seem like individualism in a world dominated by the deracinated white-collar middle class." Andrew Hoberek, *The Twilight of the Middle Class: Post-World War II American Fiction and White-collar Work* (Princeton: Princeton University Press, 2005), 96.
95 "The seeds of Motes' religious rebellion are planted in his youth," writes Srigley, "and the decisive emphasis on sin in relation to Jesus makes Hazel wary of both." Srigley, *Flannery*, 67.
96 O'Connor, *Wise*, 22.
97 O'Connor, *Wise*, 20–21.
98 Ibid., 24.
99 Ibid.
100 Flannery O'Connor and Kelly Gerald, *Flannery O'Connor: The Cartoons* (Seattle: Fantagraphics, 2012), vii. For this point, I am indebted to Rachel Austring, who wrote a graduate seminar paper on these cartoons and their implications for O'Connor's use of negative space.
101 O'Connor, *Mystery*, 117–18.
102 Ibid., 45.
103 Ibid., 118.
104 O'Connor, *Wise*, 54.
105 Ibid., 104.
106 Ibid., 105.
107 Ibid., 165.
108 Ibid., 152.
109 Bacon, *Flannery*, 64.
110 O'Connor, *Wise*, 152.
111 Ibid., 119.
112 Ibid.
113 Ibid., 63.
114 Quoted in Scott and Streight, eds., *Flannery*, xxii.

115 O'Connor, *Collected*, 897.
116 O'Connor, *Wise*, 203.
117 Ibid., 204.
118 "Haze will brook no compromise with godliness or mortality," the literary critic Ihab Hassan has observed, and "he murders a fake prophet used by a rival preacher to deceive the credulous." Hassan is half-right when he characterizes Hazel Motes as the "victim of a grotesque nihilism" who nonetheless "remains the pinpoint of light in a society too smug both in its skepticism and belief." In my reading, Motes's fanaticism is meant as a reproach for smug believers and skeptics. But Hassan could not refrain from turning O'Connor's critique of religious complacency into an indictment of religious fanaticism: "When theology runs wild, as it so often does in the South, worship and heresy become indistinguishable." Ihab Hassan, *Radical Innocence: Studies in the Contemporary American Novel* (Princeton: Princeton University Press, 1961), 79–80.
119 Ibid., 207.
120 Brian Wilkie, "Flannery O'Connor (1925–1964): *Wise Blood*," *Encyclopedia of Catholic Literature* Vol. 2, ed. Mary R. Reichardt (Westport: Greenwood Press, 2004), 528.
121 O'Connor, *Collected*, 923.
122 Connor, *Wise*, no page number.
123 Cheryl Walker, *God and Elizabeth Bishop: Meditations on Religion and Poetry* (New York: Palgrave, 2005), 20.
124 Michael Mears Bruner, *A Subversive Gospel: Flannery O'Connor and the Reimagining of Beauty, Goodness, and Truth* (Westmont: InterVarsity Press, 2017), 5.
125 "When you write about backwoods prophets, it is very difficult to get across to the modern reader that you take these people seriously, that you are not making fun of them, but that their concerns are your own and, in your judgment, central to human life." O'Connor, *Mystery*, 204.
126 Thomas Hill Schaub, *American Fiction in the Cold War* (Madison: University of Wisconsin Press, 1991), 134.
127 Flannery O'Connor, *The Complete Stories* (New York: Farrar, Straus and Giroux, 1971), 152.
128 Ibid., 132.

129 In one of the first full-length studies of O'Connor, Miles Orvell writes: "The Misfit evinces a distinguishing gentility of manner, which the old lady, with her desperate equation of manners and morals, mistakes for goodness." Miles Orvell, *Invisible Parade: The Fiction of Flannery O'Connor* (Philadelphia: Temple University Press, 1972), 132.
130 O'Connor, *Complete*, 29.
131 O'Connor, *Mystery*, 111–12.
132 O'Connor, *Collected*, 1121.
133 O'Connor, *Mystery*, 112.
134 Schaub, *American Fiction*, 135.
135 David Williams, "Flannery O'Connor (1925–1964): Short Stories," *Encyclopedia of Catholic Literature*, ed. Mary R. Reichardt (Westport: Greenwood Press, 2004), 535.
136 O'Connor, *Habit*, 219.
137 O'Connor, *Collected*, 1127.
138 O'Connor, *Mystery*, 96.
139 O'Connor, *Habit*, 436.
140 O'Connor, *Collected*, 1148.
141 Ibid., 1148–49.
142 Ibid., 1076, 1149.
143 O'Connor, *Habit*, 582. In a letter written after a visit to Wesleyan University in 1959, O'Connor defends her rather impish replies to a couple of over-eager professors when they wrote to ask her about the story: "There were a couple of young teachers there and one of them, an earnest type, started asking questions. 'Miss O'Connor,' he said, 'why was the Misfit's hat *black*?' I said most countrymen in Georgia wore black hats. He looked pretty disappointed. Then he said, 'Miss O'Connor, the Misfit represents Christ, does he not?' 'He does not,' I said. He looked crushed. 'Well, Miss O'Connor,' he said, 'what is the significance of the Misfit's hat?' I said it was to cover his head; and after that he left me alone. Anyway, that's what's happening to the teaching of literature." O'Connor, *Collected*, 1098.
144 O'Connor, *Habit*, 411.
145 Williams, "Flannery O'Connor," 533.
146 O'Connor, *Collected*, 1000.
147 O'Connor, *Complete*, 281.

148 The passage also alludes to the sacrament of marriage in Catholic theology, where both partners enter into a state of interdependence, renouncing individuality for the sake of their union in holy matrimony. See Lake, *Incarnational*, 131.
149 O'Connor, *Complete*, 283.
150 Some critics read the ending more positively than I do. For instance, Lake argues that when Manley Pointer runs off with Hulga's artificial leg, "he leaves her with the much more precious gift of self-knowledge." Lake, *Incarnational*, 132.
151 O'Connor, *Habit*, 350.
152 O'Connor, *Collected*, 376.
153 Ibid., 224.
154 Ibid., 1108.
155 Ibid., 332.
156 Ibid., 1152.
157 Srigley, *Flannery*, 32.
158 O'Connor, *Mystery*, 227.
159 O'Connor, *Collected*, 393.
160 Ibid., 399.
161 Ibid., 392.
162 Ibid., 379, 402.
163 Ibid., 438.
164 Ibid., 437–38.
165 Quoted in Gooch, *Flannery*, 310.
166 In "The Lame Shall Enter First" (1962), published in *The Sewanee Review*, O'Connor stages a similar confrontation between atheism and fundamentalism in which the latter emerges victorious, if ambiguously so. The story features a protagonist named Sheperd who volunteers his time on weekends to help juvenile delinquents, but like George Rayber's his altruism is undercut by his presumption to eradicate their religious "ignorance" and drag them willingly or unwillingly into "the space age." O'Connor, *Complete*, 451, 474.
167 The title comes from Matthew 11:12: "The Kingdom of heaven suffereth violence, and the violent bear it away." The phrase is from the Darby translation of 1884, which closely follows the King James Version (KJV), but Darby differs from the KJV in this verse, which reads

"the violent take it by force." O'Connor interestingly follows Darby's phrasing rather than KJV.
168 O'Connor, *Collected*, 463, 468.
169 Ibid., 473.
170 Ibid., 476.
171 Ibid., 478.
172 Ibid., 478–79.
173 Ibid., 478.
174 Jill Palaez Baumgaertner, *Flannery O'Connor: A Proper Scaring* (Chicago: Cornerstone Press, 1999), 15.
175 O'Connor, *Collected*, 506.
176 Ibid.
177 Ibid., 505.
178 In "Parker's Back," the protagonist Obadiah Elihue Parker has a vision of the words, "GOD ABOVE!" In response, he decides to have a Byzantine image of Christ tattooed on his back. Flannery O'Connor, *Everything That Rises Must Converge* (New York: Noonday, 1965), 232.
179 O'Connor, *Collected*, 523.
180 Ibid.
181 Ibid., 524.
182 Quoted in Kreyling, ed., *New Essays*, 3, 20.
183 Harold Bloom, "Introduction," *Flannery O'Connor: Modern Critical Views* (New York: Chelsea House Publishers, 1986), 8. Writer Reynolds Price bemoans the fact that, as he puts it, "the spectacle of belief is so radiant as to be potentially lethal. God in O'Connor seems almost like a nuclear plant out of control." Quoted in Susan Ketchin, *The Christ-haunted Landscape: Faith and Doubt in Southern Fiction* (Jackson: University Press of Mississippi, 1994), 77–78.
184 O'Connor, *Habit*, 147.
185 O'Connor, *Mystery*, 109.
186 Joyce Carol Oates, "The Parables of Flannery O'Connor," *New York Review of Books* April 9, 2009. Accessed July 13, 2014.
187 O'Connor, *Habit*, 124–25.
188 Wilkie, "Flannery O'Connor," 522.
189 "Mutual suspicion between Catholics and secular intellectuals," David Hollinger points out, "was rapidly diminishing in the wake of Vatican II

and of Kennedy's election as president in 1960, but the large-scale entry of Catholics into American intellectual life had scarcely begun." David Hollinger, *Science, Jews, and Secular Culture: Studies in Mid-twentieth-century American Intellectual History* (Princeton: Princeton University Press, 1996), 5.

190 Hilton Als, "This Lonesome Place: Flannery O'Connor on Race and Religion in the Unreconstructed South," *The New Yorker* January 29, 2001. Accessed May 6, 2019.

191 For an insightful reading of this occasion, see Roger Lundin, *Beginning with the Word: Modern Literature and the Question of Belief* (Grand Rapids: Baker Academic, 2014), 207–08.

192 O'Connor, *Mystery*, 161–62.

193 Robert Coles, *Flannery O'Connor's South* (Baton Rouge: Louisiana State University Press, 1980), xxxvi.

194 Lake, *Incarnational*, 240.

195 Pippa Norris and Ronald Inglehart, "Uneven Secularization in the U.S. and Western Europe," *Democracy and the New Religious Pluralism*, ed. Thomas Banchoff (Oxford: Oxford University Press, 2007), 31–58.

196 Christian Smith, *Religion: What It Is, How It Works, and Why It Matters* (Princeton: Princeton University Press, 2017), 249.

197 Ibid., 254.

198 J. Hillis Miller, *The Disappearance of God: Five Nineteenth-century Writers* (Cambridge: Belknap Press/Harvard University Press, 1963), 2.

199 Cleanth Brooks, *The Hidden God: Studies in Hemingway, Faulkner, Yeats, Eliot, and Warren* (New Haven: Yale University Press, 1963), 5, 131.

200 Howard Mumford Jones, *Belief and Disbelief in American Literature* (Chicago: University of Chicago Press, 1967), 2, 23, 147.

201 Ross Douthat, *Bad Religion: How a Nation Became a Nation of Heretics* (New York: Free Press, 2012), 29.

202 Roger Finke and Rodney Stark, *The Churching of America 1776–2005: Winners and Losers in Our Religious Economy* (New Brunswick: Rutgers University Press, 2007), 254.

203 O'Connor, *Mystery*, 166.

204 Ibid.

205 Ibid., 159.

206 Blodgett, *Protestant*, 34.

207 O'Connor, *Collected*, 1131.

208 Ibid., 858–59.
209 O'Connor, *Habit*, 451.
210 Ibid., 477.
211 Ibid., 477–78.
212 O'Connor, *A Prayer Journal*, 25. This was the sole entry that O'Connor recorded in her journal on January 2, 1947.

Chapter 2

1   Brad Gooch, *Flannery: A Life of Flannery O'Connor* (New York: Little, Brown, 2009), 334.
2   Flannery O'Connor, *Collected Works* (New York: Library of America, 1988), 1094–95.
3   O'Connor, *Collected*, 1095.
4   Hilton Als, "Genius Breaking Through," *The New York Review of Books* August 14, 2014: 6–8.
5   O'Connor, *Collected*, 1095.
6   Ibid.
7   O'Connor also politely declined to meet John Howard Griffin, a white journalist whose book *Black Like Me* (1961) chronicled his travels through the South in blackface: "If I had been one of them white ladies Griffin sat down by on the bus, I would have got up PDQ preferring to sit by a genuine Negro." Gooch, *Flannery*, 333.
8   Flannery O'Connor, *The Habit of Being*, ed. Sally Fitzgerald (New York: Farrar, Straus and Giroux, 1979), 253, 541.
9   Ibid., 195.
10 O'Connor, *Collected*, 139.
11 Ibid., 409.
12 Ibid., 543.
13 Joyce Carol Oates, "The Parables of Flannery O'Connor," *The New York Review of Books* April 9, 2009. Accessed July 20, 2014.
14 This previously unpublished letter is quoted in Ralph C. Wood, *Flannery O'Connor and the Christ-haunted South* (Grand Rapids: Eerdmans, 2005), 103.
15 O'Connor, *Habit*, 537.
16 Ibid.

17 O'Connor, *Collected*, 1208.
18 O'Connor, *Habit*, 193.
19 James Baldwin, *Collected Essays* (New York: Library of America, 1998), 211–12.
20 Richard Wright, *12 Million Black Voices* (New York: Thunder's Mouth Press, 1988), 142. Of course, Wright was born on a farm in rural Mississippi. In his autobiography *Black Boy* (1945), Wright memorably recalls leaving the South for "the warmth of other sons." The phrase comes from a section Wright added to his autobiography, then titled *American Hunger*, when the Book-of-the-Month Club agreed to adopt the book, but only if he retitled it *Black Boy* and cut the second part. Wright agreed to the changes and added a section that read in part: "I was leaving the South to fling myself into the unknown. ... So, in leaving the South, I was taking a part of the South to transplant in alien soil, to see if it could grow differently, if it could drink of new and cool rains, bend in strange winds, respond to the warmth of other suns, and, perhaps, to bloom." Richard Wright, *Later Works* (New York: Library of America, 1991), 880.
21 Baldwin, *Collected*, 63–64.
22 Ibid., 197.
23 Ibid.
24 Ibid., 199. Isabel Wilkerson also notes similarities between African Americans who migrated to the North in the Great Migration and immigrants who came to the New World: "A central argument of this book has been that the Great Migration was an unrecognized immigration within this country. ... My parents bore the subtle hallmarks of the immigrant psyche, except they were Americans who had taken part in an internal migration whose reach and nuances are still little understood." Isabel Wilkerson, *The Warmth of Other Suns: The Epic Story of America's Great Migration* (New York: Random House, 2011), 540.
25 Toni Morrison, *Song of Solomon* (New York: Plume, 1977), 159. Morrison offers one reason why when she writes that the Southern soil was "soggy with black people's blood." Ibid. Baldwin similarly recounts that while flying "over the rust-red earth of Georgia" in an airplane, he "could not suppress the thought that this earth had acquired its color from the blood that had dripped down from these trees." Baldwin, *Collected*, 198.

26 Critics who read *Go Tell It* as a Great Migration novel include Charles Scruggs, *Sweet Home: Invisible Cities in the Afro-American Novel* (Baltimore: Johns Hopkins University Press, 1993); Farah Jasmine Griffin, *"Who Set You Flowin'?": The African-American Migration Narrative* (Oxford: Oxford University Press, 1995); and Lawrence Rodgers, *Canaan Bound: The African-American Great Migration Novel* (Urbana: University of Illinois Press, 1997).

27 Richard C. Sernett points out that many migrants "thought of themselves as recapitulating the exodus of the children of Israel out of Egypt," and prominent preachers like Reverend C.M. Tanner proclaimed that the hand of God was at work: "the scripture is being fulfilled every day in our very sight, and it is certainly the intention of divine providence to make our people in this movement profit by it." Richard C. Sernett, *Bound for the Promised Land: African American Religion and the Great Migration* (Durham: Duke University Press, 1997), 57, 70.

28 In the *Chicago Defender*, publisher Robert S. Abbott promoted spirituals like "Bound for the Promised Land" and "Going into Canaan" as anthems for the movement, which "pounded home a comparison to the events described in the Book of Exodus for his audience of extremely religious children of slaves." Nicholas Lemann, *The Promised Land: The Great Black Migration and How It Changed America* (New York: Vintage, 1991), 16.

29 Albert J. Raboteau, *Canaan Land: A Religious History of African Americans* (Oxford: Oxford University Press, 2001), 85–86.

30 Jill Watts, *God, Harlem USA: The Father Divine Story* (Berkeley: University of California Press, 1992).

31 Baldwin knows that syncretism is a significant feature of African American religion: "what the Blacks achieved and it cannot, now be undone, ... was to dig through the rubble, in Africa, in the Caribbean, and in North America, to find their ancestors, their gods, and themselves." James Baldwin, *The Evidence of Things Not Seen* (New York: Henry Holt, 1985), 83.

32 In a classic work of religious history, E. Franklin Frazier argued that the "'storefront' church represents an attempt on the part of migrants, especially from the rural areas of the South, to re-establish a type of church in the urban environment to which they are accustomed." E. Franklin Frazier, *The Negro Church in America* (New York: Schocken Books, 1974), 58, 76.

33 In one 1924 survey, six out of ten African Americans in Philadelphia said they went to church in the South but no longer attended. Sernett, *Bound*, 147.
34 Richard Wright, *Black Boy (American Hunger)/The Outsider* (New York: Library of America, 1991), 844–45.
35 Wright, *12 Million*, 142.
36 Ibid., 131, 135.
37 Baldwin, *Collected*, 710.
38 Ibid., 293.
39 Ibid., 6.
40 James Baldwin, *The Amen Corner* (New York: Samuel French, 1968), xiv.
41 Baldwin, *Collected*, 6.
42 Notable exceptions include Cheryl F. Sanders, *Saints in Exile: The Holiness-Pentecostal Experience in African American Religion* (Oxford: Oxford University Press, 1996); James W. Coleman, *Faithful Vision: Treatments of the Sacred, Spiritual, and Supernatural in Twentieth-century African American Fiction* (Baton Rouge: Louisiana State University Press, 2006); and Christopher Z. Hobson, *James Baldwin and the Heavenly City: Prophecy, Apocalypse, and Doubt* (East Lansing: Michigan State University Press, 2018).
43 The titles of his works alone testify to this: "Many Thousands Gone," "Down at the Cross," *The Devil Finds Work*, "Sermons and Blues," and *Evidence of Things Not Seen* (the latter is Paul's definition of faith). See Michael F. Lynch, "Staying Out of the Temple: Baldwin, the African American Church, and *The Amen Corner*," *Re-viewing James Baldwin: Things Not Seen*, ed. D. Quentin Miller (Philadelphia: Temple University Press, 2000), 33–34.
44 Baldwin, *Collected*, 306.
45 Ibid., 314.
46 Ivy G. Wilson, *Specters of Democracy: Blackness and the Aesthetics of Politics in the Antebellum US* (Oxford: Oxford University Press, 2011), 7.
47 Baldwin, *Collected*, 220.
48 Ibid., 221.
49 Ibid., 230.
50 As Lawrie Balfour writes: "Although much of Baldwin's best writing was published in the postwar period, before the passage of the historic civil

rights legislation of this century, he anticipates the limitations of such legislation. Understanding that Americans are capable of living with far more racial injustice than they are comfortable admitting, Baldwin identifies the underlying forces that have continued to deny African Americans the enjoyment of equal citizenship even after his death." Lawrie Balfour, *The Evidence of Things Not Said: James Baldwin and the Promise of American Democracy* (Ithaca: Cornell University Press, 2001), 6.
51 Baldwin, *Collected*, 151–52.
52 "The Third Force of Christendom," *Life* June 9, 1958: 113.
53 Ibid., 124.
54 Randall J. Stephens, *The Fire Spreads: Holiness and Pentecostalism in the American South* (Cambridge: Harvard University Press, 2008), 230–32; "Global Christianity: A Report on the Size and Distribution of the World's Christian Population," *Pew Research Forum* December 19, 2011. Accessed July 15, 2014.
55 "Weird Babel of Tongues," *Los Angeles Daily Times* April 18, 1906: 1.
56 Ibid., 1.
57 David Gonzalez, "A Sliver of a Storefront, a Faith on the Rise," *The New York Times* January 14, 2007. Accessed May 6, 2019. See also Gaston Espinosa, *William J. Seymour and the Origins of Global Pentecostalism: A Biography and Documentary History* (Durham: Duke University Press, 2014).
58 On the African roots of these religious practices, see Ann Taves, *Fits, Trances, and Visions: Experiencing Religion and Explaining Experience from Wesley to James* (Princeton: Princeton University Press, 1999), 79–80.
59 Stephens, *The Fire Spreads*, 10.
60 Grant Wacker, *Heaven Below: Early Pentecostals and American Culture* (Cambridge: Harvard University Press, 2001), 1.
61 Ibid., 1, 14.
62 Sernett, *Bound*, 4.
63 Robert A. Orsi, "Introduction: Crossing the City Line," *Gods of the City: Religion and the American Urban Landscape*, ed. Robert A. Orsi (Bloomington: Indiana University Press, 1999), 46.
64 Baldwin, *Collected*, 48.
65 Ibid.

66 Ibid., 74.
67 Ibid., 48. David Levering Lewis observes that storefront churches "served as a psychological safety net," because they allowed migrants to preserve some of "the old, reassuring ways." David Levering Lewis, *When Harlem Was in Vogue* (New York: Penguin, 1997), 221.
68 Ralph Ellison, *Invisible Man* (New York: Vintage, 1995), 495.
69 Ibid., 496.
70 Ibid., 497.
71 Ibid., 498.
72 In *Black Manhattan* (1930), the writer James Weldon Johnson observed that because storefront churches were not "regularly organized or systematically administered," they were susceptible to "bootleggers of religion," "parasitical fakers," or "even downright scoundrels" who might start a church, take up a collection, and then disappear. James Weldon Johnson, *Black Manhattan* (New York: DeCapo Press, 1991), 163–65.
73 Ellison, *Invisible*, 499.
74 Ibid., 496–97.
75 James Baldwin, *Go Tell It on the Mountain* (New York: Dell, 2000), 6, 149.
76 Early in the Pentecostal movement, Charles Parham began to insist that speaking in tongues "must be part of any experience of the baptism of the Holy Spirit for it to be deemed genuine." Douglas Jacobsen, *Thinking in the Spirit: Theologies of the Early Pentecostal Movement* (Bloomington: Indiana University Press, 2003), 19.
77 M.M. Bakhtin, *Problems of Dostoevsky's Poetics*, ed. and trans. Caryl Emerson (Minneapolis: University of Minnesota Press, 1984).
78 Baldwin, *Go Tell It*, 56.
79 Ibid., 69. As Sanders writes, "Both the sanctified and the black Protestant Churches in the rural South have historically practiced water baptism outdoors in creeks and rivers … as a necessary act of ritual obedience that identifies the believer with the church." Sanders, *Saints in Exile*, 59.
80 Baldwin, *Go Tell It*, 69.
81 Ibid., 93.
82 Ibid., 97.
83 Ibid., 102.
84 Ibid.
85 Ibid., 104.

86 Ian MacRobert, "The Black Roots of Pentecostalism," *African American Religion: Interpretive Essays in History and Culture*, eds. Timothy E. Fulop and Albert J. Raboteau (New York: Routledge, 1997), 301.
87 Baldwin, *Go Tell It*, 103.
88 Ibid., 46.
89 Ibid., 45–46.
90 Baldwin, *Collected*, 481.
91 Ihab Hassan, *Radical Innocence: Studies in the Contemporary American Novel* (Princeton: Princeton University Press, 1961), 81.
92 Baldwin, *Go Tell It*, 116.
93 Ibid., 122.
94 Ibid., 140–41.
95 Ibid., 141.
96 Philip Dray, *At the Hands of Persons Unknown: The Lynching of Black America* (New York: Random House, 2002), 223.
97 Baldwin, *Collected*, 792.
98 Baldwin, *Go Tell It*, 70.
99 Ibid.
100 Griffin, *"Who Set You Flowin'?"* 34.
101 Baldwin, *Go Tell It*, 68.
102 Ibid., 73.
103 Ibid., 59.
104 Ibid., 59, 61.
105 Ibid., 60.
106 Ibid., 162.
107 Ibid., 163.
108 Ibid., 158.
109 Ibid., 162.
110 Horace A. Porter, *Stealing the Fire: The Art and Protest of James Baldwin* (Middletown: Wesleyan University Press, 1989), 104.
111 Baldwin, *Go Tell It*, 164.
112 Ibid.
113 Ibid., 158.
114 Sanders, *Saints in Exile*, 123.
115 Baldwin, *Collected*, 138.
116 Ibid., 690.

117 One testament to the richness of this language is Toni Morrison's tribute in her eulogy at Baldwin's funeral in New York City, "You gave me a language to dwell in." Toni Morrison, "James Baldwin: His Voice Remembered; Life in His Language," *The New York Times Book Review* December 20, 1987: 27. Accessed May 16, 2006.
118 Baldwin, *Collected*, 755.
119 Ibid., 57.
120 Frazier, *The Negro Church*, 59.
121 Lemann, *The Promised Land*, 77–78.
122 David W. Dunlap, *From Abyssinian to Zion* (New York: Columbia University Press, 2004), 6.
123 Eric Metaxas, *Bonhoeffer: Pastor, Martyr, Prophet, Spy* (New York: Thomas Nelson, 2010), 108.
124 "Dietrich Bonhoeffer: German Martyr Transformed by Experience with Harlem's Abyssinian Baptist Church," DDayMedia January 16, 2012. Accessed July 23, 2014.
125 Baldwin, *Collected*, 499. The younger Powell later became the first African American from New York to be elected to the United States House of Representatives in 1947, where he served as a senator until 1971.
126 Baldwin clearly held Rosa Artimas Horn in high esteem, yet she is also the basis for his much less sympathetic character Margaret in *The Amen Corner*. See Clarence E. Hardy, III, *James Baldwin's God: Sex, Hope, and Crisis in Black Holiness Culture* (Knoxville: The University of Tennessee Press, 2003), 4–5; and Joanna Brooks, "From Edwards to Baldwin: Heterodoxy, Discontinuity, and New Narratives of American Religious-literary History," *Early American Literature* Vol. 45, No. 2 (2010): 431–33.
127 Baldwin, *Collected*, 303.
128 Ibid., 303, 305.
129 David Leeming, *James Baldwin: A Biography* (New York: Henry Holt, 1994), 25.
130 Baldwin, *Go Tell It*, 45.
131 Baldwin, *Collected*, 224.
132 Baldwin, *Go Tell It*, 4.
133 According to Ann Douglas, Harlem in the 1920s was "the most exciting entertainment scene America had ever boasted." Ann Douglas, *Terrible*

Honesty: Mongrel Manhattan in the 1920s (New York: Farrar, Straus and Giroux, 1995), 74.
134 Arnold Rampersad, *Ralph Ellison: A Biography* (New York: Knopf, 2007), 87.
135 Lewis, *When Harlem Was in Vogue*, 211.
136 Sanders, *Saints in Exile*, 123.
137 Ibid., 6, 123.
138 Baldwin, *Go Tell It*, 27–28.
139 Ibid., 32.
140 Ibid., 34.
141 Ibid.
142 Baldwin, *Collected*, 296.
143 Orsi, "Introduction," 44, 53.
144 Hassan, *Radical Innocence*, 81.
145 Baldwin, *Collected*, 299.
146 Ibid.
147 Lynch, "Staying Out of the Temple," 54.
148 Baldwin, *Go Tell It*, 9.
149 Ibid., 56.
150 Ibid., 11.
151 Ibid., 199.
152 Sanders, *Saints in Exile*, 4, 20.
153 Vinson Synan, *The Holiness-Pentecostal Tradition: Charismatic Movements in the Twentieth Century* (Grand Rapids: Eerdmans, 1997), 55.
154 Stephens, *The Fire Spreads*, 182.
155 Baldwin, *Go Tell It*, 9.
156 Jordan Elgrably, "James Baldwin: The Art of Fiction 78," *The Paris Review* Vol. 91 (Spring 1984). Accessed July 23, 2014.
157 Baldwin, *Go Tell It*, 6–7.
158 Ibid., 7.
159 Ibid., 8.
160 Ibid.
161 Ibid., 7.
162 Ibid., 7–8.
163 Lynch, "Staying Out of the Temple," 33.
164 Baldwin, *Collected*, 792.

165 As David L. Chappell persuasively argues, the "civil right movement succeeded for many reasons," but "one reason that has received insufficient attention" is that "black southern activists got strength from old-time religion, and white supremacists failed, at the same moment, to muster the cultural strength that conservatives traditionally get from religion." David L. Chappell, *A Stone of Hope: Prophetic Religion and the Death of Jim Crow* (Chapel Hill: University of North Carolina Press, 2004), 8.
166 Baldwin, *Collected*, 12.
167 Ibid., 12–13.
168 Ibid., 18.
169 Sanders, *Saints in Exile*, 112.
170 Leeming, *James Baldwin*, 89.
171 Baldwin, *Collected*, 304.
172 Ibid.
173 Taves, *Fits, Trances, and Visions*, 334.
174 Baldwin, *Collected*, 304–05.
175 Ibid., 301.
176 Ibid., 308.
177 Ibid., 309.
178 Ibid., 309–10.
179 Ibid., 80.
180 Ibid., 307.
181 Ibid.
182 Ibid., 308.
183 Ibid.
184 Ibid.
185 Leeming, *James Baldwin*, 133.
186 Barbara K. Olson, "'Come-to-Jesus Stuff' in James Baldwin's *Go Tell It on the Mountain* and *The Amen Corner*," *African American Review* Vol. 31, No. 2 (Summer 1997): 299, 301.
187 Griffin, *Who Set You Flowin'?* 90–91.
188 Lynch, "Staying Out of the Temple," 57–58. Lynch argues further that in his play *The Amen Corner* "Baldwin saw his opportunity to demonstrate why within a few years fourteen-year-old John, now in the person of eighteen-year-old David, would have to revolt." Lynch, "Staying Out of the Temple," 47.

189 Fred Standley and Louis H. Pratt, eds., *Conversations with James Baldwin* (Jackson: University Press of Mississippi, 1989), 240.
190 Ibid., 238.
191 Ibid.
192 Baldwin, *Go Tell It*, 56.
193 Ibid., 74–75.
194 Ibid., 75.
195 Ibid.
196 Ibid., 76.
197 Ibid.
198 Ibid., 143.
199 Ibid., 192.
200 Ibid. Notably, Gabriel perceives what is happening to John in very different terms. At the end of Gabriel's prayer, while Elisha is speaking in tongues, John and his father exchange a glance that is especially charged: "Gabriel had never seen such a look on John's face before; Satan, at that moment, stared out of John's eyes while the Spirit spoke. … And John did not drop his eyes, but seemed to want to stare forever into the bottom of Gabriel's soul." Ibid., 149–50.
201 Baldwin, *Collected*, 565.
202 Baldwin, *Go Tell It*, 195–96.
203 Ibid., 203.
204 Ibid.
205 Ibid.
206 Ibid., 212.
207 Ibid., 205.
208 Ibid., 207.
209 Ibid.
210 Ibid., 209.
211 Ibid., 210.
212 Baldwin is open-minded about the experience of spirit possession, as a comment he once made about seeing the film *The Exorcist* suggests: "I tried to be absolutely open to it, suspending judgment as totally as I could. For, after all, if I had once claimed to be 'filled' with the Holy Ghost, and had once really believed … that the Holy Ghost spoke through me, I could not, out of hand, arbitrarily sneer at the notion

of demonic possession. The fact that I had been an adolescent boy when I believed all this did not really get me off the hook." Baldwin, *Collected*, 567.
213 Baldwin, *Go Tell It*, 225.
214 Ibid., 225.
215 Ibid., 221.
216 Ibid., 207.
217 Baldwin, *Collected*, 840.
218 Baldwin, *Go Tell It*, 214.
219 James Baldwin, *Giovanni's Room* (New York: Dial, 1956), 224.
220 Hassan, *Radical Innocence*, 182.
221 Darryl Pinckney, "James Baldwin: The Risks of Love," *The New York Review of Books* April 13, 2000: 81–82.
222 Baldwin, *Go Tell It*, 226.
223 Craig Hansen Werner, *Playing the Changes: From Afro-Modernism to the Jazz Impulse* (Urbana: University of Illinois Press, 1994), 212.
224 Baldwin, *Collected*, 565.
225 Dwight McBride, ed., *James Baldwin Now* (New York: New York University Press, 1999); Douglas Field, ed., *A Historical Guide to James Baldwin* (Oxford: Oxford University Press, 2009); Michele Elam, ed., *The Cambridge Companion to James Baldwin* (Cambridge: Cambridge University Press, 2015).
226 Pinckney, "James Baldwin," 81–82.
227 Taves, *Fits, Trances, and Visions*, 353.
228 Hortense Spillers, "Afterword," *James Baldwin: America and Beyond*, eds. Cora Kaplan and Bill Schwarz (Ann Arbor: University of Michigan Press, 2011), 242.
229 Baldwin, *Collected*, 48.
230 Standley and Pratt, eds., *Conversations*, 48.
231 Ibid., 48.
232 Baldwin, *Collected*, 567.
233 Ibid., 571.
234 Ibid., 714.
235 Leeming, *James Baldwin*, xiii.
236 A week before his death, he confided to his biographer that religion still furnished the "inner vocabulary" of his mind: "During the night, he

wanted to talk about religion. He realized that the church's role in his life had been significant, especially with respect to what he called his 'inner vocabulary'. As for the larger questions, he did not 'believe' in God, but he felt—especially when he was alone, that there was 'something out there.'" Leeming, *James Baldwin*, 384.

237 Baldwin, *Collected*, 572.
238 Emmanuel Levinas, *Alterity and Transcendence*, trans. Michael B. Smith (New York: Columbia University Press, 1999).
239 Robert D. Putnam and David E. Campbell, *American Grace: How Religion Divides and Unites Us* (New York: Simon and Schuster, 2010); Paul Maltby, *Christian Fundamentalism and the Culture of Disenchantment* (Charlottesville: University of Virginia Press, 2013).
240 Baldwin, *Collected*, 784.
241 Ibid., 785.
242 Ibid., 784.
243 Leeming, *James Baldwin*, 353.
244 Ibid.
245 Ibid.
246 Ibid.
247 Chinua Achebe, "The Day I Finally Met James Baldwin," PEN America January 8, 2007. Accessed July 28, 2014.
248 Baldwin, *Collected*, 796.
249 Ibid., 778.
250 Ibid., 839.
251 Ibid., 571.
252 Baldwin recalls the first time he heard Martin Luther King speak in Montgomery, Alabama: "When King rose to speak—to preach—I began to understand how the atmosphere of this church differed from that of all the other churches I had known. At first, I thought that the great emotional power and authority of the Negro church was being put to a new use, but this is not exactly the case. The Negro church was playing the same role which it had always played in Negro life, but it had acquired a new power." Ibid., 643.
253 Ibid., 838.
254 McBride, ed., *James Baldwin Now*, 273.

Chapter 3

1. James Baldwin, *Collected Essays* (New York: Library of America, 1998), 308.
2. Ibid.
3. Ibid., 307.
4. Ibid., 308.
5. Ibid.
6. Ibid., 317.
7. Ibid.
8. "What we had set out to do," the authors write in a preface, "was nothing less than to explain why humanity, instead of entering a truly human state, is sinking into a new kind of barbarism." Theodor Adorno and Max Horkheimer, *The Dialectic of Enlightenment*, ed. Gunzelin Schmid Noerr, trans. Edmund Jephcott (Stanford: Stanford University Press, 2002), xiv.
9. Baldwin, *Collected*, 317. Eric J. Sundquist argues that African Americans "responded more knowingly to the Holocaust than did other Americans prior to the upsurge in public discussion in the 1960s," for they "instinctively" understood Hitler's use of pseudo-science and racial ideology to implement segregation in Nazi Germany as a "conceptual framework for reinterpreting both the ordeal of slavery and its legacy in racial discrimination and violence." Eric J. Sundquist, *Strangers in the Land: Blacks, Jews, Post-Holocaust America* (Cambridge: Harvard University Press, 2009), 5–6.
10. Arthur Koestler, *The Yogi and the Commissar, and Other Essays* (New York: Macmillan, 1945), 89.
11. Fred L. Standley and Louis H. Pratt, eds., *Conversations with James Baldwin* (Jackson: University Press of Mississippi, 1989), 266.
12. Alfred Kazin, *New York Jew* (New York: Knopf, 1978), 30.
13. Ibid., 34.
14. Ibid., 27.
15. Ibid., 142.
16. Ibid., 26.
17. Ibid., 194.
18. Ibid., 34.

19 Richard H. Crossman, ed., *The God That Failed* (New York: Columbia University Press, 2001), 55. See also Andrew Delbanco, "'The Only Permanent State': Belief and the Culture of Incredulity," *Invisible Conversations: Religion in the Literature of America*, ed. Roger Lundin (Waco: Baylor University Press, 2009), 150.

20 Robert Alter, "Confronting the Holocaust," *After the Tradition: Essays on Modern Jewish Writing* (New York: Dutton, 1969), 163–80; Alan L. Berger, *Crisis and Covenant: The Holocaust in American Fiction* (Albany: State University of New York Press, 1985); Emily Miller Budick, "The Holocaust in the Jewish American Literary Imagination," *The Cambridge Companion to Jewish American Literature*, eds. Hana Wirth-Nesher and Michael P. Kramer (Cambridge: Cambridge University Press, 2003), 212–30; Amy Hungerford, *The Holocaust of Texts: Genocide, Literature, and Personification* (Chicago: University of Chicago Press, 2003); Efraim Sicher, *The Holocaust Novel* (New York: Routledge, 2005); and Eric J. Sundquist, "The Historian's Anvil, the Novelist's Crucible," *The Literature of the Holocaust*, ed. Alan Rosen (Cambridge: Cambridge University Press, 2013), 252–67.

21 Quoted in Edward Mendelson, "New York Everyman," *The New York Review of Books* June 12, 2009. Accessed June 6, 2011.

22 Talal Asad, *Formations of the Secular: Christianity, Islam, Modernity* (Stanford: Stanford University Press, 2003); Jose Casanova, "The Secular, Secularization, Secularisms," *Rethinking Secularism*, eds. Craig Calhoun, Mark Juergensmeyer, and Jonathan VanAntwerpen (Oxford: Oxford University Press, 2013), 54–74.

23 Michael Warner, "Secularism," *Keywords for American Cultural Studies*, eds. Bruce Burgett and Glenn Hendler (New York: New York University Press, 2007), 209.

24 Janet R. Jakobsen and Ann Pellegrini, eds., *Secularisms* (Durham: Duke University Press, 2008).

25 Craig Calhoun, Mark Juergensmeyer, and Jonathan VanAntwerpen, eds., *Rethinking Secularism* (Oxford: Oxford University Press, 2011), 5.

26 Jonathon Freedman argues that while literary critics have returned again and again to "the much-vexed questions of Jewish identity," "assimilation," and "the nature of historical memory," the "conflict between religion and secularism" in Jewish literature has gotten very little attention. Jonathan

Freedman, *The Temple of Culture: Assimilation and Anti-Semitism in Literary Anglo-America* (Oxford: Oxford University Press, 2000), 5.
27 "A Portrait of Jewish Americans," Pew Research Center October 1, 2013. Accessed September 25, 2014.
28 Dietrich Bonhoeffer, *Prisoner for God* (New York: Macmillan, 1959), 123.
29 Thomas A. Indinopulos, "The Holocaust and the Death of God," *The Death of God Movement and the Holocaust: Radical Theology Encounters the Shoah*, eds. Stephen R. Haynes and John K. Roth (Westport: Greenwood Press, 1999), 64.
30 Kathryn Lofton, "Cosmology," *Religion in American History*, eds. Amanda Porterfield and John Corrigan (Malden: Wiley-Blackwell, 2010), 277.
31 John K. Roth, "If God Was Silent, Absent, Dead, or Nonexistent, What about Philosophy and Theology: Some Aftereffects and Aftershocks of the Holocaust," *After the Holocaust: Challenging the Myth of Silence*, eds. David Cesarini and Eric J. Sundquist (New York: Routledge, 2012), 143.
32 Richard L. Rubenstein, *After Auschwitz: Radical Theology and Contemporary Judaism* (Indianapolis: Bobbs Merrill, 1966), 153.
33 Jacob Neusner, *Stranger at Home: "The Holocaust," Zionism, and American Judaism* (Chicago: University of Chicago Press, 1981), 71.
34 Michael L. Morgan, *Beyond Auschwitz: Post-Holocaust Jewish Thought in America* (Oxford: Oxford University Press, 2001), 69.
35 Ibid., 70.
36 Quoted in Berger, *Crisis and Covenant*, 3.
37 Timothy A. Bennett and Rochelle L. Millen, "Christians and Pharisees: Jewish Responses to Radical Theology," *The Death of God Movement and the Holocaust: Radical Theology Encounters the Shoah*, eds. Stephen R. Haynes and John K. Roth (Westport: Greenwood Press, 1999), 118.
38 Rubenstein, *After Auschwitz*, 294.
39 David G. Roskies, *Against the Apocalypse: Responses to Catastrophe in Modern Jewish Culture* (New York: Syracuse University Press, 1984, 1999), 8–9.
40 Michael Goldberg, *Why Should the Jews Survive? Looking Past the Holocaust toward a Jewish Future* (Oxford: Oxford University Press, 1995), 4–5.
41 Philip Roth, *Reading Myself and Others* (New York: Vintage, 2001), 195.
42 Chaim Potok, *The Chosen* (New York: Balantine Books, 1995), 190.

43 Ibid., 192.
44 Ibid.
45 Ibid., 228.
46 Ibid., 191.
47 Andrew Hoberek, *The Twilight of the Middle Class: Post-World War II American Fiction and White-collar Work* (Princeton: Princeton University Press, 2005), 70–71.
48 David Hollinger, *Post-ethnic America: Beyond Multiculturalism* (New York: Basic Books, 1995).
49 Hana Wirth-Nesher and Michael P. Kramer, eds., *The Cambridge Companion to Jewish American Literature* (Cambridge: Cambridge University Press, 2003), 7.
50 Murray Baumgarten, "American Midrash: Urban Jewish Writing and the Reclaiming of Judaism," *The Cambridge Companion to American Judaism*, ed. Dana Evan Kaplan (Cambridge: Cambridge University Press, 2005), 360.
51 Morris Dickstein, *Gates of Eden: American Culture in the Sixties* (Cambridge: Harvard University Press, 1997), 36.
52 Leslie Fiedler, *A New Fiedler Reader* (Amherst: Prometheus Books, 1999), 386, 389, 401.
53 Cynthia Ozick, *Art and Ardor* (New York: Knopf, 1983), 169.
54 Alfred Kazin, *Alfred Kazin's Journals*, ed. Richard M. Cook (New Haven: Yale University Press, 2011), 375.
55 Saul Bellow, "A Jewish Writer in America, Part II," *The New York Review of Books* November 10, 2011. Accessed March 28, 2013.
56 Ibid.
57 Ibid.
58 Roth, *Reading*, 106.
59 Ibid.
60 Kazin, *Alfred Kazin's Journals*, 560.
61 Roth, *Reading*, 279.
62 Ibid.
63 Gloria L. Cronin and Ben Siegel, eds., *Conversations with Saul Bellow* (Oxford: University Press of Mississippi, 1994), 222.
64 Saul Bellow, *It All Adds Up* (New York: Viking, 1994), 173.
65 Cronin and Siegel, eds., *Conversations*, 90.
66 Ibid., 103.

67 Quoted in Michael P. Kramer, ed., *New Essays on Seize the Day* (Cambridge: Cambridge University Press, 1998), 9.
68 Saul Bellow, "A Jewish Writer in America, Part I," *The New York Review of Books* October 27, 2011. Accessed March 28, 2013.
69 Ibid.
70 Ibid.
71 Ibid.
72 Bellow, "A Jewish Writer in America, Part II."
73 Tony Tanner, *Saul Bellow* (New York: Barnes and Noble, 1965), 2.
74 Saul Bellow, "A Jewish Writer in America, Part II."
75 Ibid.
76 Ibid.
77 Saul Bellow, *Novels 1944–1953* (New York: Library of America, 2003), 260.
78 Ibid.
79 Ibid., 260–61.
80 Ibid., 393.
81 Ibid., 392–93.
82 Saul Bellow, *Novels 1956–1964* (New York: Library of America, 2007), 626. As Patrick O'Donnell points out, "*Herzog* may not necessarily be the source of the term 'midlife crisis,' but it certainly is one of the most penetrating portrayals of the fabled condition that seems to afflict American males between the ages of 45 and 55." Patrick O'Donnell, *The American Novel Now* (Oxford: Wiley-Blackwell, 2010), 26.
83 Bellow, *Novels 1956–1964*, 659.
84 Louis Menand, "Introduction," *Civilization and Its Discontents*, ed. Sigmund Freud (New York: Norton, 2005), 22. On the therapeutic ethos of spirituality in the 1960s and 1970s, see Robert N. Bellah, et al., *Habits of the Heart: Individualism and Commitment in American Life* (Berkeley: University of California Press, 2007).
85 Bellow, *Novels 1956–1964*, 508. Moses Herzog takes his first name from the great Jewish patriarch who led his people out of Egypt, and his middle name derives from another patriarch, the father of Samuel in the Hebrew Bible whose name means "God has purchased" or "Praise God" in Hebrew. Daniel Fuchs, "Identity and the Postwar Temper in American Jewish Fiction," *A Concise Companion to Postwar American Literature and Culture*, ed. Josephine G. Hendin (Oxford: Blackwell, 2004), 241.
86 Saul Bellow, *Herzog* (New York: Viking, 1961), 436.

87 Bellow, *Novels 1956–1964*, 650.
88 Ibid., 748.
89 Ibid., 442.
90 Ibid., 737–38; Timothy Snyder, *Bloodlands: Europe between Hitler and Stalin* (New York: Basic Books, 2010), xviii.
91 Bellow, *Novels 1956–1964*, 710.
92 Ibid.
93 Ibid., 711.
94 Hungerford, *The Holocaust of Texts*, 128.
95 Saul Bellow, *Mr. Sammler's Planet* (New York: Viking, 1970), 137.
96 Ibid., 197.
97 Primo Levi, *The Drowned and the Saved* (New York: Vintage, 1989), 82.
98 Bellow, *Mr. Sammler's Planet*, 92.
99 Ibid., 137.
100 Ibid.
101 Ibid., 273.
102 Theodor W. Adorno, *Negative Dialectics*, trans. E.B. Ashton (New York: Continuum, 2005), 362–63; Theodor W. Adorno, *Prisms*, trans. Samuel and Shierry Weber (Cambridge: MIT Press, 1981), 34.
103 Adorno, *Prisms*, 34.
104 Bellow, *Mr. Sammler's Planet*, 236.
105 Ibid., 236–37.
106 Ibid., 237.
107 Ibid., 313.
108 Alan L. Berger, *Crisis and Covenant: The Holocaust in American Jewish Fiction* (Albany: State University of New York Press, 1985), 101, 106.
109 Hungerford, *The Holocaust of Texts*, 132.
110 Saul Bellow, *Letters*, ed. Benjamin Taylor (New York: Viking, 2010), 438–39. Leslie Fiedler admitted that he was compelled "begrudgingly and at long last … to recognize the full scope and horror of the Holocaust, of which I had for so long remained at least half-deliberately unaware." Fiedler, *A New Fiedler Reader*, 392.
111 Morris Dickstein, *Leopards in the Temple: The Transformation of American Fiction, 1945–1970* (Cambridge: Harvard University Press, 2002), 63.
112 Bellow, "A Jewish Writer in America, Part II."

113 David L. Ulin, "Imagined Hells of Philip Roth," *Los Angeles Times* October 3, 2010: E1, E11.
114 *Philip Roth: Unmasked*, directed by William Karel and Livia Manera (PBS, 2013).
115 Amy Hungerford, *Postmodern Belief: American Literature and Religion after 1960* (Princeton: Princeton University Press, 2010), 138.
116 Roth, *Reading*, 67.
117 Ibid., no page number.
118 George J. Searles, *Conversations with Philip Roth* (Oxford: University Press of Mississippi, 1992), 12.
119 Ibid., 13.
120 Ibid., 66.
121 Ibid., 74.
122 Ibid., 12.
123 Philip Roth, *Goodbye, Columbus* (New York: Vintage, 1987), 114.
124 Ibid.
125 Ibid., 122.
126 Ibid., 123.
127 Searles, *Conversations*, 5, 55, 85.
128 Roth, *Goodbye*, 100.
129 Ibid., 88.
130 Ibid.
131 Searles, *Conversations*, 2.
132 Ibid., 88.
133 Ibid., 89.
134 Ibid., 100.
135 Roth, *Goodbye*, 100.
136 Ibid., 98.
137 Philip Roth, *Portnoy's Complaint* (New York: Random House, 1969), 61.
138 Ibid., 72.
139 Philip Roth, *Everyman* (London: Jonathan Cape, 2006), 51.
140 Ibid.
141 Roth, *Portnoy's Complaint*, 76.
142 Philip Roth, *Novels 1993–1995* (New York: Library of America, 2010), 118.
143 Ibid., 286–87.
144 Charles McGrath, "Interview: Zukerman's Alter Brain," *The New York Times Book Review* May 7, 2000. Accessed October 22, 2014.

145 Philip Roth, *American Pastoral* (New York: Knopf, 1997), 40.
146 Ibid., 41.
147 Ibid., 85.
148 Ibid.
149 Ibid., 311.
150 Ibid., 386.
151 Ibid., 69.
152 Ibid., 85–86.
153 Philip Jenkins, *Mystics and Messiahs: Cults and New Religions in American History* (Oxford: Oxford University Press, 2000), 197.
154 Philip Roth, *The Plot Against America* (London: Jonathan Cape, 2004), 3.
155 Ibid., 4, 220.
156 Ibid., 220.
157 Ibid., 4.
158 Ibid., 4, 5.
159 Hungerford, *The Holocaust of Texts*, 3.
160 Philip Roth, *The Ghost Writer* (New York: Vintage, 1995), 125.
161 Ibid., 150.
162 Roth, *Novels 1993–1995*, 231.
163 Michael Rothberg, "Roth and the Holocaust," *The Cambridge Companion to Philip Roth*, ed. Timothy Parrish (Cambridge: Cambridge University Press, 2007), 53.
164 Roth, *Novels 1993–1995*, 218.
165 Ibid., 9, 49.
166 Ibid., 186.
167 Ibid., 187.
168 Ibid.
169 Ibid., 188, 191.
170 Philip Roth, "Pictures of Malamud," *The New York Times Book Review* April 20, 1986. Accessed October 20, 2014.
171 Roth, *Novels 1993–1995*, 117.
172 Ibid., 116.
173 Ibid., 25.
174 Ibid., 287. In a review of the novel for *The New Yorker*, John Updike complained: "Yet, once they have been so vividly introduced, the characters turn out to be talking heads, faces attached to tirades.

The novel is an orgy of argumentation." John Updike, "Recruiting Raw Nerves," *The New Yorker* March 15, 1993: 110.
175 Searles, *Conversations*, 121–22. Recall that the subtitle is *Operation Shylock: A Confession*.
176 Claudia Roth Pierpont, *Roth Unbound: A Writer and His Books* (New York: Farrar, Straus and Giroux, 2013), 316.
177 Philip Roth, *Nemesis* (New York: Harcourt Brace, 2010), 76.
178 Ibid., 74.
179 Ibid., 75.
180 Ibid., 74–75.
181 Ibid., 127.
182 Ibid., 170.
183 Ibid., 154.
184 Ibid., 264.
185 Ibid., 264–65.
186 Ibid., 265.
187 Ibid., 275.
188 Ibid., 261.
189 In a perceptive review of *Nemesis* in *The New York Review of Books*, novelist J.M. Coetzee writes that in trying "to grasp God's mysterious designs," Bucky "takes humanity, and the reach of human understanding, seriously," and he "keeps an ideal of human dignity alive in the face of fate, Nemesis, the gods, God." J.M. Coetzee, "On the Moral Brink," *The New York Review of Books* October 28, 2010. Accessed October 28, 2014.
190 Susan Jacoby, "The Blessings of Atheism," *The New York Times* January 5, 2013: 6.
191 Ibid.
192 Ibid.
193 Ibid.
194 Ibid.
195 Ibid.
196 Ibid.
197 Philip Roth, *The Human Stain* (Boston: Houghton Mifflin, 2000), 242–43.
198 Pierpont, *Roth Unbound*, 218.
199 David Brauner, *Post-war Jewish Fiction: Ambivalence, Self-explanation and Transatlantic Connections* (New York: Palgrave, 2001), 6.

200 Michelle M. Tokarczyk, *E.L. Doctorow's Skeptical Commitment* (New York: Peter Lang, 2000), 2.
201 E.L. Doctorow, *Reporting the Universe* (Cambridge: Harvard University Press, 2003), 21, 119, 67.
202 Ibid., 113.
203 Christopher D. Morris, ed., *Conversations with E.L. Doctorow* (Jackson: University Press of Mississippi, 1999), 157.
204 Ibid., 270.
205 E.L. Doctorow, *City of God* (New York: Random House, 2000), 42, 25.
206 Ibid., 4.
207 "The major shift in American spirituality over the past half century has been toward a God who is not only vividly present but deeply kind. He is no longer the benign but distant sovereign of the old mainstream church; nor is he the harsh tyrant of the Hebrew Bible. He is personal and intimate." T.M. Luhrmann, *When God Talks Back: Understanding the American Evangelical Relationship with God* (New York: Random House, 2012), xvi.
208 Doctorow, *City*, 25.
209 Quoted in Corey S. Powell, *God in the Equation: How Einstein Became the Prophet of the New Religious Era* (New York: The Free Press, 2002), 13.
210 Ibid., 252. See also the essay on Albert Einstein in E.L. Doctorow, *Creationists: Selected Essays 1993–2006* (New York: Random House, 2006).
211 Doctorow, *City*, 15.
212 Ibid., 48.
213 Ibid., 49.
214 Morris, ed., *Conversations*, 112.
215 Ibid., 94.
216 Ibid., 101–02.
217 Ibid., 121.
218 Ibid., 122.
219 Daniel Mendelsohn writes about the burden of Holocaust memory for the descendants of survivors and victims in his brilliant memoir *The Lost: A Search for Six of Six Million* (New York: HarperCollins, 2006).
220 Doctorow, *City*, 80.
221 Ibid., 30.

222 Ibid., 266.
223 Ibid., 255.
224 Doctorow, *Reporting*, 115.
225 Ibid., 92–93.
226 Ibid., 259.
227 E.L. Doctorow, *Sweet Land Stories* (New York: Random House, 2004), 90.
228 Ibid., 101.
229 Ibid., 90.
230 Ibid.
231 Ibid., 111.
232 Ibid., 111–12.
233 Ibid., 113.
234 Ibid., 116.
235 Ibid.
236 "During the Age of Evangelicalism," writes Stephen P. Miller, "born-again Christianity provided alternately a language, a medium, and a foil by which millions of Americans came to terms with … a society that, by almost any measure, had grown more religiously pluralistic and, in certain circles, more self-consciously secular." Stephen P. Miller, *The Age of Evangelicalism: America's Born-again Years* (Oxford: Oxford University Press, 2014), 5–6.
237 Doctorow, *Sweet*, 97, 100, 105.
238 Hal Lindsey, *The Late Great Planet Earth* (Grand Rapids: Zondervan, 1970), 43.
239 Ibid.
240 Compare Philip Roth's assessment of Israel's victory in the Six-day War, albeit delivered in the voice of the half-mad character George Ziad, that it was a confirmation of "Jewish *might*," justifying "Israeli military expansionism as historically just by joining it to the memory of Jewish victimization; to rationalize—as historical justice, as just retribution, as nothing more than self-defense—the gobbling up of the Occupied Territories and the driving of the Palestinians off their land once again." Roth, *Novels 1993–1995*, 119.
241 Lindsey, *The Late Great Planet Earth*, 42–43.
242 "The evangelical right was not only part of Reagan's coalition; it was also one of its pillars." Miller, *The Age of Evangelicalism*, 66–67.

243 Morris, ed., *Conversations*, 71.
244 See, for example, E.L. Doctorow, *Citizen Doctorow, Notes on Art and Politics: The Nation Essays 1978-2012*, ed. Richard Lingeman (Washington, DC: The Nation, 2014).
245 Morris, ed., *Conversations*, 81–82.
246 David A. Hollinger, *Science, Jews, and Secular Culture: Studies in Mid-twentieth-century American Intellectual History* (Princeton: Princeton University Press, 1996).
247 According to Andrea Most, many American Jews discovered that the "tacitly Protestant cultural and social sphere ... made it almost impossible to become fully accepted Americans without giving up public signs of religious difference." Andrea Most, "The Birth of Theatrical Liberalism," *After Pluralism: Reimagining Religious Engagement*, eds. Courtney Bender and Pamela E. Klassen (New York: Columbia University Press, 2010), 145.
248 George Marsden, *The Twilight of the American Enlightenment: The 1950s and the Crisis of Liberal Belief* (New York: Basic Books, 2014); Darren Dochuk, *From Bible Belt to Sunbelt: Plainfolk Religion, Grassroots Politics, and the Rise of Evangelical Conservatism* (New York: Norton, 2011); Kevin Kruse, *One Nation under God: How Corporate America Invented Christian America* (New York: Basic Books, 2015).
249 Dana Evan Kaplan, "Trends in American Judaism from 1945 to the Present," *The Cambridge Companion to American Judaism*, ed. Dana Evan Kaplan (Cambridge: Cambridge University Press, 2005), 75.
250 Bruce Phillips, "American Judaism in the Twenty-first Century," *The Cambridge Companion to American Judaism*, ed. Dana Evan Kaplan (Cambridge: Cambridge University Press, 2005), 399.
251 Philip Roth, *The Counterlife* (New York: Vintage, 1996), 283, 310.
252 Of course, it is important to remember that this is Nathan Zuckerman view, not the author's. "Being Zuckerman is one long performance and the very opposite of what is thought of as *being oneself*," Zuckerman says. "All I can tell you with certainty is that I, for one, have no self, and that I am unwilling or unable to perpetrate upon myself the joke of a self." Ibid., 324.
253 Morris, ed., *Conversations*, 82–83.

Chapter 4

1. Don DeLillo, *Underworld* (New York: Knopf, 1997), 544.
2. Ibid., 628.
3. Ibid., 633.
4. Claudia Roth Pierpont, *Roth Unbound: A Writer and His Books* (New York: Farrar, Straus and Giroux, 2013), 306.
5. Don DeLillo, "The Power of History," *The New York Times Magazine* September 7, 1997. Accessed April 29, 2019.
6. Don DeLillo, *Mao II* (New York: Penguin, 1991), 7.
7. "Toward a Hidden God," *Time* April 8, 1966. Accessed May 20, 2008.
8. DeLillo, *Mao II*, 8.
9. Susan L. Mizruchi, "Introduction," *Religion and Cultural Studies*, ed. Susan L. Mizruchi (Princeton: Princeton University Press, 2001), ix; John A. McClure, "Postmodern/Post-secular: Contemporary Fiction and Spirituality," *Modern Fiction Studies* Vol. 41, No. 1 (Spring 1995): 142.
10. Rhonda Byrne, *The Secret* (New York: Simon and Schuster, 2006); Kathryn Lofton, *The Gospel of O* (Berkeley: University of California Press, 2011).
11. Richard W. Fox, *Jesus in America: Personal Savior, Cultural Hero, National Obsession* (San Francisco: Harper San Francisco, 2004), 15.
12. Charles Taylor, *A Secular Age* (Cambridge: Belknap Press/Harvard University Press, 2007), 3.
13. Ibid., 11.
14. Quoted in Anthony DeCurtis, "'An Outsider in This Society': An Interview with Don DeLillo," *Introducing Don DeLillo*, ed. Frank Lentricchia (Durham: Duke University Press, 1996), 63.
15. Don DeLillo, *White Noise: Text and Criticism*, ed. Mark Osteen (New York: Penguin, 1985), 37. For a reading of the supermarket and other sites in DeLillo's fiction, see David J. Alworth, *Site Reading: Fiction, Art, Social Form* (Princeton: Princeton University Press, 2015).
16. John A. McClure, *Partial Faiths: Postsecular Fiction in the Age of Pynchon and Morrison* (Athens: University of Georgia Press, 2007), 65, 77.
17. Amy Hungerford, "Don DeLillo's Latin Mass," *Contemporary Literature* Vol. 47, No 3 (Fall 2006): 343.
18. Dan Cryer, "Low Profile," interview with Don DeLillo, *Newsday* October 23, 1997: B06. Accessed February 17, 2006. According to a Pew Forum survey,

"roughly one-third of those who were raised Catholic have left the Church, and approximately one-in-ten American adults are former Catholics." "U.S. Catholics Tilt Left, Pew Survey Finds," *Catholic World News* June 30, 2008. Accessed May 21, 2009.

19 DeLillo, *Underworld*, 490, 683.
20 DeCurtis, "An Outsider in This Society," 66.
21 Ibid., 65–66.
22 Elizabeth K. Rosen, *Apocalyptic Transformation: Apocalypse and the Postmodern Imagination* (Lanham: Lexington Books, 2008); Joseph Dewey, *In a Dark Time: The Apocalyptic Temper in the American Novel of the Nuclear Age* (West Lafayette: Purdue University Press, 1990); Joseph Dewey, "DeLillo's Apocalyptic Satires," The Cambridge Companion to Don DeLillo, ed. John N. Duvall (Cambridge: Cambridge University Press, 2008), 53–65; Timothy Parrish, *From the Civil War to the Apocalypse: Postmodern History and American Fiction* (Amherst: University of Massachusetts Press, 2008).
23 DeCurtis, "An Outsider in Society," 65.
24 Diana Eck, *A New Religious America: How a Christian Country Has Now Become the World's Most Religiously Diverse Nation* (San Francisco: Harper San Francisco, 2001).
25 "We are now living in a spiritual super-nova, a kind of galloping pluralism on the spiritual plane." Taylor, *A Secular Age*, 300.
26 Christopher Lasch describes this therapeutic sensibility as follows: "People today hunger not for personal salvation, let alone for the restoration of an earlier golden age, but for the feeling, the momentary illusion, of personal well-being, health, and psychic security. … To live for the moment is the prevailing passion—to live for yourself, not for your predecessors or posterity." Christopher Lasch, *The Culture of Narcissism: American Life in an Age of Diminishing Expectations* (New York: Norton, 1979), 30, 33.
27 Morris Dickstein, *Gates of Eden: American Culture in the Sixties*, 2nd edition (Cambridge: Harvard University Press, 1997), xiv–xv.
28 Robert Bellah, et al., *Habits of the Heart* (Berkeley: University of California Press, 1985), 228.
29 Donald E. Miller, *Reinventing American Protestantism: Christianity in the New Millennium* (Berkeley: University of California Press, 1997), 4; George Gallup, Jr., and D. Michael Lindsey, *Surveying the Religious Landscape: Trends in U.S. Beliefs* (Harrisburg: Morehouse, 1999), 3, 8.

30 Following Randall Balmer, I will use the term "evangelical" "to refer broadly to conservative Protestants—including fundamentalists, evangelicals, Pentecostals, and charismatics—who insist on some sort of spiritual rebirth as a criterion for entering the kingdom of heaven, who often impose exacting behavioral standards on the faithful, and whose beliefs, institutions, and folkways comprise the evangelical subculture in America." Randall Balmer, *Mine Eyes Have Seen the Glory: A Journey into the Evangelical Subculture in America*, 4th edition (Oxford: Oxford University Press, 2006), xvi.

31 Charles Taylor, *Varieties of Religion Today: William James Revisited* (Cambridge: Harvard University Press, 2002), 38; Eck, *A New Religious America*, 4–5.

32 The U.S. Religious Landscape Survey, Pew Forum on Religion and Public Life: March 4, 2008. Accessed April 14, 2011.

33 Don DeLillo, *The Names* (New York: Knopf, 1982), 173.

34 Harvey Cox, *Fire from Heaven: The Rise of Pentecostalism and the Reshaping of Religion in the 21st Century* (New York: Da Capo Press, 2001); Allan Anderson, *An Introduction to Pentecostalism: Global Charismatic Christianity* (Cambridge: Cambridge University Press, 2004).

35 DeLillo, *The Names*, 337, 339.

36 Ibid., 339.

37 Ibid., 304–05.

38 Ibid., 304.

39 Ibid., 306.

40 Ibid.

41 Ibid., 150.

42 Ibid., 92, 146.

43 Ibid., 92.

44 Ibid.

45 On Jack's multiple marriages and the complex genealogy of his children, see Thomas Ferraro, "Whole Families Shopping at Night!" *New Essays on White Noise*, ed. Frank Lentricchia (Cambridge: Cambridge University Press, 1991), 16–17.

46 DeLillo, *White Noise*, 86.

47 Ibid., 87.

48 Robert Wuthnow, *After Heaven: Spirituality in America since the 1950s* (Berkeley: University of California Press, 1998), 3.

49 Ibid., 286.
50 Ibid.
51 Ibid., 72.
52 Ibid., 12.
53 Ibid., 65.
54 Emily Ogden has shown how mesmerists in the nineteenth century deliberately courted incredulity and thereby produced a new form of credulity in which skeptical viewers suspend their disbelief. Emily Ogden, *Credulity: A Cultural History of US Mesmerism* (Chicago: University of Chicago Press, 2018). Michael F. Brown argues that in much New Age spirituality, "unorthodox beliefs open a philosophical space that lends plausibility to views once regarded as odd or threatening." Michael F. Brown, *The Channeling Zone: American Spirituality in an Anxious Age* (Cambridge: Harvard University Press, 1997), 7–8.
55 Ibid., 27.
56 DeLillo, *White Noise*, 142, 144.
57 Ibid., 144, 145.
58 Circulation of tabloids is difficult to estimate, because most readers buy them at supermarket checkout counters; subscriptions account for less than 10 percent of total circulation for most tabloids. See Richard Davis and Diana Marie Owen, *New Media and American Politics* (Oxford: Oxford University Press, 1998), 97.
59 DeLillo, *White Noise*, 326.
60 John Updike, *Self-consciousness: Memoirs* (New York: Knopf, 1989), 226–27.
61 Mark Osteen, *American Magic and Dread: Don DeLillo's Dialogue with Culture* (Philadelphia: University of Pennsylvania Press, 2000), 166, 179.
62 DeLillo, *White Noise*, 23–24.
63 Ibid., 20, 34, 155, 79, 154.
64 Ibid., 117.
65 Ibid., 154.
66 Ibid., 154–55.
67 Ibid., 79.
68 Ibid., 242.
69 Ibid., 127.
70 Ibid., 227.
71 Ibid., 322–23.

72 Catherine Morley, "Don DeLillo's Transatlantic Dialogue with Sergei Eisenstein," *Journal of American Studies* Vol. 40, No. 1 (April 2006): 17–34.
73 DeLillo, *White Noise*, 322.
74 Mark Conroy, "From Tombstone to Tabloid: Authority Figured in *White Noise*," *Critique: Studies in Contemporary Fiction* Vol. 35, No. 2 (Winter 1994): 110.
75 Taylor, *A Secular Age*, 38.
76 DeLillo, *White Noise*, 46.
77 Taylor, *Varieties*, 39–40.
78 Andrew Delbanco, *The Real American Dream: A Meditation on Hope* (Cambridge: Harvard University Press, 1999), 3, 5.
79 Thomas DePietro, ed., *Conversations with Don DeLillo* (Jackson: University Press of Mississippi, 2005), 81.
80 DeLillo, *White Noise*, 47.
81 Ibid., 100.
82 Ibid., 37.
83 Ibid., 38.
84 Ibid., 251.
85 Ibid., 103.
86 DePietro, ed., *Conversations*, 167.
87 DeLillo, *White Noise*, 135.
88 Ibid., 137.
89 Grant Wacker, *America's Pastor: Billy Graham and the Shaping of a Nation* (Cambridge: Belknap Press/Harvard University Press, 2014), 45–47.
90 Matthew Avery Sutton, *American Apocalypse: A History of Modern Evangelicalism* (Cambridge: Belknap Press/Harvard University Press, 2014), 327. See also Robert Wuthnow, *Be Very Afraid: The Cultural Response to Terror, Pandemics, Environmental Devastation, Nuclear Annihilation, and Other Threats* (Oxford: Oxford University Press, 2010).
91 DeLillo, *White Noise*, 123.
92 Ibid., 147–48.
93 DeLillo, *Underworld*, 88–89.
94 Ibid., 88.
95 Ibid., 127.
96 Ibid., 140.

97 Ibid., 270.
98 DeLillo, *Mao II*, 3.
99 Dereck Daschke and W. Michael Ashcraft, eds., *New Religious Movements: A Documentary Reader* (New York: New York University Press, 2005), 140–41.
100 DeLillo, *Mao II*, 6.
101 Ibid., 15.
102 John Duvall, *Don DeLillo's Underworld: A Reader's Guide* (New York: Continuum, 2002), 15.
103 DeLillo, *The Names*, 276.
104 DePietro, ed., *Conversations*, 80.
105 DeLillo, *Mao II*, 7.
106 Ibid., 8.
107 Ibid., 69.
108 Ibid.
109 Rodney Stark and Roger Finke, *Acts of Faith: Explaining the Human Side of Religion* (Berkeley: University of California Press, 2000), 46.
110 DeLillo, *Mao II*, 163.
111 Ibid., 78.
112 McClure, *Partial Faiths*, 142.
113 DeLillo, *Mao II*, 69.
114 DeLillo, *White Noise*, 315.
115 Ibid., 318.
116 Ibid., 318–19.
117 DeLillo, *Mao II*, 69.
118 DePietro, ed., *Conversations*, 81.
119 DeLillo, *White Noise*, 310.
120 Osteen, *American*, 188.
121 DePietro, ed., *Conversations*, 106. Critics are unanimous about DeLillo's place in the paranoid school of contemporary fiction, less so about the significance of that school. In a review of *Underworld*, James Wood wrote that it "proves, once and for all, the incompatibility of paranoid history with great fiction," since the novel "surrenders fiction to the mysticism it should repel." James Wood, *The Broken Estate: Essays on Literature and Belief* (New York: Random House, 1999), 181.
122 Don DeLillo, *Running Dog* (New York: Knopf, 1978), 111.

123 DeLillo, *Underworld*, 826.
124 Quoted in Peter Knight, *Conspiracy Culture: From the Kennedy Assassination to the* X-Files (London: Routledge, 2000), 226.
125 Don DeLillo, *Libra* (New York: Viking, 1988), 181.
126 Ibid., 458.
127 Ibid.
128 Ibid., 259.
129 DeLillo, *Underworld*, 802.
130 DePietro, ed., *Conversations*, 106.
131 DeLillo, *Underworld*, 241.
132 Ibid., 280.
133 Cryer, "Low Profile."
134 Knight, *Conspiracy Culture*, 230.
135 DeLillo, *Underworld*, 173, 251, 354, 405, 436, 620.
136 Ibid., 289.
137 Ibid., 801.
138 Ibid., 559.
139 Ibid., 573.
140 Ibid., 826.
141 Ibid., 557.
142 Patrick O'Donnell, "*Underworld*," *The Cambridge Companion to Don DeLillo*, ed. John Duvall (Cambridge: Cambridge University Press, 2009), 109.
143 DeLillo, "Power."
144 Karl Marx, *The Marx-Engels Reader*, ed. Robert C. Tucker (New York: Norton, 1978), 594.
145 DeLillo, *Underworld*, 132.
146 David H. Evans, "Taking out the Trash: Don DeLillo's *Underworld*, Liquid Modernity, and the End of Garbage," *Cambridge Quarterly* Vol. 35, No. 2 (2006): 3.
147 DeLillo, *Underworld*, 365.
148 Ibid.
149 Colleen McDannell, *Material Christianity: Religion and Popular Culture in America* (New Haven: Yale University Press, 1998).
150 Duvall, *Don DeLillo's* Underworld, 8.
151 Tom LeClair, "An Interview with Don DeLillo," *Contemporary Literature* Vol. 23, No. 1 (Winter 1982): 26.

152 DeLillo, *Underworld*, 717.
153 Irving Marlin and Joseph Dewey, "'What Beauty, What Power': Speculations on the Third Edgar," *Underworlds: Perspectives on Don DeLillo's Underworld*, eds. Joseph Dewey, Steven G. Kellman, and Irving Malin (Newark: University of Deleware Press, 2002), 21.
154 DeLillo, *Underworld*, 717.
155 The Baltimore Catechism was commissioned by the Third Plenary Council of Baltimore in 1884 and revised in 1941, which enlarged the text to 499 questions from its original 421. The 1941 revision also added an Appendix titled "Why I Am a Catholic." The Baltimore Catechism was widely used in parochial schools. See Ira Nadel, "The Baltimore Cathechism; or Comedy in *Underworld*," *Underworlds: Perspectives on Don DeLillo's Underworld*, eds. Joseph Dewey, Steven G. Kellman, and Irving Malin (Newark: University of Delaware Press, 2002), 197–98.
156 Ibid., 716.
157 Ibid., 718.
158 Ibid., 727–28.
159 Ibid., 242.
160 Ibid., 249.
161 Ibid., 811.
162 Ibid., 815.
163 Ibid., 817.
164 John Patrick Shanley's play *Doubt: A Parable* (2005) features an old-fashioned nun in a nearly identical Bronx Catholic School who experiences a similar crisis of faith. John Patrick Shanley, *Doubt: A Parable* (New York: Theater Communications Group, 2005).
165 DeLillo, *Underworld*, 819.
166 Ibid., 821.
167 Ibid.
168 Evans notes the irony that "it is to this benighted individual, with all her superstition and pettiness, rather than to her enlightened companion Sister Gracie, that the novel vouchsafes its final manifestation of grace, the appearance of the murdered girl Esmeralda in a billboard ad for Minute Maid Orange Juice." Evans, "Taking," 27–28.
169 DeLillo, *Underworld*, 822.
170 DePietro, ed., *Conversations*, 158.
171 DeLillo, *Underworld*, 824.

172 Ibid., 822. Malin and Dewey write about her epiphany in similar terms: "She is suddenly infused with certainty in a world she had begun to consign to chaos, had begun to doubt was in the control of any benevolent Creator, was in fact deeply, undeniably spiritual." Malin and Dewey, "What Beauty, What Power," 24.
173 DeLillo, *Underworld*, 824.
174 Ibid.
175 Ibid., 613.
176 Ibid., 282.
177 Duvall, *Don DeLillo's* Underworld, 24.
178 DeLillo, *Underworld*, 88.
179 Ibid., 809.
180 Ibid., 295.
181 Ibid., 825.
182 Ibid., 826.
183 Ibid.
184 Ibid., 807.
185 Ibid., 808.
186 Ibid., 303.
187 Tony Tanner, "Afterthoughts on Don DeLillo's *Underworld*," *Raritan* Vol. 17, No. 4 (Spring 1998): 70; John Leonard quoted in Duvall, *Don DeLillo's* Underworld, 73.
188 Don DeLillo, *Falling Man* (New York: Scribner, 2007), 60–61.
189 Ibid., 61.
190 Ibid., 62.
191 Robert A. Ferguson, *Alone in America: The Stories That Matter* (Cambridge: Harvard University Press, 2013), 215.
192 DeLillo, *Falling Man*, 61.
193 Ibid., 156.
194 Ibid., 112.
195 Ibid., 62–63.
196 Ibid., 233.
197 Ibid., 156.
198 Ibid., 89.
199 Ibid., 90.
200 Ibid., 234–35.

201 Ibid., 65.
202 Amy Hungerford, *Postmodern Belief: American Literature and Religion since 1960* (Princeton: Princeton University Press, 2010), 111.
203 Christian Smith, *Religion: What It Is, How It Works, and Why It Matters* (Princeton: Princeton University Press, 2017), 251.

Bibliography

Achebe, Chinua. "The Day I Finally Met James Baldwin." PEN America January 8, 2007. Accessed July 28, 2014.

Adorno, Theodor, and Max Horkheimer. *The Dialectic of Enlightenment*. Ed. Gunzelin Schmid Noerr. Trans. Edmund Jephcott. Stanford: Stanford University Press, 2002.

Adorno, Theodor W. *Negative Dialectics*. Trans. E.B. Ashton. New York: Continuum, 2005.

Adorno, Theodor W. *Prisms*. Trans. Shierry Weber Nicholsen and Samuel Weber. Cambridge: MIT Press, 1983.

Ahlstrom, Sydney E. *A Religious History of the American People*. New Haven: Yale University Press, 1971.

Alan Lloyd-Smith, Alan. *American Gothic Fiction: An Introduction*. New York: Continuum, 2004.

Als, Hilton. "Genius Breaking Through." *The New York Review of Books* August 14, 2014: 6–8.

Als, Hilton. "This Lonesome Place: Flannery O'Connor on Race and Religion in the Unreconstructed South." *The New Yorker* January 29, 2001. Accessed May 6, 2019.

Alter, Robert. "Confronting the Holocaust." *After the Tradition: Essays on Modern Jewish Writing*. New York: Dutton, 1969. 163–80.

Alworth, David J. *Site Reading: Fiction, Art, Social Form*. Princeton: Princeton University Press, 2015.

Anderson, Allan. *An Introduction to Pentecostalism: Global Charismatic Christianity*. Cambridge: Cambridge University Press, 2004.

Asad, Talal. *Formations of the Secular: Christianity, Islam, and Modernity*. Stanford: Stanford University Press, 2003.

Bacon, Jon Lance. *Flannery O'Connor and Cold War Culture*. Cambridge: Cambridge University Press, 1993.

Bakhtin, M.M. *Problems of Dostoevsky's Poetics*. Ed. and trans. Caryl Emerson. Minneapolis: University of Minnesota Press, 1984.

Baldwin, James. *The Amen Corner*. New York: Samuel French, 1968.

Baldwin, James. *Collected Essays*. New York: Library of America, 1998.

Baldwin, James. *The Evidence of Things Not Seen*. New York: Henry Holt, 1985.

Baldwin, James. *Giovanni's Room*. New York: Dial, 1956.

Baldwin, James. *Go Tell It on the Mountain*. New York: Dell, 2000.

Balfour, Lawrie. *The Evidence of Things Not Said: James Baldwin and the Promise of American Democracy*. Ithaca: Cornell University Press, 2001.

Balmer, Randall. *Mine Eyes Have Seen the Glory: A Journey into the Evangelical Subculture in America*. 4th edition. Oxford: Oxford University Press, 2006.

Barkun, Michael. *A Culture of Conspiracy: Apocalyptic Visions in Contemporary America*. Berkeley: University of California Press, 2006.

Baumgaertner, Jill Palaez. *Flannery O'Connor: A Proper Scaring*. Chicago: Cornerstone Press, 1999.

Baumgarten, Murray. "American Midrash: Urban Jewish Writing and the Reclaiming of Judaism." *The Cambridge Companion to American Judaism*. Ed. Dana Evan Kaplan. Cambridge: Cambridge University Press, 2005. 345–62.

Bellah, Robert N., et al. *Habits of the Heart: Individualism and Commitment in American Life*. Berkeley: University of California Press, 2007.

Bellow, Saul. *Herzog*. New York: Viking, 1961.

Bellow, Saul. *It All Adds Up*. New York: Viking, 1994.

Bellow, Saul. "A Jewish Writer in America, Part I." *The New York Review of Books* October 27, 2011. Accessed March 28, 2013.

Bellow, Saul. "A Jewish Writer in America, Part II." *The New York Review of Books* November 10, 2011. Accessed March 28, 2013.

Bellow, Saul. *Letters*. Ed. Benjamin Taylor. New York: Viking, 2010.

Bellow, Saul. *Mr. Sammler's Planet*. New York: Viking, 1970.

Bellow, Saul. *Novels 1944–1953*. New York: Library of America, 2003.

Bellow, Saul. *Novels 1956–1964*. New York: Library of America, 2007.

Bennett, Jane. *The Enchantment of Modern Life: Attachments, Crossings, and Ethics*. Princeton: Princeton University Press, 2001.

Bennett, Timothy A., and Rochelle L. Millen. "Christians and Pharisees: Jewish Responses to Radical Theology." *The Death of God Movement and the Holocaust: Radical Theology Encounters the Shoah*. Eds. Stephen R. Haynes and John K. Roth. Westport: Greenwood Press, 1999. 111–30.

Berger, Alan L. *Crisis and Covenant: The Holocaust in American Jewish Fiction*. Albany: State University of New York Press, 1985.

Berger, Peter L., ed. *The Desecularization of the World: Resurgent Religion and World Politics*. Grand Rapids: Eerdmans, 1999.

Blodgett, Jan. *Protestant Evangelical Literary Culture and Contemporary Society*. Westport: Greenwood Press, 1997.

Bloom, Harold. "Introduction." *Flannery O'Connor: Modern Critical Views.* New York: Chelsea House Publishers, 1986. 1–8.

Bonhoeffer, Dietrich. *Prisoner for God.* New York: Macmillan, 1959.

Brauner, David. *Post-war Jewish Fiction: Ambivalence, Self-explanation and Transatlantic Connections.* New York: Palgrave, 2001.

Brooks, Cleanth. *The Hidden God: Studies in Hemingway, Faulkner, Yeats, Eliot, and Warren.* New Haven: Yale University Press, 1963.

Brooks, Joanna. "From Edwards to Baldwin: Heterodoxy, Discontinuity, and New Narratives of American Religious-literary History." *Early American Literature* Vol. 45, No. 2 (2010): 431–33.

Brown, Michael F. *The Channeling Zone: American Spirituality in an Anxious Age.* Cambridge: Harvard University Press, 1997.

Bruner, Michael Mears. *A Subversive Gospel: Flannery O'Connor and the Reimagining of Beauty, Goodness, and Truth.* Westmont: InterVarsity Press, 2017.

Budick, Emily Miller. "The Holocaust in the Jewish American Literary Imagination." *The Cambridge Companion to Jewish American Literature.* Eds. Hana Wirth-Nesher and Michael P. Kramer. Cambridge: Cambridge University Press, 2003. 212–30.

Butler, Jon. *Awash in a Sea of Faith: Christianizing the American People.* Cambridge: Harvard University Press, 1990.

Byrne, Rhonda. *The Secret.* New York: Simon and Schuster, 2006.

Calhoun, Craig, Mark Juergensmeyer, and Jonathan VanAntwerpen, eds. *Rethinking Secularism.* Oxford: Oxford University Press, 2011.

Casanova, Jose. "The Secular, Secularization, Secularisms." *Rethinking Secularism.* Eds. Craig Calhoun, Mark Juergensmeyer, and Jonathan VanAntwerpen. Oxford: Oxford University Press, 2013. 54–74.

Chappell, David L. *A Stone of Hope: Prophetic Religion and the Death of Jim Crow.* Chapel Hill: University of North Carolina Press, 2004.

Coetzee, J.M. "On the Moral Brink." *The New York Review of Books* October 28, 2010. Accessed October 28, 2014.

Coleman, James W. *Faithful Vision: Treatments of the Sacred, Spiritual, and Supernatural in Twentieth-century African American Fiction.* Baton Rouge: Louisiana State University Press, 2006.

Coles, Robert. *Flannery O'Connor's South.* Baton Rouge: Louisiana State University Press, 1980.

Conroy, Mark. "From Tombstone to Tabloid: Authority Figured in *White Noise.*" *Critique: Studies in Contemporary Fiction* Vol. 35, No. 2 (Winter 1994): 97–110.

Cox, Harvey. *Fire from Heaven: The Rise of Pentecostalism and the Reshaping of Religion in the 21st Century*. New York: Da Capo Press, 2001.

Cronin, Gloria L., and Ben Siegel, eds. *Conversations with Saul Bellow*. Oxford: University Press of Mississippi, 1994.

Crossman, Richard H., ed. *The God That Failed*. New York: Columbia University Press, 2001.

Cryer, Dan. "Low Profile." Interview with Don DeLillo. *Newsday* October 23, 1997: B06. Accessed February 17, 2006.

Daschke, Dereck, and W. Michael Ashcraft, eds. *New Religious Movements: A Documentary Reader*. New York: New York University Press, 2005.

Davis, Richard, and Diana Marie Owen. *New Media and American Politics*. Oxford: Oxford University Press, 1998.

DeCurtis, Anthony. "'An Outsider in This Society': An Interview with Don DeLillo." *Introducing Don DeLillo*. Ed. Frank Lentricchia. Durham: Duke University Press, 1996. 43–66.

Delbanco, Andrew. "'The Only Permanent State': Belief and the Culture of Incredulity." *Invisible Conversations: Religion in the Literature of America*. Ed. Roger Lundin. Waco: Baylor University Press, 2009. 149–55.

Delbanco, Andrew. *The Real American Dream: A Meditation on Hope*. Cambridge: Harvard University Press, 1999.

DeLillo, Don. *Falling Man*. New York: Scribner, 2007.

DeLillo, Don. *Libra*. New York: Viking, 1988.

DeLillo, Don. *Mao II*. New York: Penguin, 1991.

DeLillo, Don. *The Names*. New York: Knopf, 1982.

DeLillo, Don. "The Power of History." *The New York Times Magazine* September 7, 1997. Accessed April 29, 2019.

DeLillo, Don. *Running Dog*. New York: Knopf, 1978.

DeLillo, Don. *Underworld*. New York: Knopf, 1997.

DeLillo, Don. *White Noise: Text and Criticism*. Ed. Mark Osteen. New York: Penguin, 1985.

DePietro, Thomas, ed. *Conversations with Don DeLillo*. Jackson: University Press of Mississippi, 2005.

Desmond, John. *Risen Sons: Flannery O'Connor's Vision of History*. Athens: University of Georgia Press, 1987.

Dewey, Joseph. "DeLillo's Apocalyptic Satires." *The Cambridge Companion to Don DeLillo*. Ed. John N. Duvall. Cambridge: Cambridge University Press, 2008. 53–65.

Dewey, Joseph. *In a Dark Time: The Apocalyptic Temper in the American Novel of the Nuclear Age*. West Lafayette: Purdue University Press, 1990.

Dickstein, Morris. *Gates of Eden: American Culture in the Sixties*. 2nd edition. Cambridge: Harvard University Press, 1997.

Dickstein, Morris. *Leopards in the Temple: The Transformation of American Fiction, 1945–1970*. Cambridge: Harvard University Press, 2002.

"Dietrich Bonhoeffer: German Martyr Transformed by Experience with Harlem's Abyssinian Baptist Church." DDayMedia January 16, 2012. Accessed July 23, 2014.

Dochuk, Darren. *From Bible Belt to Sunbelt: Plainfolk Religion, Grassroots Politics, and the Rise of Evangelical Conservatism*. New York: Norton, 2011.

Doctorow, E.L. *Citizen Doctorow, Notes on Art and Politics: The Nation Essays 1978–2012*. Ed. Richard Lingeman. Washington, DC: The Nation, 2014.

Doctorow, E.L. *City of God*. New York: Random House, 2000.

Doctorow, E.L. *Creationists: Selected Essays 1993–2006*. New York: Random House, 2006.

Doctorow, E.L. *Reporting the Universe*. Cambridge: Harvard University Press, 2003.

Doctorow, E.L. *Sweet Land Stories*. New York: Random House, 2004.

Doherty, Thomas. *Cold War, Cool Medium: Television, McCarthyism, and American Culture*. New York: Columbia University Press, 2003.

Douglas, Ann. *Terrible Honesty: Mongrel Manhattan in the 1920s*. New York: Farrar, Straus and Giroux, 1995.

Douthat, Ross. *Bad Religion: How a Nation Became a Nation of Heretics*. New York: Free Press, 2012.

Dray, Philip. *At the Hands of Persons Unknown: The Lynching of Black America*. New York: Random House, 2002.

Dunlap, David W. *From Abyssinian to Zion*. New York: Columbia University Press, 2004.

During, Simon. *Modern Enchantments: The Cultural Power of Secular Magic*. Cambridge: Harvard University Press, 2002.

Duvall, John. *Don DeLillo's Underworld: A Reader's Guide*. New York: Continuum, 2002.

Eck, Diana. *A New Religious America: How a Christian Country Has Now Become the World's Most Religiously Diverse Nation*. San Francisco: Harper San Francisco, 2001.

Elam, Michele, ed. *The Cambridge Companion to James Baldwin*. Cambridge: Cambridge University Press, 2015.

Elgrably, Jordan. "James Baldwin: The Art of Fiction 78." *The Paris Review* Vol. 91 (Spring 1984). Accessed July 23, 2014.

Ellison, Ralph. *Invisible Man*. New York: Vintage, 1995.
English, James F. "Everywhere and Nowhere: The Sociology of Literature after 'The Sociology of Literature,'" *New Literary History* Vol. 41, No. 2 (Spring 2010): v–xxiii.
Espinosa, Gaston. *William J. Seymour and the Origins of Global Pentecostalism: A Biography and Documentary History*. Durham: Duke University Press, 2014.
Evans, David H. "Taking Out the Trash: Don DeLillo's *Underworld*, Liquid Modernity, and the End of Garbage." *Cambridge Quarterly* Vol. 35, No. 2 (2006): 103–32.
Feldman, Noah. *Divided by God: America's Church-state Problem and What We Should Do about It*. New York: Farrar, Straus and Giroux, 2005.
Ferguson, Robert A. *Alone in America: The Stories That Matter*. Cambridge: Harvard University Press, 2013.
Ferraro, Thomas Ferraro. "Whole Families Shopping at Night!" *New Essays on* White Noise. Ed. Frank Lentricchia. Cambridge: Cambridge University Press, 1991. 15–38.
Fessenden, Tracy. *Culture and Redemption: Religion, the Secular, and American Literature*. Princeton: Princeton University Press, 2007.
Fiedler, Leslie. *A New Fiedler Reader*. Amherst: Prometheus Books, 1999.
Field, Douglas, ed. *A Historical Guide to James Baldwin*. Oxford: Oxford University Press, 2009.
Finke, Roger, and Rodney Stark. *The Churching of America 1776–2005: Winners and Losers in Our Religious Economy*. New Brunswick: Rutgers University Press, 2007.
Fogel, Robert W. *The Fourth Great Awakening and the Future of Egalitarianism*. Chicago: University of Chicago Press, 2000.
Fox, Richard W. *Jesus in America: Personal Savior, Cultural Hero, National Obsession*. San Francisco: Harper San Francisco, 2004.
Frazier, E. Franklin. *The Negro Church in America*. New York: Schocken Books, 1974.
Freedman, Jonathan. *The Temple of Culture: Assimilation and Anti-Semitism in Literary Anglo-America*. Oxford: Oxford University Press, 2000.
Frykholm, Amy Johnson. *Rapture Culture: Left Behind and Evangelical America*. Oxford: Oxford University Press, 2004.
Fuchs, Daniel. "Identity and the Postwar Temper in American Jewish Fiction." *A Concise Companion to Postwar American Literature and Culture*. Ed. Josephine G. Hendin. Oxford: Blackwell, 2004. 238–62.

Fuller, Robert C. *Spiritual, but Not Religious: Understanding Unchurched America*. Oxford: Oxford University Press, 2001.

Gallup, George, Jr. "Religion: In America: Will the Vitality of Churches Be the Surprise of the Next Century?" *U.S. Society and Values* Vol. 2, No. 1 (March 1997). Accessed April 27, 2005.

Gallup, George, Jr., and D. Michael Lindsey. *Surveying the Religious Landscape: Trends in U.S. Beliefs*. Harrisburg: Morehouse, 1999.

Geertz, Clifford. *The Interpretation of Cultures*. New York: Basic Books, 1973.

"Global Christianity: A Report on the Size and Distribution of the World's Christian Population." Pew Research Forum December 19, 2011. Accessed July 15, 2014.

Goldberg, Michael. *Why Should the Jews Survive? Looking Past the Holocaust toward a Jewish Future*. Oxford: Oxford University Press, 1995.

Gonzalez, David. "A Sliver of a Storefront, a Faith on the Rise." *The New York Times* January 14, 2007. Accessed May 6, 2019.

Gooch, Brad. *Flannery: A Life of Flannery O'Connor*. New York: Little, Brown, 2009.

Gregory, Brad. *The Unintended Reformation: How a Religious Revolution Secularized Society*. Cambridge: Harvard University Press, 2012.

Griffin, Farah Jasmine. *"Who Set You Flowin'?": The African-American Migration Narrative*. Oxford: Oxford University Press, 1995.

Guardini, Romano. *The End of the Modern World: A Search for Orientation*. Trans. Joseph Theman and Herbert Burke. New York: Sheed and Ward, 1956.

Hall, David L., ed. *Lived Religion in America: Toward a History of Practice*. Princeton: Princeton University Press, 1997.

Hardy, Clarence E., III. *James Baldwin's God: Sex, Hope, and Crisis in Black Holiness Culture*. Knoxville: University of Tennessee Press, 2003.

Hassan, Ihab. *Radical Innocence: Studies in the Contemporary American Novel*. Princeton: Princeton University Press, 1961.

Hatch, Nathan. *The Democratization of American Christianity*. New Haven: Yale University Press, 1989.

Hawkes, John. "Flannery O'Connor's Devil." *Sewanee Review* 70 (1962): 395–407.

Herberg, Will. *Protestant-Catholic-Jew: An Essay in American Religious Sociology*. Garden City: Doubleday Anchor, 1955, 1960.

Hoberek, Andrew. *The Twilight of the Middle Class: Post-World War II American Fiction and White-collar Work*. Princeton: Princeton University Press, 2005.

Hobson, Christopher Z. *James Baldwin and the Heavenly City: Prophecy, Apocalypse, and Doubt*. East Lansing: Michigan State University Press, 2018.

Hollinger, David. *Post-ethnic America: Beyond Multiculturalism*. New York: Basic Books, 1995.

Hollinger, David. *Science, Jews, and Secular Culture: Studies in Mid-twentieth-century American Intellectual History*. Princeton: Princeton University Press, 1996.

Hungerford, Amy. "Don DeLillo's Latin Mass." *Contemporary Literature* Vol. 47, No. 3 (Fall 2006): 343–80.

Hungerford, Amy. *The Holocaust of Texts: Genocide, Literature, and Personification*. Chicago: University of Chicago Press, 2003.

Hungerford, Amy. *Postmodern Belief: American Literature and Religion after 1960*. Princeton: Princeton University Press, 2010.

Hunter, James Davidson. *To Change the World: The Irony, Tragedy, and Possibility of Christianity in the Late Modern World*. Oxford: Oxford University Press, 2010.

Indinopulos, Thomas A. "The Holocaust and the Death of God." *The Death of God Movement and the Holocaust: Radical Theology Encounters the Shoah*. Eds. Stephen R. Haynes and John K. Roth. Westport: Greenwood Press, 1999. 63–68.

Isserman, Maurice, and Michael Kazin. *America Divided: The Civil War of the 1960s*. 3rd edition. Oxford: Oxford University Press, 2008.

Jacobsen, Douglas. *Thinking in the Spirit: Theologies of the Early Pentecostal Movement*. Bloomington: Indiana University Press, 2003.

Jacoby, Susan. "The Blessings of Atheism." *The New York Times* January 5, 2013: 6.

Jacoby, Susan. *The Great Agnostic: Robert Ingersoll and American Freethought*. New Haven: Yale University Press, 2013.

Jakobsen, Janet R., and Ann Pellegrini, eds. *Secularisms*. Durham: Duke University Press, 2008.

Jenkins, Philip. *Mystics and Messiahs: Cults and New Religions in American History*. Oxford: Oxford University Press, 2000.

Johnson, James Weldon. *Black Manhattan*. New York: DeCapo Press, 1991.

Jones, Howard Mumford. *Belief and Disbelief in American Literature*. Chicago: University of Chicago Press, 1967.

Kakutani, Michiko. "Intuitive and Precise, a Relentless Updike Mapped America's Mysteries." *The New York Times* January 28, 2009: A22.

Kaplan, Dana Evan. "Trends in American Judaism from 1945 to the Present." *The Cambridge Companion to American Judaism*. Ed. Dana Evan Kaplan. Cambridge: Cambridge University Press, 2005. 61–78.

Kazin, Alfred. *Alfred Kazin's Journals*. Ed. Richard M. Cook. New Haven: Yale University Press, 2011.

Kazin, Alfred. *New York Jew*. New York: Knopf, 1978.

Ketchin, Susan. *The Christ-haunted Landscape: Faith and Doubt in Southern Fiction*. Jackson: University Press of Mississippi, 1994.

Kilcourse, George A., Jr. *Flannery O'Connor's Religious Imagination: A World with Everything Off Balance*. New York: Paulist Press, 2001.

Knight, Peter. *Conspiracy Culture: From the Kennedy Assassination to the X-Files*. London: Routledge, 2000.

Koestler, Arthur. *The Yogi and the Commissar, and Other Essays*. New York: Macmillan, 1945.

Kramer, Michael P., ed. *New Essays on* Seize the Day. Cambridge: Cambridge University Press, 1998.

Kreyling, Michael, ed. *New Essays on* Wise Blood. Cambridge: Cambridge University Press, 1995.

Kruse, Kevin. *One Nation under God: How Corporate America Invented Christian America*. New York: Basic Books, 2015.

Lake, Cristina Bieber. *The Incarnational Art of Flannery O'Connor*. Macon: Mercer University Press, 2005.

Landy Joshua. *How to Do Things with Fictions*. Oxford: Oxford University Press, 2012.

LaPorte, Charles, and Sebastian Lecourt. "Introduction: Nineteenth-century Literature, New Religious Movements, and Secularization." *Nineteenth-century Literature* Vol. 73, No. 2 (September 2018): 147–60.

Larsen, Timothy. *Crisis of Doubt: Honest Faith in Nineteenth Century England*. Oxford: Oxford University Press, 2006.

Lasch, Christopher. *The Culture of Narcissism: American Life in an Age of Diminishing Expectations*. New York: Norton, 1979.

LeClair, Tom. "An Interview with Don DeLillo." *Contemporary Literature* Vol. 23, No. 1 (Winter 1982): 19–31.

Leeming, David. *James Baldwin: A Biography*. New York: Henry Holt, 1994.

Lemann, Nicholas. *The Promised Land: The Great Black Migration and How It Changed America*. New York: Vintage, 1991.

Levi, Primo. *The Drowned and the Saved*. New York: Vintage, 1989.

Levinas, Emmanuel. *Alterity and Transcendence*. Trans. Michael B. Smith. New York: Columbia University Press, 1999.

Levine, Caroline. *Forms: Whole, Rhythm, Hierarchy, Network*. Princeton: Princeton University Press, 2015.

Lewis, David Levering. *When Harlem Was in Vogue*. New York: Penguin, 1997.

Lewis, Pericles. *Religious Experience in the Modernist Novel*. Cambridge: Cambridge University Press, 2010.

Lindberg, Anne Morrow. *Gift from the Sea*. New York: Pantheon, 1955, 2005.

Lindsey, Hal. *The Late Great Planet Earth*. Grand Rapids: Zondervan, 1970.

Lofton, Kathryn. "Cosmology." *Religion in American History*. Eds. Amanda Porterfield and John Corrigan. Malden: Wiley-Blackwell, 2010. 266–84.

Lofton, Kathryn. *The Gospel of O*. Berkeley: University of California Press, 2011.

Luhrmann, T.M. "C.S. Lewis: Evangelical Rock Star." *The New York Times* June 26, 2013: A23.

Luhrmann, T.M. *When God Talks Back: Understanding the American Evangelical Relationship with God*. New York: Knopf, 2012.

Lundin, Roger. *Beginning with the Word: Modern Literature and the Question of Belief*. Grand Rapids: Baker Academic, 2014.

Lynch, Michael F. "Staying Out of the Temple: Baldwin, the African American Church, and *The Amen Corner*." *Re-viewing James Baldwin: Things Not Seen*. Ed. D. Quentin Miller. Philadelphia: Temple University Press, 2000. 8–71.

MacRobert, Ian. "The Black Roots of Pentecostalism." *African American Religion: Interpretive Essays in History and Culture*. Eds. Timothy E. Fulop and Albert J. Raboteau. New York: Routledge, 1997. 295–310.

Maltby, Paul. *Christian Fundamentalism and the Culture of Disenchantment*. Charlottesville: University of Virginia Press, 2013.

Marlin, Irving, and Joseph Dewey. "'What Beauty, What Power': Speculations on the Third Edgar." *Underworlds: Perspectives on Don DeLillo's Underworld*. Eds. Joseph Dewey, Steven G. Kellman, and Irving Malin. Newark: University of Delaware Press, 2002. 19–27.

Marsden, George. *The Twilight of the American Enlightenment: The 1950s and the Crisis of Liberal Belief*. New York: Basic Books, 2014.

Marx, Karl. *The Marx-Engels Reader*. Ed. Robert C. Tucker. New York: Norton, 1978.

Masuzawa, Tomoko. *The Invention of World Religions: Or, How European Universalism Was Preserved in the Language of Pluralism*. Chicago: University of Chicago Press, 2005.

McBride, Dwight, ed. *James Baldwin Now*. New York: New York University Press, 1999.

McClure, John A. *Partial Faiths: Postsecular Fiction in the Age of Pynchon and Morrison*. Athens, GA: University of Georgia Press, 2007.

McClure, John A. "Postmodern/Post-secular: Contemporary Fiction and Spirituality." *Modern Fiction Studies* Vol. 41, No. 1 (Spring 1995): 141–63.

McDannell, Colleen. *Material Christianity: Religion and Popular Culture in America*. New Haven: Yale University Press, 1998.

McGrath, Charles. "Interview: Zukerman's Alter Brain." *New York Times Book Review* May 7, 2000. Accessed October 22, 2014.

McGurl, Mark. *The Program Era: Postwar Fiction and the Rise of Creative Writing*. Cambridge: Harvard University Press, 2010.

Menand, Louis. "Introduction." *Civilization and Its Discontents*. Ed. Sigmund Freud. New York: Norton, 2005. 9–32.

Mencken, H.L. *The Philosophy of Friedrich Nietzsche*. Boston: Luce and Company, 1908.

Mendelsohn, Daniel. *The Lost: A Search for Six of Six Million*. New York: HarperCollins, 2006.

Mendelson, Edward. "New York Everyman." *The New York Review of Books* June 12, 2009. Accessed June 6, 2011.

Metaxas, Eric. *Bonhoeffer: Pastor, Martyr, Prophet, Spy*. New York: Thomas Nelson, 2010.

Milbank, John. *Theology and Social Theory: Beyond Secular Reason*. 2nd edition. New York: Blackwell, 2006.

Miller, Donald E. *Reinventing American Protestantism: Christianity in the New Millennium*. Berkeley: University of California Press, 1997.

Miller, J. Hillis. *The Disappearance of God: Five Nineteenth-century Writers*. Cambridge: Belknap Press/Harvard University Press, 1963.

Miller, Stephen P. *The Age of Evangelicalism: America's Born-again Years*. Oxford: Oxford University Press, 2014.

Mizruchi, Susan L. "Introduction." *Religion and Cultural Studies*. Ed. Susan L. Mizruchi. Princeton: Princeton University Press, 2001. ix–xxv.

Morgan, Michael L. *Beyond Auschwitz: Post-Holocaust Jewish Thought in America*. Oxford: Oxford University Press, 2001.

Morley, Catherine. "Don DeLillo's Transatlantic Dialogue with Sergei Eisenstein." *Journal of American Studies* Vol. 40, No. 1 (April 2006): 17–34.

Morris, Christopher D., ed. *Conversations with E.L. Doctorow*. Jackson: University Press of Mississippi, 1999.

Morrison, Toni. "James Baldwin: His Voice Remembered; Life in His Language." *The New York Times Book Review* December 20, 1987: 27. Accessed May 16, 2006.

Morrison, Toni. *Song of Solomon*. New York: Plume, 1977.

Most, Andrea. "The Birth of Theatrical Liberalism." *After Pluralism: Reimagining Religious Engagement*. Eds. Courtney Bender and Pamela E. Klassen. New York: Columbia University Press, 2010. 127–55.

Nadel, Ira. "The Baltimore Cathechism; or Comedy in *Underworld*." *Underworlds: Perspectives on Don DeLillo's Underworld*. Eds. Joseph Dewey, Steven G. Kellman, and Irving Malin. Newark: University of Delaware Press, 2002. 176–98.

Neusner, Jacob. *Stranger at Home: "The Holocaust," Zionism, and American Judaism*. Chicago: University of Chicago Press, 1981.

Niebuhr, Reinhold. *Pious and Secular America*. New York: Scribner's, 1958.

Nietzsche, Friedrich. *The Gay Science*. Trans. Walter Kaufman. New York: Vintage, 1974.

Norris, Pippa, and Ronald Inglehart. "Uneven Secularization in the U.S. and Western Europe." *Democracy and the New Religious Pluralism*. Ed. Thomas Banchoff. Oxford: Oxford University Press, 2007.

O'Connor, Flannery. *Collected Works*. New York: Library of America, 1983.

O'Connor, Flannery. *Collected Works*. New York: Library of America, 1988.

O'Connor, Flannery. *The Complete Stories*. New York: Farrar, Straus and Giroux, 1971.

O'Connor, Flannery. *Everything That Rises Must Converge*. New York: Noonday, 1965.

O'Connor, Flannery. *The Habit of Being: Letters of Flannery O'Connor*. Ed. Sally Fitzgerald. New York: Farrar, Straus and Giroux, 1979.

O'Connor, Flannery. *Mystery and Manners: Occasional Prose*. Eds. Sally Fitzgerald and Robert Fitzgerald. New York: Farrar, Straus and Giroux, 1969.

O'Connor, Flannery. *A Prayer Journal*. New York: Farrar, Straus and Giroux, 2013.

O'Connor, Flannery. *The Presence of Grace and Other Book Reviews*. Athens: University of Georgia Press, 1983.

O'Connor, Flannery. *Wise Blood*. New York: Farrar, Straus and Giroux, 1967.
O'Connor, Flannery, and Kelly Gerald. *Flannery O'Connor: The Cartoons*. Seattle: Fantagraphics, 2012.
O'Donnell, Patrick. *The American Novel Now*. Oxford: Wiley-Blackwell, 2010.
O'Donnell, Patrick. "*Underworld.*" *The Cambridge Companion to Don DeLillo*. Ed. John Duvall. Cambridge: Cambridge University Press, 2009. 108–22.
O'Gorman, Farrell. *Peculiar Crossroads: Flannery O'Connor, Walker Percy, and Catholic Vision in Postwar Southern Fiction*. Baton Rouge: Louisiana State University Press, 2004.
Oates, Joyce Carol. "The Parables of Flannery O'Connor." *New York Review of Books* April 9, 2009. Accessed July 13, 2014.
Ogden, Emily. *Credulity: A Cultural History of US Mesmerism*. Chicago: University of Chicago Press, 2018.
Olsen, Barbara K. "'Come-to-Jesus Stuff' in James Baldwin's *Go Tell It on the Mountain* and *The Amen Corner*." *African American Review* Vol. 31, No. 2 (Summer 1997): 295–301.
Orsi, Robert A. "Introduction: Crossing the City Line." *Gods of the City: Religion and the American Urban Landscape*. Ed. Robert A. Orsi. Bloomington: Indiana University Press, 1999. 1–78.
Orsi, Robert A. *The Madonna of 115th Street: Faith and Community in Italian Harlem, 1880–1950*. 2nd edition. New Haven: Yale University Press, 2002.
Orvell, Miles. *Invisible Parade: The Fiction of Flannery O'Connor*. Philadelphia: Temple University Press, 1972.
Osteen, Mark. *American Magic and Dread: Don DeLillo's Dialogue with Culture*. Philadelphia: University of Pennsylvania Press, 2000.
Owen, Alex. *The Place of Enchantment: British Occultism and the Culture of the Modern*. Chicago: University of Chicago Press, 2004.
Ozick, Cynthia. *Art and Ardor*. New York: Knopf, 1983.
Parrish, Timothy. *From the Civil War to the Apocalypse: Postmodern History and American Fiction*. Amherst: University of Massachusetts Press, 2008.
Pecora, Vincent P. *Secularization and Cultural Criticism: Religion, Nation, and Modernity*. Chicago: University of Chicago Press, 2006.
Philip Roth: Unmasked. Directed by William Karel and Livia Manera. PBS, 2013.
Phillips, Bruce. "American Judaism in the Twenty-first Century." *The Cambridge Companion to American Judaism*. Ed. Dana Evan Kaplan. Cambridge: Cambridge University Press, 2005. 397–416.
Pierpont, Claudia Roth. *Roth Unbound: A Writer and His Books*. New York: Farrar, Straus and Giroux, 2013.

Pinckney, Darryl. "James Baldwin: The Risks of Love." *The New York Review of Books* April 13, 2000: 81–82.

Pinsker, Sanford. "Restlessness in the 1950s: What Made Rabbit Run?" *New Essays on Rabbit, Run.* Ed. Stanley Trachtenberg. Cambridge: Cambridge University Press, 1993. 53–76.

Porter, Horace A. *Stealing the Fire: The Art and Protest of James Baldwin.* Middletown: Wesleyan University Press, 1989.

"A Portrait of Jewish Americans." Pew Research Center October 13, 2013. Accessed September 25, 2014.

Potok, Chaim. *The Chosen.* New York: Balantine, 1995.

Powell, Corey S. *God in the Equation: How Einstein became the Prophet of the New Religious Era.* New York: The Free Press, 2002.

Prothero, Stephen. *Religious Literacy: What Every American Needs to Know—and Doesn't.* San Francisco: HarperCollins, 2007.

Putnam, Robert D., and David E. Campbell. *American Grace: How Religion Divides and Unites Us.* New York: Simon and Schuster, 2010.

Raboteau, Albert J. *Canaan Land: A Religious History of African Americans.* Oxford: Oxford University Press, 2001.

Rampersad, Arnold. *Ralph Ellison: A Biography.* New York: Knopf, 2007.

Rivett, Sarah. *The Science of the Soul in Colonial New England.* Chapel Hill: University of North Carolina Press, 2011.

Robinson, Marilynne. "Credo." *Harvard Divinity School Bulletin* Vol. 36, No. 2 (Spring 2008). Accessed May 6, 2019.

Robinson, Marilynne. *Gilead.* New York: Farrar, Straus and Giroux, 2004.

Rodgers, Daniel T. *Age of Fracture.* Cambridge: Belknap Press/Harvard University Press, 2011.

Rodgers, Lawrence. *Canaan Bound: The African-American Great Migration Novel.* Urbana: University of Illinois Press, 1997.

Roof, Wade Clark. *Spiritual Marketplace: Baby Boomers and the Remaking of American Religion.* Princeton: Princeton University Press, 1999.

Rosen, Elizabeth K. *Apocalyptic Transformation: Apocalypse and the Postmodern Imagination.* Lanham: Lexington Books, 2008.

Roskies, David G. *Against the Apocalypse: Responses to Catastrophe in Modern Jewish Culture.* New York: Syracuse University Press, 1984, 1999.

Roth, John K. "If God Was Silent, Absent, Dead, or Nonexistent, What About Philosophy and Theology: Some Aftereffects and Aftershocks of the Holocaust." *After the Holocaust: Challenging the Myth of Silence.* Eds. David Cesarini and Eric J. Sundquist. New York: Routledge, 2012. 139–51.

Roth, Philip. *American Pastoral*. New York: Knopf, 1997.
Roth, Philip. *The Counterlife*. New York: Vintage, 1996.
Roth, Philip. *Everyman*. London: Jonathan Cape, 2006.
Roth, Philip. *The Ghost Writer*. New York: Vintage, 1995.
Roth, Philip. *Goodbye, Columbus*. New York: Vintage, 1987.
Roth, Philip. *The Human Stain*. Boston: Houghton Mifflin, 2000.
Roth, Philip. *Nemesis*. New York: Harcourt Brace, 2010.
Roth, Philip. *Novels 1993–1995*. New York: Library of America, 2010.
Roth, Philip. "Pictures of Malamud." *New York Times Book Review* April 20, 1986. Accessed October 20, 2014.
Roth, Philip. *The Plot Against America*. London: Jonathan Cape, 2004.
Roth, Philip. *Portnoy's Complaint*. New York: Random House, 1969.
Roth, Philip. *Reading Myself and Others*. New York: Vintage, 2001.
Rothberg, Michael. "Roth and the Holocaust." *The Cambridge Companion to Philip Roth*. Ed. Timothy Parrish. Cambridge: Cambridge University Press, 2007.
Rubenstein, Richard L. *After Auschwitz: Radical Theology and Contemporary Judaism*. Indianapolis: Bobbs Merrill, 1966.
Sanders, Cheryl F. *Saints in Exile: The Holiness-Pentecostal Experience in African American Religion*. Oxford: Oxford University Press, 1996.
Schaub, Thomas Hill. *American Fiction in the Cold War*. Madison: University of Wisconsin Press, 1991.
Scott, R. Neil, and Irwin H. Streight, eds. *Flannery O'Connor: The Contemporary Reviews*. Cambridge: Cambridge University Press, 2009.
Scruggs, Charles. *Sweet Home: Invisible Cities in the Afro-American Novel*. Baltimore: Johns Hopkins University Press, 1993.
Searles, George J. *Conversations with Philip Roth*. Oxford: University Press of Mississippi, 1992.
Sernett, Richard C. *Bound for the Promised Land: African American Religion and the Great Migration*. Durham: Duke University Press, 1997.
Shanley, John Patrick. *Doubt: A Parable*. New York: Theater Communications Group, 2005.
Sicher, Efraim. *The Holocaust Novel*. New York: Routledge, 2005.
Smith, Christian. *Religion: What It Is, How It Works, and Why It Matters*. Princeton: Princeton University Press, 2017.
Smith, Wilfred Cantwell. *Believing: An Historical Perspective*. Oxford: Oneworld, 1998.

Snyder, Timothy. *Bloodlands: Europe between Hitler and Stalin*. New York: Basic Books, 2010.

Spillers, Hortense. "Afterword." *James Baldwin: America and Beyond*. Eds. Cora Kaplan and Bill Schwarz. Ann Arbor: University of Michigan Press, 2011. 241–45.

Srigley, Susan. *Flannery O'Connor's Sacramental Art*. South Bend: University of Notre Dame, 2004.

Standley, Fred L., and Louis H. Pratt, eds. *Conversations with James Baldwin*. Jackson: University Press of Mississippi, 1989.

Stark, Rodney, and Roger Finke. *Acts of Faith: Explaining the Human Side of Religion*. Berkeley: University of California Press, 2000.

Stephens, Randall J. *The Fire Spreads: Holiness and Pentecostalism in the American South*. Cambridge: Harvard University Press, 2008.

Sundquist, Eric J. "The Historian's Anvil, the Novelist's Crucible." *The Literature of the Holocaust*. Ed. Alan Rosen. Cambridge: Cambridge University Press, 2013. 252–67.

Sundquist, Eric J. *Strangers in the Land: Blacks, Jews, Post-Holocaust America*. Cambridge: Harvard University Press, 2009.

Sutton, Matthew Avery. *American Apocalypse: A History of Modern Evangelicalism*. Cambridge: Belknap Press/Harvard University Press, 2014.

Synan, Vinson. *The Holiness-Pentecostal Tradition: Charismatic Movements in the Twentieth Century*. Grand Rapids: Eerdmans, 1997.

Tanner, Tony. "Afterthoughts on Don DeLillo's *Underworld*." *Raritan* Vol. 17, No. 4 (Spring 1998): 48–71.

Tanner, Tony. *Saul Bellow*. New York: Barnes and Noble, 1965.

Taves, Ann. *Fits, Trances, and Visions: Experiencing Religion and Explaining Experience from Wesley to James*. Princeton: Princeton University Press, 1999.

Taylor, Charles. *A Secular Age*. Cambridge: Belknap Press/Harvard University Press, 2007.

Taylor, Charles. *Varieties of Religion Today: William James Revisited*. Cambridge: Harvard University Press, 2002.

"The Third Force of Christendom." *Life* June 9, 1958: 113.

Tillich, Paul. *The Courage to Be*. New Haven: Yale University Press, 1952, 2000.

Tillich, Paul. *The Essential Tillich*. Ed. R. Forrester Church. Chicago: University of Chicago Press, 1987.

Tokarczyk, Michelle M. *E.L. Doctorow's Skeptical Commitment*. New York: Peter Lang, 2000.

"Toward a Hidden God," *Time* April 8, 1966. Accessed May 20, 2008.
Ulin, David L. "Imagined Hells of Philip Roth." *Los Angeles Times* October 3, 2010: E1, E11.
Updike, John. *Due Considerations: Essays and Criticism*. New York: Knopf, 2007.
Updike, John. *In the Beauty of the Lilies*. New York: Knopf, 1996.
Updike, John. *Rabbit, Run*. New York: Random House, 1996.
Updike, John. "Recruiting Raw Nerves." *The New Yorker* March 15, 1993: 110.
Updike, John. "Religion and Literature." *The Religion Factor: An Introduction to How Religion Matters*. Eds. William Scott Green and Jacob Neusner. Louisville: Westminster John Knox Press, 1996. 227–42.
Updike, John. *Self-consciousness: Memoirs*. New York: Knopf, 1989.
Updike, John. "A Special Message for the First Edition." *In the Beauty of the Lilies*. Franklin Center, PA: Franklin Library, 1996. ii.
Urban, Hugh B. *The Church of Scientology: A History of a New Religion*. Princeton: Princeton University Press, 2011.
"US Catholics Tilt Left, Pew Survey Finds." *Catholic World News* June 30, 2008. Accessed May 21, 2009.
US Religious Landscape Survey, Pew Forum on Religion and Public Life: March 4, 2008. Accessed April 14, 2011.
Viswanathan, Gauri. *Outside the Fold: Conversion, Modernity, and Belief*. Princeton: Princeton University Press, 1998.
Wacker, Grant. *America's Pastor: Billy Graham and the Shaping of a Nation*. Cambridge: Belknap Press/Harvard University Press, 2014.
Wacker, Grant. *Heaven Below: Early Pentecostals and American Culture*. Cambridge: Harvard University Press, 2001.
Walker, Cheryl. *God and Elizabeth Bishop: Meditations on Religion and Poetry*. New York: Palgrave, 2005.
Warner, Michael, Jonathan VanAntwerpen, and Craig Calhoun, eds. *Varieties of Secularism in a Secular Age*. Cambridge: Harvard University Press, 2010.
Warner, Michael. "Secularism." *Keywords for American Cultural Studies*. Eds. Bruce Burgett and Glenn Hendler. New York: New York University Press, 2007. 209–12.
Warner, W. Lloyd. *The Family of God*. New Haven: Yale University Press, 1961.
Watson, Jay. "Flannery O'Connor." *The Cambridge Companion to American Fiction after 1945*. Ed. John N. Duvall. Cambridge: Cambridge University Press, 2012. 207–19.
Watts, Jill. *God, Harlem USA: The Father Divine Story*. Berkeley: University of California Press, 1992.

Weber, Max. "Science as Vocation." *From Max Weber: Essays in Sociology*. Ed. and trans. H.H. Gerth and C. Wright Mills. London: Routledge, 1948. 129–56.

"Weird Babel of Tongues." *Los Angeles Daily Times* April 18, 1906: 1.

Werner, Craig Hansen. *Playing the Changes: From Afro-Modernism to the Jazz Impulse*. Urbana: University of Illinois Press, 1994.

Whitfield, Stephen J. *The Culture of the Cold War*. Baltimore: Johns Hopkins University Press, 1991.

Wilkerson, Isabel. *The Warmth of Other Suns: The Epic Story of America's Great Migration*. New York: Random House, 2011.

Wilkie, Brian. "Flannery O'Connor (1925–1964): *Wise Blood*." *Encyclopedia of Catholic Literature* Vol. 2. Ed. Mary R. Reichardt. Westport: Greenwood Press, 2004.

Williams, David. "Flannery O'Connor (1925–1964): Short Stories." *Encyclopedia of Catholic Literature*. Ed. Mary R. Reichardt. Westport: Greenwood Press, 2004.

Williams, Raymond. *Marxism and Literature*. Oxford: Oxford University Press, 1977.

Wilson, A.N. *God's Funeral*. New York: Norton, 1999.

Wilson, Ivy G. *Specters of Democracy: Blackness and the Aesthetics of Politics in the Antebellum US*. Oxford: Oxford University Press, 2011.

Wirth-Nesher, Hana, and Michael P. Kramer, eds. *The Cambridge Companion to Jewish American Literature*. Cambridge: Cambridge University Press, 2003.

Wood, James. "Acts of Devotion." *The New York Times* November 2, 2005. Accessed May 28, 2013.

Wood, James. *The Broken Estate: Essays on Literature and Belief*. New York: Random House, 1999.

Wood, Ralph C. *Flannery O'Connor and the Christ-haunted South*. Grand Rapids: Eerdmans, 2005.

Worthen, Molly. *Apostles of Reason: The Crisis of Authority in American Evangelicalism*. Oxford: Oxford University Press, 2013.

Wright, Richard. *Black Boy (American Hunger)/The Outsider*. New York: Library of America, 1991.

Wright, Richard. *Later Works*. New York: Library of America, 1991.

Wright, Richard. *12 Million Black Voices*. New York: Thunder's Mouth Press, 1988.

Wuthnow, Robert. *After Heaven: Spirituality in America since the 1950s*. Berkeley: University of California Press, 1998.

Wuthnow, Robert. *Be Very Afraid: The Cultural Response to Terror, Pandemics, Environmental Devastation, Nuclear Annihilation, and Other Threats*. Oxford: Oxford University Press, 2010.

Index

Abyssinian Baptist Church 73–5, 84
Achebe, Chinua 108–9, 109
  Things Fall Apart 108
Adorno, Theodor 112, 129–30
  Dialectic of Enlightenment, The 112
  Prisms 129
Adventism 8
African American
  gospel music 90–2
  largest congregation 84
  religious culture 61, 65–7, 73–4, 82–3, 89–90, 101, 105
Ahlstrom, Sidney, E, *A Religious History of the American People* 11
Allbee, Kirby 126
Als, Hilton 55, 61
Altizer, Thomas J.J., *Radical Theology and the Death of God* 117
American Jewish writers 112, 114–17, 119, 122–4, 128, 138, 141, 147, 156–7. *See also* Holocaust; specific writers
American writers. *See also* specific writers
  religion, perception 14–17, 20, 23, 27–8, 34–5, 198
apostasy 5–7, 14–15, 38, 41, 45, 48–9, 51, 71, 82, 105, 126, 136
Appelfeld, Aharon 139
Aquinas, Thomas 22
Arendt, Hannah, *Eichmann in Jerusalem* 28
Asad, Talal 3, 115, 201 n.18
atheism 1–2, 12, 21, 36, 38, 50, 145, 190
atheists 52, 57, 59, 126, 130, 145
Azusa Street Revival 66, 72, 90. *See also* Pentecostalism

Bakhtin, M.M. 76
Baldwin, James. *See also* Great Migration; Pentecostalism
  Amen Corner, The 68, 226 n.126, 228 n.188
  "American Dream and the American Negro" (essay) 106
  association with church 85–93
  "Autobiographical Notes" (essay) 68, 95
  black liberation theology 95
  character's crisis of faith 66–8, 71–2, 75–81, 93–4
  conversion experience 85
  Crying Holy, change of name 68
  "Dark Days" 109
  Devil Finds Work, The 106–7
  "Down at the Cross" 68, 85, 88
  "Everybody's Protest Novel" 93
  "Every Good-bye Ain't Gone" 109
  Fire Next Time, The 68, 111
  first novel, subject matter 97–105, 97–106
  Go Tell It on the Mountain 61, 65, 67–8, 70, 75, 83, 85–6, 88, 92–4, 97, 104, 155, 168
  "Harlem Ghetto, The" 73
  jazz, affinities with 90, 97
  lecture at Kalamazoo College 69
  on murder of Jews 113
  "Nobody Knows My Name: A Letter from the South" (essay) 64
  Nobody Knows My Name: More Notes of a Native Son 64, 93, 95
  "Notes for a Hypothetical Novel" 70
  Notes of a Native Son 64, 73, 95
  "Open Letter to the Born Again" 107
  own conversion experience 94–5
  Price of the Ticket, The 110

Temple of the Fire Baptized
(fictional) 76, 82–6, 89–90, 98
When Harlem Was in Vogue 87
Baumgarten, Murray 122
Bellah, Robert, *Habits of the Heart* 7
Bellow, Saul
  Adventures of Augie March, The
    125–6
  "A Jewish Writer in America" 122,
    124
  Herzog 125–8, 130
  letter to Ozick, Cynthia 130
  Mr. Sammler's Planet 125, 128–9
  rejection of labels 123–4
  religious belief and practices 15,
    111, 114, 116, 122–8, 130–2,
    148, 157–8
  Victim, The 125–6, 131
Berger, Alan L. 130
Bloom, Harold 53–4
Bonhoeffer, Dietrich 84, 116
  Prisoner for God 116
Branch Davidians 8–9, 14
Brooks, Cleanth 25, 55, 57
  Hidden God, The 57
  Understanding Fiction 25
Brotherhood 74–5
Bruner, Michael Mears 43

Calhoun, Craig, *Rethinking Secularism*
  115
Campbell, David E. 11
Capouya, Emile 96–7, 111
Casanova, Jose 115
Catholicism 16, 27, 29–30, 33–4,
  41–2, 55, 57, 133, 137, 161, 164,
  167, 176
Church of Scientology, 31
Civil Rights movement 67, 70, 93, 108
Cold War 30, 182
Coleman, James W. 146
Coles, Robert 56
Conroy, Mark 176
conversion 9–10, 15, 50, 53

Crossman, Richard, *God That Failed,*
  The 114
Cullen, Countee 95

Daddy Grace 66, 96
death of God movement 117–19
DeCurtis, Anthony 164
Delbanco, Andrew 176
DeLillo, Don
  apocalyptic themes 165–6
  character's crisis of faith 164, 167–95
  on conspiracy theories 182–4, 186
  on extravagant forms of religion
    162–4, 173–4
  Falling Man 163, 195, 197
  Libra 183
  Mao II 162–3, 179–80, 182
  Names, The 163, 167–9, 180
  on new religious America 166–73
  Running Dog 182
  Underworld 161, 163–4, 178–9,
    182–8, 194–5
  White Noise 163, 170, 172–3,
    175–7, 181–2
Dickstein, Morris 122, 131, 166
Divne, Father 66
Doctorow, E.L.
  character's crisis of faith 149–59
  City of God 17, 148, 150–2
  Massey lectures at Harward
    University 147, 151
  religious belief and practices 116
  religious pluralism 147, 151, 153,
    157–9
  Reporting the Universe 17, 151
  Sweet Land Stories 153
Dray, Philip, *At the Hands of Persons*
  Unknown 79
DuBois, W.E.B. 65, 197
Duvall, John 180, 193

Eisenhower, Dwight D. 30, 210 n.57
Eisenstein, Sergei 175
  Battleship Potemkin 176

Ellison, Ralph 74, 76, 86
  Invisible Man 74–5
English, James F 16, 46
eschatology 15, 155, 165, 178, 186
Evangelicalism 148, 155, 162, 167, 170
Evans, David H. 187
Exodus 66, 70, 119, 221 n.28

Fackenheim, Emile L.
  God's Presence in History 118
  "On the Self-exposure of Faith to the Modernsecular World" 118
Ferguson, Robert A., *Alone in America: The Stories That Matter* 196
Feuerbach, Ludwig, *The Essence of Christianity* 12
Fiedler, Leslie 122
Fink, Roger, *Acts of Faith: Exploring the Human Side of Religion* 181
Fitzgerald, Robert 21, 34, 55
Fitzgerald, Sally 21, 55
Fox, Richard Wightman 163
Freedman, Jonathan 133

Gallup, George, Jr. 30, 166
Gilman, Richard 51
Goldberg, Michael 119, 121
  Why Should the Jews Survive? Looking Past the Holocaust toward a Jewish Future 119
Gooch, Brad 34, 61
Gordon, Caroline 55
  Malefactors, The 23
Graham, Billy 30–1, 38, 178, 211 n.65
Great Migration 64–7, 73, 75–6, 82–3, 93, 220 n.24
Griffin, Farah Jasmine 80, 97
Guardini, Romano, *The End of the Modern World: A Search for Orientation* 27

Hamilton, William, *Radical Theology and the Death of God* 117
Hardwick, Elizabeth 54–5

Hardy, Clarence E. 85
Harlem, religious life. *See* Baldwin, James
Hassan, Ihab 88
Hawkes, John 53
Herberg, Will 29, 33, 57
  Protestant-Catholic-Jew: An Essay in American Sociology 29, 121, 210 n.55
Herberg, Will 29, 33, 57
Herbert, George 13
Hester, Betty 26, 54
Higher Criticism 1–2
Hoberek, Andrew 121
Hofstadter, Richard 186
Hollinger, David 121
Holocaust 16, 28–9, 112–14, 117–22, 125–6, 128, 130–1, 138–41, 148–51, 156. *See also* American Jewish writers
Horkheimer, Max, *Dialectic of Enlightenment, The* 112
Horn, Rosa Artimas 85
Hubbard, L. Ron 32
  Dianetics: The Modern Science of Mental Health 31
Hungerford, Amy 128, 131, 164, 198

Ingersoll, Robert G. 2
  Some Mistakes of Moses 1
  "Why Am I Agnostic?" 2
Irwin, B.H. 90

Jacoby, Susan 145–6
Jenkins, Jerry B., *Left Behind: A Novel of the Earth's Last Days* 155–6, 165
Jewish intellectuals 113–15
  secular theodicy 115–16
JFK (film) 183
Jones, Howard Mumford, *Belief and Disbelief in American Literature* 57
Juergensmeyer, Mark, *Rethinking Secularism* 115

Kazin, Alfred 55
  Journals 123
  New York Jew 112
  relationship to Judaism 112–14
King, Jr. Martin Luther 110
  "I Have a Dream Speech" 63
Knight, Peter 184
Koestler, Arthur 112, 114
  "On Disbelieving Atrocities" 112
Koresh, David 8, 155

LaHaye, Timothy, *Left Behind: A Novel of the Earth's Last Days* 155–6, 165
Lake, Cristina Bieber 56
Lee, Maryat 61
Leeming, David 106, 108
Leman, Nicholas, *Promised Land, The* 83
Levi, Primo 128
Levinas, Emmanuel 107
Lewis, David Levering, *When Harlem Was in Vogue* 87
Lewis, Sinclair, *Elmer Gantry* 38
Lindberg, Anne Morrow, *Gift from the Sea* 32
Lindsey, Hal 155, 156
  Late Great Planet Earth, The 155, 165, 178
Lofton, Kathryn 117
Lowell, Robert 54–5
Luhrmann, T.M. 6, 202 n.29, 203 n.35, 209 n.38
Lynch, Michael F. 93, 97

Marx, Karl 135
McAffrey, Larry 156
McCarthy, Cormac 161
McCarthy, Mary 54–5
McClure, John A. 164
McGurl, Mark 25
Menand, Louis 127
Mencken, H.L., *Philosophy of Friedrich Nietzsche, The* 2

Metaxas, Eric 84
Methodists 66–7, 73, 166–7
Miller, J. Hillis, *Disappearance of God, The* 57
Miller, William 8
Morrison, Toni, *Song of Solomon* 65

National Jewish Population Survey (NJPS) 157
New Age religions 162
New Age spirituality 7, 11, 199, 247 n.54
New Criticism 25, 42, 131
new religious movements 9, 31–2, 58, 66–7, 180–1, 183, 186, 199
Niebuhr, Reinhold 4, 57, 84
  Pious and Secular America 4
Nietzsche, Friedrich 2, 117, 127, 162, 200 n.8

Oates, Joyce Carol 54, 62
O'Connor, Flannery
  approach to fiction 24–5
  "Artificial Nigger, The" 62–3
  as a cartoonist 37
  "Catholic Novelist in the Protestant South, The" 19
  character's crisis of faith 28–9, 35–53
  Christian readers 26–7, 34
  "Church and the Fiction Writer, The" 24
  "Displaced Person, The" 28
  on doctrine of Incarnation 26
  Emory University lecture 22
  Everything That Rises Must Converge 52, 217 n.178
  "Good Country People" 47
  A Good Man Is Hard to Find 28, 42–3, 47, 62
  "Greenleaf" 52
  on institutional religion 21
  intellectual difficulties 59
  letter to Greene, Helen 40

letter to Hester, Betty 26
letter to Lee, Maryat 63
literary friends 55
modern readers 49
Mystery and Manners: Occasional Prose 20
"Novelist and Believer" 20, 23, 56
A Prayer Journal 25, 59
race investigations 62
religious beliefs 19, 21–4
"Revelation" 52
Sweet Briar College, lecture at 20–1, 33, 207 n.17
Violent Bear It Away, The 48, 50–2
Wise Blood 21, 35–6, 38–40, 42, 45, 48, 51, 61, 108
O'Donnell, Patrick 186
Orsi, Robert A. 16, 73, 88
Gods of the City: Religion and the American Urban Landscape 73
Osteen, Mark 182
Ozick, Cynthia 122, 130

Peal, Norman Vincent, *Power of Positive Thinking, The* 39
Pelatowski, Theodore 68
Pentecostalism 50, 61, 66–7, 70–2, 74, 76, 78, 88, 90, 155, 167, 169, 199
Phillips, Bruce 157
Pierpont, Claudia Roth 142, 161
Pinckney, Darryl 104–5
Porter, Horace A. 55, 81
Potok, Chaim, *Chosen, The* 120
Powell, Corey S. 84
Powell, Sr., Adam Clayton 84
Protestantism 16, 29, 33–4, 121–2, 157, 164, 166–7, 170
Putnam, Robert D. 11

Raboteau, Albert J. 66
Rampersad, Arnold 87
religion. *See also* new religious movements; US religious history
current usage 3–4
evolution over time 12
national revival 31, 34
religious studies 105, 126–7
key-terms and concepts 15–16
Revelation 8, 52, 153–6, 165, 187–99
Rinehart, B.P. 74–5
Robinson, Marilynne 14, 16
Gilead 12–15
Roof, Wade Clark 4
Roskies, David G., *Against the Apocalypse:Responses to Catastrophe in Modern Jewish Culture* 119
Roth, John K. 117
Roth, Philip 15, 111, 114, 116, 120, 122–3, 131–3, 136, 138–48, 157–8, 161
American Pastoral 136–7
Everyman 136
fictional homages to Jewish community 188
Ghost Writer 139
Goodbye, Columbus 132–3, 135
Human Stain, The 146
"Imagining Jews" 123
irreverent approach to religion 132–46
Nemesis 142
Operation Shylock 136, 139, 141
Plot Against America 138
Portnoy's Complaint 135
Reading Myself and Others 120, 132
religious belief and practices 116
Rothberg, Michael 139
Rubenstein, Richard
After Auschwitz: Radical Theology and Contemporary Judaism 117, 119–20
"God after the Death of God" 119
Rubenstein, Richard L. 117–20

Sanders, Cheryl F. 82, 87, 94
Schaub, Thomas Hill 43, 45, 214 n.126
Secret, The 163

secularization 26, 56–7, 93, 115, 157, 166
  scholars on 3
  Western nations 4
Seventh-Day Adventist 8, 67, 73
Simon, John W. 40
Smith, Christian 56
Smith, Wilfred Cantwell 4
Snyder, Timothy 127
Soyinka, Wole 110
Spillers, Hortense 105
Spiritualists 66, 73
Srigley, Susan 49
Stark, Rodney, *Acts of Faith: Exploring the Human Side of Religion* 181
Steiner, George, *Language and Silence* 118
Stephens, Randall J. 72, 90
  The Fire Spreads: Holiness and Pentecostalism in the American South 72
Sunday, Billy 31
Sutton, Matthew Avery 178

Tanner, Tony 195
Taves, Ann 94, 105
  Fits, Trances, and Visions 94
Taylor, Charles 3, 6, 20, 163, 166, 176, 179
  A Secular Age 3, 20, 163
theodicy 15, 28, 114, 117, 121, 125–8, 139–40, 142–5, 148–9, 191, 195
Thompson, Francis, *Hound of Heaven, The* 40, 43
Tillich, Paul 34
  Courage to Be, The 33
  "Lost Dimension in Religion, The" 33

Uncle Tom's Cabin 93
Updike, John 1–17, 32, 172, 198
  character's crisis of faith 1–3, 5–8, 10–11
  "Future of Faith, The" (essay) 2
  Higher Gossip (essays) 5
  In the Beauty of the Lilies 1, 5–6, 9–11, 14, 41, 155, 200 n.1

  A Month of Sundays 5
  predicament of religion 1–3
  Rabbit, Run 5
  Roger's Version 5
  on secularism and scientific materialism 6
  Self-Consciousness 172
  teleology verses genealogy 9
  twentieth century, religious status 14
Urban, Hugh B. 31, 73
US religious history 166–73. *See also* American writers
  churchgoers, demography 166–7
  Jewish literary renaissance 122

Vahanian, Gabriel, *Death of God, The* 117
VanAntwerpen, Jonathan, *Rethinking Secularism* 115

Wacker, Grant 72–3
Walker, Cheryl 43
Warner, Michael 4, 115
Warren, Robert Penn, *Understanding Fiction* 25
Watson, Jay 22
Watts, Jill 36
Weber, Max 175
Welty, Eudora, "Where Is the Voice Coming From?" 63
Wiesel, Elie 118
Wilkie, Brian 41
Williams, David 45, 47
Williams, Raymond 14
Wilson, Ivy G. 69
Winfrey, Oprah 163
Wood, James 13
Wright, Richard, *12 Million Black Voices* 64, 67
Wuthnow, Robert 170

Zionist movement 120

www.ingramcontent.com/pod-product-compliance
Lightning Source LLC
Chambersburg PA
CBHW050323020526
44117CB00031B/1664